STUDIES PRESENTED TO
The International Commission for the History
of Representative & Parliamentary Institutions

XXII

REPRESENTATIVE INSTITUTIONS
In Renaissance France

REPRESENTATIVE INSTITUTIONS
In Renaissance France
1421–1559

J. RUSSELL MAJOR

GREENWOOD PRESS, PUBLISHERS
WESTPORT, CONNECTICUT

Library of Congress Cataloging in Publication Data

Major, J. Russell (James Russell), 1921-
    Representative institutions in Renaissance France,
1421-1559.

    Reprint. Originally published: Madison : University
of Wisconsin Press, 1960. (Studies presented to the
International Commission for the History of Representative & Parliamentary Institutions ; 22)
    Includes bibliographical references and index.
    1. France. États généraux.   2. France--Politics
and government--1328-1589.   3. Representative government
and representation--France--History.   I. Title.
II. Series: Etudes présentées à la Commission inter-
nationale pour l'histoire des assemblées d'états ; 22.
JN2413.M32 1983   328.44'09033   82-25305
ISBN 0-313-23569-4 (lib. bdg.)

To my mother

Reprinted in 1983 by Greenwood Press
A division of Congressional Information Service, Inc.
88 Post Road West, Westport, Connecticut 06881

Printed in the United States of America

10 9 8 7 6 5 4 3 2 1

PREFACE

This is a history of French representative institutions from the beginning of the reign of Charles VII until the death of Henry II just before the outbreak of the Wars of Religion. It is intended to demonstrate the popular, consultative nature of the Renaissance Monarchy, not to give a detailed description of each assembly. To do so would be impossible because the "Estates General" or the "assembly of the three estates" [1] was only one of many representative institutions that flourished in France. There were often local assemblies of the three estates in viscounties, provostships, dioceses, bailiwicks, and seneschalsies. Above these local estates there were provincial or governmental estates in Brittany, Normandy, Languedoc, Burgundy, and elsewhere. Still larger were the regional assemblies like the estates of Languedoïl. Finally there were assemblies to which only one estate was summoned. There were local, provincial, regional, and national assemblies of the Catholic clergy, the Protestants, the nobility, and the towns. No work, however long, could hope to do justice to this variant and luxuriant growth. Therefore, I have dealt with all the assemblies in a cursory fashion except for the Estates General of 1484 which I have treated at length to show the problems faced by the government officials and deputies during the period. It is my intention at a later date to carry the narra-

[1] These two terms were used interchangeably during the sixteenth and seventeenth centuries, but there was a marked preference for calling the institution an "assembly of the three estates" in the fifteenth century. However, examples of the use of the term "Estates General" may be found at this time. (See Mayer, IX, 212; *Archives historiques du Rouergue*, VII [1930], 381–82; and Gustave Dupont-Ferrier, *Études sur les institutions financières de la France à la fin du moyen âge* [Paris, 1932], II, 24.) Neither the number of people who attended nor the way in which they were chosen affected the nomenclature. Even the small assembly held at Paris in 1558 was occasionally referred to as being an Estates General. (See AD, Côte d'Or, C 3,469, and for the comparable phrase of "a general assembly of the estates of France," see AD, Côte d'Or, C 3,062, fol. 255.)

tive to the middle of the seventeenth century in the hope of explaining why representative institutions decayed in France just before the English Parliament insured forever its position in the government of the nation.

It is also my intention to make an analytical study of the Estates General. The first volume in this project, *The Deputies to the Estates General in Renaissance France,* has just been published. It is a study of the deputies to the Estates General: who they were, how they were elected, how they lived during the sessions, and how they were paid. This involves a long account of the composition and procedures used in the local and provincial estates that elected deputies to the Estates General. It also contains evidence to support my interpretation of the nature of the Renaissance Monarchy in France. It was largely through the study of these oft-neglected local institutions that I felt forced to adopt the position I have taken in this volume. Later, I plan to publish studies on the procedures used in the Estates General and on French public opinion as seen in the local, provincial, and national cahiers. A bibliography will be included in one of these works.

This study has been made possible by the generous assistance of many foundations and individuals. Fulbright and John Simon Guggenheim Memorial fellowships enabled me to spend the years 1952–54 in France, locating and microfilming unpublished material, and a three-year Faculty Research Fellowship of the Social Science Research Council gave me the time to write this volume. In addition, funds granted by the Carnegie Foundation and the University Center in Georgia made it possible for me to do research in the Harvard University libraries during the summers of 1951 and 1955. To Emory University I am indebted for additional financial assistance and for the readiness with which leaves of absence from my normal academic duties have been granted.

To numerous librarians and archivists both in Paris and in the departments, I wish to express my gratitude for the assistance they have given me in locating and microfilming manuscripts and other materials. Without their help there would be many more omissions and errors in this volume. To Professors Helmut Koenigsberger of the University of Manchester, Gaines Post of the University of Wisconsin, Gordon Griffiths of the University of Washington, and Walter Love of Emory University, I give thanks for their careful criticisms of the entire volume. To the many scholars at Princeton, Emory, and elsewhere who have assisted me in various ways, to the library staff of Emory University, to our departmental secretaries, and to the graduate students who have participated in phases of this work, I also wish to express my appreciation. Above all others, I must thank my wife who not only assumed the usual chores of typist, proofreader, and critic, but also followed me on my wanderings through France with four small children and found time to copy some of the microfilmed manuscripts we brought home. Indeed, as I look back on the past few years, I realize more and more how much this book is a family project that has been made possible through the co-operative efforts of generous foundations, helpful librarians and archivists, and able historians.

CONTENTS

REPRESENTATIVE INSTITUTIONS
In Renaissance France

ONE

The Renaissance Monarchy in France

General Considerations

"Francis I was an absolute monarch." [1] So wrote Henry Lemonnier in one of the volumes of that splendid history edited by Ernest Lavisse. How often this statement has been made; but does it give a true picture of the Renaissance Monarchy of France? Any study of representative institutions during the period must consider this question.

Although Burckhardt recognized the nature of the government of the Italian states as one of the principal causative factors that produced the Italian Renaissance, his successors have tended to disregard the insight of the brilliant Swiss scholar in favor of economic-social considerations. There are many political histories, but neither for Italy nor for the kingdoms to the north has sufficient effort been made to define the underlying characteristics of the government of the monarchs who played such a large role during the transitional period that was the Renaissance. [2]

There were no dynastic changes to aid in developing the concept of a Renaissance Monarchy for France, yet it seems undeniable that there was considerable difference between the monarchies of, let us say, Philip IV, Francis I, and Louis XIV; between the Medieval, the Renaissance, and the Baroque. The reigns of Charles VII and Louis XI were the formative period of the Renaissance Monarchy. During the following century it matured and developed, and during the reigns of Henry IV and Louis XIII it declined. The intervening century with its religious, intellectual, and economic revolutions marked the height of the Renaissance Monarchy.

The Characteristics of the Renaissance Monarchy

The first and most pronounced characteristic of this monarchy was its feudal-dynastic structure and motivation. States were enlarged by marriage and wars of conquest were undertaken to secure claimed in-

3

heritances rather than strategic boundaries. The marital activities of the Habsburgs, the Burgundian dukes, and the royal houses of the Spanish kingdoms are but the most famous examples of a general European phenomenon. The French again and again invaded Italy in the hope of winning Naples or Milan to which the Valois had some claim, but at the same time neglected the Rhineland and other areas nearer home.[3] A feudal characteristic of the Renaissance state was the escheating of lordships to the crown when a noble family became extinct. It was by this natural process that the title to so many duchies, counties, and lesser territories was won, especially during the reign of Louis XI. Much of that wily king's policy was dedicated to taking full advantage of this aspect of feudal law. He was not above plotting to gain the lands of the House of Orléans by marrying its last male heir to his daughter who could have no children. The dynastic and feudal character of the Renaissance state became as one when the Valois turned to the question of the marriage of the Breton heiress. Two kings had to win her hand before the duchy could be permanently reunited with the crown.

Since territorial aggrandizement at the expense of foreign states or local nobles depended on dynastic claims and feudal law, legitimacy and legality had to be stressed to an unusual degree. The Renaissance prince has often been pictured as a highly individualistic ruler with little respect for aught save wit and power, but in fact even the Italian potentate was ever anxious to find legal justification for the authority he wielded, and elsewhere rulers were still less subject to challenge on this score.

This stress on legitimacy by the Renaissance Monarchs was not limited to their own rights, it involved a respect for the rights of their subjects. When a new king came to the throne, he invariably confirmed the privileges of the various individuals and corporate groups within his kingdom. When a princely or feudal domain fell to a king, he at once recognized the privileges its inhabitants had been granted by their previous rulers. Thus the growth of the royal domain in France and elsewhere did not mean the consolidation of power in the hands of the king as much as it marked the acceptance of the diversified and decentralized conglomeration of duchies, counties, seigneuries, and towns that was the Renaissance Monarchy.

The acceptance of the ideas of legitimacy and privilege made necessary a decentralized form of government that was carried to the point of creating separate sovereign courts for different semiautonomous regions. Dynasticism, feudalism, legitimacy, and privilege had all been incorporated into the medieval state, but whereas medieval decentralization was derived primarily from the power wielded by the greater and lesser seigneurs, Renaissance decentralization came more from a surrender of the centralized authority of the king who had become both monarch and seigneur to provincial estates and sovereign courts, administrative organs of government, and semisovereign officials. These royal officials in turn were checked by the survival of seigneurial, municipal, and provincial rights, and by the very fact that they were too few in number to regulate the actions of the people in a day before rapid transportation and mass communication. Around 1505 there were approximately 12,000 royal officials in France, a nation of 15,000,000 inhabitants and 480,000 square kilometers; or one official for each 1,250 inhabitants and one for each 40 square kilometers. The number of royal officials increased during the course of the century, but at no time could they have interfered with the actions of the people to the degree found in the modern democracy. France in 1934 had one official for each seventy inhabitants and 56 for each 40 square kilometers.[4]

The bulk of the transition from the Medieval to the Renaissance type of decentralization took place during the reign of Charles VII. At first Charles showed a preference for centralized institutions like those of his Capetian predecessors. When he came to the throne there were two Parlements, or sovereign judicial courts, in unoccupied France. One at Poitiers served the northern part of his realm, and the other, established in 1420 at Toulouse, was for the benefit of the southern region. By 1428 communication between Poitou and Languedoc had improved sufficiently to make possible the reunion of the two Parlements at Poitiers. With the recapture of Paris in 1436, the now united Parlement returned to the capital. The financial courts underwent a similar experience. The *Chambre des comptes* was transferred from Bourges to Paris, and the *Cour des aides*, from Poitiers immediately after the reconquest of the capital. The sovereign courts, united, returned to their former home.

A few years later the policy of centralization began to be exchanged for one of decentralization. The king's advisors ceased to uphold the doctrine that the sovereign courts and the essential services of the administration were indivisible organisms which exercised their authority over the whole kingdom. Instead they began to advocate the creation of sovereign provincial institutions. The new policy resulted in part from the difficulties of ruling so large a kingdom, but perhaps more from the advisability of satisfying the particularistic desires of newly acquired provinces that had usually enjoyed separate institutions under their feudal rulers.[5] Local royal Parlements were created at Toulouse in 1443 at the request of the estates of Languedoc, at Bordeaux in 1451 with the reconquest of Guyenne, at Grenoble and at Dijon with the annexation of Dauphiné and Burgundy, at Aix in 1501, and at Rouen with the accession of Francis I when existing feudal institutions were modified. Still later, additional Parlements were created for Brittany, for the Italian possessions, and for those in the Empire.

In a similar manner the financial courts were gradually decentralized. Provincial *Chambres des comptes* were established at Montpellier, Rouen, Dijon, Grenoble, Nantes, and Aix during the century following the reconquest of France. The jurisdiction of the *Cour des aides* at Paris was reduced by Charles VII; local sovereign bodies were formed in Languedoc, Guyenne, Normandy, and other provinces, though in some instances the new courts were attached to other provincial institutions. In 1445 the same king divided the older parts of the royal domain into four sections, each under a *trésorier de France,* but a central *Chambre du trésor* was retained at Paris.[6]

Decentralization was furthered in still another way. In 1454 it was decided to hold local assemblies of the three estates to codify the customs of the various provinces, bailiwicks, and other localities. Once these local customs were definitely established and put in writing, it became virtually impossible to develop a common law for the entire country by any means other than revolution. The unifying effect of Roman Law in the minds of some judges who presided over the meetings was of limited importance because the customs were actually determined by those who attended the assemblies. The crown and the judges respected the customs and privileges of the people too much to engage in any large scale interference.[7]

The administrative and military, like the judicial and financial institutions of the crown, were also decentralized during the latter part of the fifteenth century when the kings decided to appoint governors for many of the former great feudal dependencies. This practice spread to the older parts of the domain until all France was divided into about twelve jurisdictions ruled by princes or great nobles. These governors exercised, or sought to exercise, nearly every nonjudicial prerogative of the crown. By 1499 it became necessary to deny them such regalian powers as to pardon, ennoble, and legitimize, but during the Wars of Religion the monarchs were in no condition to impose any checks. Governors did not hesitate to raise armies, convoke the provincial estates, publish ordonnances, appropriate royal revenue, and in general to conduct themselves as independent rulers. Even greater authority in the form of appanages was given by the kings to members of their families. France was indeed fortunate that few royal princes reached middle age or left heirs.[8]

The creation of provincial sovereign courts for justice and finance and the division of the kingdom into governments were contributions towards a decentralized administration by the Renaissance Monarchs.

Other factors also made for decentralization, but these were present in the older Medieval Monarchy. France was too large a country to be supervised carefully by the king and his council in an age of slow transportation and communication. Many decisions had to be made at the bailiwick level. Here officials could legally interpret royal ordonnances in the light of local custom, but many went further. Directives were often honored more in their breach than in their observance. Ordonnance after ordonnance was issued on the same subject, but compliance was far from universal. The growing practice of permitting officials to buy their offices weakened royal control, for these officials could not easily be removed. The performance of the intendant under Louis XIV mitigated rather than solved these difficulties, though it was with the reign of the Sun King that the Renaissance Monarchy came to an end.

The seigneurs, towns, and villages still exercised many governmental functions and this made for decentralization just as during the Middle Ages. The Renaissance Monarchs generally respected the privileges of these individuals and corporate groups, though the gradual extinction of many of the great feudal families and the activities of power-hungry local crown officials were not without affect. The towns resisted with fair success until the reign of Henry IV, even Louis XI being generally content with strengthening the hold of the friendly, local oligarchy in the municipal governments. The villages actually improved their position. In the Middle Ages they had been controlled by their seigneurs, but during the late fifteenth and sixteenth centuries they constituted themselves as legal communities with elected syndics to look after their interests. The influence of the seigneurs waned and that of the crown was hardly felt except in demands for taxes. The survival of the power of independent action by these three groups is amply testified to by their activities during the Wars of Religion and to a lesser extent during the Fronde.[9]

Closely associated with the decentralization of the Renaissance Monarchy was the confusion over boundaries, privileges, rights, and jurisdictions. This situation was not greatly improved until the Revolution itself.

In the remarkable introduction to his *Atlas des bailliages*,[10] Armand Brette showed that the France of 1789 was still far from being a national and ordered state. Her boundaries were nowhere clearly defined except along the sea. Elsewhere much land was in dispute. Territories, independent, or with strong claim to independence, such as the duchy of Bouillon, the principalities of Montbéliard, Bidache, and Salm, the republics of Mandure and Mulhouse, the counties of Sarrverden, Venaissin, and Sault, to say nothing of the papal state of Avignon, existed along the borders and even in the interior of the country. Many of these enclaves owned smaller enclaves in France, and France, in turn, was sometimes in possession of parishes surrounded by these enclaves. There is ample evidence to show that often neither the French king, the foreign lord, nor the local magistrates could agree on what they owned. Foreigners held fiefs in France. In the bailiwick of Gex and perhaps elsewhere they sought to vote in the elections of 1789. Ecclesiastical boundaries rarely coincided with those of the nation and the dioceses of many foreign archbishops and bishops included parishes in France. Two of these prelates were actually elected deputies to the Estates General in 1789. Great fiefs which had long ago reverted to the crown still sought to preserve a theoretical independence. Provence talked of the king as being her count, Béarn had delusions of sovereignty, and because of its presumed independent status, the kingdom of Navarre would no more take part in the Estates General of 1789 than in those convoked during the seventeenth century.

More serious was the confusion about the boundaries of the administrative subdivisions of the kingdom. Nearly every bailiwick had jurisdiction over parishes completely surrounded by neighboring bailiwicks. Frequently parishes and even towns were claimed by rival royal authorities. It was impossible for any magistrate to know exactly what territory he was to administer. In 1789 there were no less than 1,800 divided or contested parishes in France. Many secondary bailiwicks claimed independence from the principal bailiwick to which they had been traditionally attached. There were quarrels about the extent and nature of the justice in countless seigneuries. Each town possessed its special privileges which more often than not differed from those of its neighbor. Royal officials sometimes had only the vaguest idea of the rights of each. The resultant confusion was so great that it was difficult for officials to govern or the law to operate. Disobedience could safely become commonplace, and one is not surprised to find an aristocrat writing after the Revolution that before 1789 people enjoyed "the most complete liberty. One was free to speak, to write, to act with the greatest independence, and one could even defy the authorities in perfect security." [11] Yet the France of 1789 was better organized and more centralized than the France of the Renaissance.

Why did the Renaissance Monarchs permit so much decentralization and confusion? Why did they respect the privileges of their subjects? The answer to these questions lies partly in the fact that the rulers were products of the climate of opinion of their age. They had been taught that a king was responsible for the well-being of his subjects, that to deprive them of their long-recognized privileges was to become a tyrant, and tyranny was as hateful in their age as it had been in the

Medieval period. There was, of course, the possibility that a ruler would recklessly break the bonds of tradition or that he would be so self-righteous that he would interpret every questionable royal prerogative in his own favor. Such kings there occasionally were, but their weakness in character was checked by their weakness in power.

It has generally been assumed that the establishment of a standing army during the reign of Charles VII furthered the growth of royal absolutism, but no one has bothered to prove exactly when and how the new military force was used to subvert existing society or institutions. Indeed, even a casual examination of the size and composition of the new army dispels any illusions as to the possibility that it could have been effectively used against the civilian population. The *compagnies d'ordonnance* or cavalry created in 1445 consisted of only 2,000 *lances* of six men each, and the *francs-archers*, an infantry militia established three years later, numbered but 16,000 men. If we assumed that these two units were kept up to strength, and they certainly were not, the new standing army and militia together would have numbered less than two modern divisions. Even with the rapid transportation and communication of today and the immense superiority of the arms and training of the modern soldier over the civilian population, such a force could hardly subject a population of 15,000,000 persons. It is true that the number of *lances* was later increased, the *francs-archers* were replaced by a more effective infantry, and mercenaries were hired, but the benefits of the improvements were reduced by leaving units under strength and by permitting half the members of the *compagnies d'ordonnance* to be on leave at one time.[12] Thus the armies of the Renaissance were too small to permit a king to hold his subjects in subjection against their will, and this was doubly true because the subjects themselves were well armed. Anne de Montmorency is reported to have brought a retinue of eight hundred horsemen when he came to court in 1560 to attend the council of Fontainebleau, and he certainly could have mustered a much larger force had there been any need. Troyes marched 3,875 men before the Duke of Orléans in 1544, Amiens had 3,000 men in 1597, and many other towns had comparable forces equipped with artillery and munitions.[13] Though a king could have taken the fortified castles of Montmorency and captured any single town in his kingdom, it was cheaper and easier to avoid offending subjects, and any sort of an attack on a large number of nobles or towns was clearly impossible.

Besides the smallness of the royal army and the presence of armed nobles and towns, there was a third check to limit the king's capacity to make war on his subjects: he could not count on the obedience and loyalty of his own troops. The *compagnies d'ordonnance* were composed almost entirely of the local nobility and captained by members of the leading families of the provinces. The *francs-archers* were bourgeois and peasants subject to call in case of war. Such an army was but a small step forward from the feudal levies of the Middle Ages. The mercenaries so numerous in time of war were no more trustworthy. These troops obeyed the orders of the officers who paid them, not those of the king. The Thirty Years War produced many examples of this phenomenon; and the Fronde, which saw armies change sides at the bidding of a Condé or a Turenne, proved all too clearly that France was no exception to the rule. Louis XIV was the first French king to establish effective control over a large military force. Earlier, troops and civilians alike obeyed their monarch if they saw fit, but not otherwise. The army had been created to deal with foreign invaders and bandits. It was also capable of handling one or two rebellious magnates or several disobedient towns, but it could not cope with a large, unwilling population composed of the relatives and neighbors of its members. In the final analysis, the Valois, like the Tudors, had to rely on the support of their more powerful subjects.

The extinction of most of the great feudal houses by the end of the reign of Louis XI has led most historians to see the crown or even the bourgeoisie as emerging into predominance. One writer of the latter school goes so far as to say that the kings "were the gaolers and hangmen hired by the bourgeoisie to over-awe the masses and . . . their quaint trappings and titles were kept as an ornament to the gay world of snobbery." [14] No more erroneous statement has ever been made by a competent historian; for if the kings of the Renaissance had a master, it was the nobility. Indeed, the repeated resurgence of the aristocracy has been one of the dominant factors in European history. Only during the last two centuries has the bourgeoisie as a class been in a position to compete in France, while in some parts of Europe the aristocracy has not yet had its final say.

The extinction of the great feudal houses and the reunion of their domains to the crown during the fifteenth century was paralleled by the growth of a new class of powerful nobles, created it is true by royal favor, but none the less capable of actions dangerous to the crown. What medieval count behaved with greater arrogance before his sovereign than Henry, Duke of Guise, or held more land than Anne, Duke of Montmorency, or revolted with as clear a conscience as Louis, Prince of Condé? It is true that the hold of the great noble on his vassals was somewhat weaker at the dawn of the sixteenth century, but this was largely offset by the advent of the client. Every great noble had a number of lesser nobles and lawyers in his service for whom he found employment and from whom he expected obedience. He used his influence to get many of them appointed to posts in the army and royal bureaucracy, but should he decide to revolt they were expected to support him, not the king.[15] The Reformation added disaffected religious elements who were willing to follow any leader who would uphold their doctrinal views. The collective importance of the lesser nobility also increased. They often elected syndics to watch after their interests and organize their resistance against any who presumed to encroach upon their privileges.

There is no better proof of the powerful position of the nobility in France than that this class alone was able to escape nearly all taxation. In the thirteenth and fourteenth centuries only those nobles who served in the army in accordance with their feudal obligations were excused from making financial contributions. During the Hundred Years War the nobility extended this concession to include their entire order whether military service was performed or not. This privilege does not appear to have been officially recognized, and early in his reign Louis XI talked of collecting taxes from the nobility as well as his other subjects. He soon abandoned the idea and not long before his death he even surrendered his better established right to tax those among them who engaged in trade. Thus the very class that Louis XI is supposed to have destroyed entrenched its privileges during his regime. The clergy was less fortunate and became a regular contributor to the royal treasury before the middle of the sixteenth century.[16]

Much has been said of the increased use of men of bourgeois origin by the early Renaissance French kings, but it is erroneous to say that this phenomenon made for a bourgeois monarchy. In the first place, one cannot assess the influence of a social class on a government merely by counting the number of officials who originated therefrom. A host of bureaucrats and lawyers had less influence upon major decisions than a few landed magnates whose aid the king needed. Great nobles held high places in the councils of Charles VII and Louis XI and received many estates and pensions.[17] The seigneurial nobility often found employment in posts of lesser importance side by side with men of bourgeois descent. Nearly half of the commissioners sent by Charles VII to the provincial estates of central France came from the nobility.[18] Even in the judicial and financial branches of the government where special training was necessary, there were men of this class. The Marillacs were seigneurs in Haute-Auvergne in the fourteenth century, but during the sixteenth some of them moved to Paris, where they became members of Parlement, the *Chambre des comptes,* and held other high government positions.[19] The Rémonds were companions of the Dukes of Burgundy in the Middle Ages, but during the Renaissance they served as officers in the bailiwick of La Montagne. Jean and Pion de Bar embarked on administrative careers under Charles VII, and the former worked his way up to the post of bailiff of Touraine largely through services rendered as a financial official.[20] A significant number of the members of the Parlement at Toulouse came from the nobility,[21] but the more common practice for a young nobleman who preferred the life of an administrator to that of a soldier was to combine a career in the church with one in the government. Here the numbers that can be cited are legion. The military-judicial post of bailiff, sometimes held in the fifteenth century by men of bourgeois origin, became in the Renaissance a virtual monopoly of the noble of the sword, albeit with diminished duties.[22]

The movement of members of the upper bourgeoisie into the ranks of the nobility should not be interpreted as marking the ascendancy of this class. The ranks of the landed aristocracy had been refilled in this manner for centuries, and the noble of late from the town quickly adopted the mores of his new estate. Nineteenth century capitalists frequently began as day laborers, but who would argue that Rockefeller or Carnegie maintained a working-class consciousness during years of wealth? If ever they had had such a consciousness, they soon abandoned it, and so it was with the new nobility of the Renaissance.

The seigneurial nobility was but the most important segment of the privileged class. There was a municipal nobility which increased rapidly in numbers during the fifteenth and sixteenth centuries as a result of individual promotion or election to one of the many town offices that carried with it ennoblement. This municipal nobility and others of the bourgeois patricians slowly consolidated their hold on the town governments. General assemblies of the inhabitants became rarer. The guilds were seldom consulted, even in an advisory capacity. From the reign of Louis XI, who favored this development, the bulk of the French towns were oligarchies in the strictest sense of the word.

During the sixteenth century the position of the municipal nobility and the bourgeois patricians was threatened by local royal officials. These officials, for the most part trained in law and often holders of titles of nobility, were not content with the various lieutenancies and other posts in the bailiwicks, but sought municipal positions as well. The typical official at Dijon prior to 1550 had been a merchant, but in 1588 and 1594 the ratio was fourteen to six in favor of the lawyers. Amiens and other localities underwent similar changes.[23] This development was by no means encouraged by the crown. Indeed, the Renaissance Monarchs made an unsuccessful effort to prevent royal officials from representing the third estate in the Norman provincial estates and the registers of their council are full of orders designed to restrain their aggressive tactics in the towns. In October, 1547, an edict was even issued forbidding them to hold municipal office, but in vain. The crown could not restrain its own officials, and it was only after this date that the greatest influx took place.[24]

The Renaissance Monarchs were no more able to control the actions of their national officials than those of their local ones. Here also one finds titled lawyers and administrators strengthening their positions. It was during the last of the fifteenth century, a time we have often been told that the kings were achieving absolute power, when the Parlement of Paris finally won the right to debate royal ordonnances and to make remonstrances, a development which gave a degree of legislative authority to that body. Even Francis I had difficulty in bridling the court's ambitions.[25] The dynamic element in French society was not the king, nor was it the bourgeoisie, whose ablest members were ever ready to desert their order; it was the seigneurial nobility and the royal officials. A Venetian ambassador reported around 1560 that "the government of the state is entirely in the hands of the nobles, that is to say, the princes and the barons, each of whom is charged by the king to govern a province. Justice is in the hands of men of the long robe who come from the third estate and are for the most part doctors of law." [26] Machiavelli maintained that principalities were governed either by a prince with a body of servants or by a prince and barons; and France, he found to be of the latter type.[27]

To summarize the situation, the government of Renaissance France was decentralized. The boundaries of its inferior jurisdictions were confused, special privileges were poorly defined but still respected, the system of taxation placed the burden on the poor and the weak, the seigneurial nobility opposed the growth of monarchial power, and the army and the bureaucracy were inadequate and difficult to control.

In addition to these practical checks on royal authority, there were theoretical limitations. Even proroyalist jurists placed the king under divine, natural, and fundamental law. Popular tracts during the Wars of Religion, the insurrections under Louis XIII, and the Fronde indicate that in the minds of the vocal elements of the population the rights and privileges of the provinces, towns, and corporations, of the clergy, nobility, and bourgeoisie were also placed beyond reach of the crown. The kings and their councils showed by their actions that they too accepted these additional checks upon their authority. Machiavelli felt sure that the French kings were bound by the law, more so than their fellow monarchs, and that the Parlements would deliver judgments against them. Indeed, Louis XII went to the length of expressly forbidding the Parlements to pay attention to any dispensation he might later grant from an ordonnance he issued in 1499.[28]

The Bases of Monarchial Power

What then were the bases of monarchial power? The answer seems clear. It had both negative and positive roots. On the negative side, discontented persons had difficulty organizing opposition to the king. There were no firmly established institutions at the national level capable of challenging his authority. The size of the kingdom, the slowness of communication, the divergent mass of provincial privileges, customs, and jealousies, the web of family alliances and rivalries reduced the probability of widespread rebellions and opened the way for a royal policy of divide and conquer should a rebellion occur. If kings usually found it best to bargain with their subjects rather than to risk driving them into rebellion, subjects generally preferred compromise to open disobedience.

On the positive side, kings were obeyed when they could get the bulk of the population to support their cause. An aim of *The Prince* was to teach how power could be won and maintained, and no one was more certain than Machiavelli that it was much more important for a ruler of his day to satisfy the people than the military because "the people are the more powerful." To secure the support of the people, the prince was advised to appear to have all the traditional virtues, to tax lightly, and when great feudal dependencies escheated to the crown, to alter neither the laws nor the taxes of the inhabitants.[29] The experienced Commynes likewise advised kings to secure the affection of their people. He praised Charles the Bold for his generosity, his desire to entertain and educate young noblemen, and for the easy access he granted to his servants and his subjects. He criticized Louis XI for trying to conquer the possessions of the dead Burgundian duke instead of seeking to gain his territories by marriage or by winning the affections of the inhabitants.[30] Even Cardinal Richelieu thought that "love is the most powerful motive which obliges one to obey."[31] The Valois were generally successful in their quest for popularity, and a Venetian ambassador described the devotion of the French people to their king as "a unique thing in the Christian world."[32] Thus the Renaissance Monarchy in France, as in England, relied more on popular support than on military power. It is no coincidence that the most popular rulers of the period were often the strongest.

The Renaissance Monarchs were supported by their subjects for a number of reasons. They were God's anointed rulers to whom obedience was taught by the Church. They were the restorers of order after a long period of warfare marked by all the horrors of pillaging and murdering by undisciplined soldiers. There was no safe, logical alternative to their rule however much town and noble alike might be opposed to further increases in royal power. Indeed, the late Valois–early Bourbon rulers accurately sensed the feelings of the people and were ever ready to support and protect the peoples' privileges even against their own officials. The registers of the king's council are full of instances of their overruling subordinates who were overzealous in extending royal, and incidentally their own, power at the expense of privileges of communities and individuals. Only when a noble, a town, or a province failed in its duty to the king were its rights likely to be infringed upon by the crown.

There was a degree of intimacy between the kings and their people which surprised the ambassadors of republican Venice. In 1561 one of them stated that he attributed the devotion of the French to the crown to:

the familiarity which exists between the monarch and his subjects all of whom he treats as his companions. No one is excluded from his presence. Lackeys and people of lowest condition dare to enter the king's private office in order to see everything that happens and to hear all that is said. If one wishes to speak of something important, he must have the patience to find a place where there are not a great many people and then talk in a low voice in order not to be heard. This great familiarity, it is true, makes subjects insolent, but at the same time it makes them faithful and devoted to their kings.[33]

When a midwife complained that the crowd of people gathered to witness the birth of the future Louis XIII got in her way, Henry IV said, "Be quiet, midwife, this child belongs to everybody. Everybody must rejoice in him." [34] We would do well to picture the Renaissance Monarch as the "first gentleman" of France rather than the "Sun King." The removal of the court to Versailles by Louis XIV was symbolic of a growing separation between the crown and the people, and the return of the court to Paris in 1789 could have had equal importance had an abler man than Louis XVI been the head of the state.

A more tangible way of winning support also lay in the power of the kings. They controlled a vast system of patronage. Most of the highest offices of the church lay at their disposal, and the wealthiest bishoprics and abbeys went to their faithful supporters. Government positions, one of the most lucrative of all forms of employment during the period, found their way into the same hands. Fiefs, patents of nobility, and nearly every type of privilege lay at the disposal of the monarch. He who served the crown loyally and ably often received untold riches. Montmorency, Sully, and Richelieu were only the most famous of those who won wealth and power through loyalty and service. Thousands of lesser names could be added. In an age when prices rose more rapidly than income from most landed estates, royal service often provided the best means for a noble to remain financially solvent.

Representative Institutions as a Basis of Monarchial Power

Representative institutions were also at the disposal of monarchs who sought to maintain their authority through popular support. It may seem strange that kings encouraged and developed assemblies of the estates, but since neither the Medieval nor the Renaissance Monarchs had ever heard of representative government, they could have foreseen no reason to fear or destroy representative assemblies. They regarded these institutions as tools for their use, like their councils and their judicial and financial courts. It is true that the estates sometimes got out of hand, but did not the council and the courts also check the king upon occasion? As long as no one thought that either the council or the estates could govern alone, one was no more dangerous than the other, and both could prove of value upon occasion. The uses of the estates were discovered during the Middle Ages, and strong monarchs like Edward I of England and Philip IV of France did not hesitate to summon large assemblies.

The barons, prelates, and townsmen seemed to have had little desire to attend the newly created national assemblies, and only the strongest rulers could force them to do so. Thus with the collapse of royal authority in Europe during the fourteenth century, there was actually a decline in the use of national assemblies. In their place sprang up countless local and provincial estates: some were organized by the crown as substitutes for the larger assemblies, others were started by feudal magnates or local royal officials, and still others were formed at the initiative of the local inhabitants to arrange for protection against the marauders that always appeared in time of royal weakness. This development was not desired by the kings. When the feudal magnates and deputies were at a national assembly, they were in the king's power; but at the provincial assemblies, the king's commissioners found themselves in the hands of nobles and townsmen who were more likely to make strong remonstrances against governmental abuses than to lend support to the royal cause. Only in England were national ties strong enough to prevent the triumph of provincialism during a time of trouble.

The revival of royal authority at the dawn of the Renaissance brought about a revival of the use of national assemblies at the insistence of the rulers themselves. Once more they felt strong enough to win formal public approval in large meetings for the innovations, especially taxation, which they thought necessary because of the political, social, economic, and religious changes taking place around them. They had no fear of the assemblies of the estates because these institutions were generally not considered to have any independent power. Indeed the prevailing argument, perhaps put forth by the kings themselves, was that representative assemblies served to increase royal power by enabling the crown to extend its influence into fields of activity ordinarily denied it. This attitude is illustrated by Philippe de Commynes; writing of a proposed invasion of the continent in 1474 by England, he said: "But things move very slowly there because the king cannot undertake such work without assembling his Parliament, which is like our three estates, and, consisting of sober and pious men, is very serviceable and a great strengthening to the king. When these estates are assembled, he declares his intention and asks his subjects for an aid. . . ." [35] According to Commynes the English Parliament did not decrease the power of the king by preventing him from levying an aid without consent. Rather Parliament increased his power by making it possible for him legally to obtain money beyond his ordinary revenue. In the same spirit Henry VIII declared to the Commons in 1543: "We at no time stand so highly in our estate royal as in time of Parliament, wherein we as head and you as members are conjoined and knit together in one body politic. . . ." [36]

In Germany, during the thirteenth century, power had passed from the emperor to the princes. During the fourteenth century the local estates came between the princes and their subjects. The latter half of the fifteenth century, however, saw a revival of the authority of the princes which provided a counterbalance to the power and divergent interests of the local estates.[37] These princes sought to persuade their subjects to abandon their narrow provincialism by creating single representative institutions for all their lands to be used as instruments "for welding together the haphazard conglomerations of domains, fiefs, counties and lordships, which were the legacy of the Middle Ages, and for restoring political unity; by forcing the separate estates to accept their position as members of one body politic, the princes created in Germany the unity of the territorial state." [38]

Nowhere can this process be seen more clearly than in the territory of the fifteenth century Burgundian dukes. When these magnates sought to become national sovereigns, they were faced with the problem of unifying many provinces which they ruled as feudal lords and not as king. The inhabitants of these provinces were bound together neither by a common language nor by common traditions. They sought only local independence. Nevertheless, the problems which faced the dukes of Burgundy were little worse than those of the neighboring Germanic princes, and they were tackled in much the same manner. The Burgundian dukes sought to strengthen their hold on the various provinces in two ways: by increasing their own authority within each province and by establishing central institutions over provincial ones. A Privy

Council was formed to look after political affairs. A Parlement was established as the highest court of justice for the provinces.[39] In addition, an Estates General was created which "not only gave the prince an opportunity to deliberate with his subjects as a whole; but it also provided the most potent of the means of unification which had brought together the seventeen Burgundian provinces." [40] The duke could appear in the Estates General before the deputies from the various towns and provinces to explain his policy, point out the need for common action, or indicate why taxes were necessary. The very existence of an Estates General weakened the power, influence, and prestige of provincial estates and furthered the unification of the various ducal lands.[41]

Spain furnishes another good example of the use of national assemblies by the Renaissance Monarchs. Ferdinand and Isabella used the Castilian Cortes to break the power of the nobles, after which they sought to avoid summoning that body because its long and glorious tradition made it a real threat to royal authority. However, between 1497 and 1516 Ferdinand had to convoke the Cortes twelve times to get money for his foreign wars.[42] The attitude of his successor was somewhat different. Charles V, through his experience in the Low Countries, was well acquainted with the various uses of the estates. Like his Burgundian ancestors he sought to make them his tool. He freely granted to the Castilian Cortes the right to appoint two deputies to watch over the fulfillment of his promises to that assembly. He tried to get the Cortes to collect taxes. Several times he sought to get the privileged orders to accept their share of the burden of taxation—a step which, if taken, would have greatly strengthened that body. Charles often explained his policy to the Cortes in hopes of winning the support of the Spanish people for his numerous projects. His attitude toward Aragon is also illuminating. This kingdom had three Cortes, those of Valencia and Catalonia as well as of Aragon proper. To help solve the problem of particularism, Charles nearly always summoned the General Cortes of all three kingdoms together in preference to holding separate meetings as had usually been done in the past.[43] His successors continued this practice and the process of centralization was finally completed in 1709 when Philip V convoked the General Cortes of Aragon with that of Castile. Only Navarre was able to retain its provincial Cortes throughout the eighteenth century.[44]

Philip II followed much the same policy as his father in both Aragon and Castile. It is true that he sought to diminish the privileges of the Castilian Cortes, but it is none the less a fact that he made full use of this institution. He not only summoned it frequently, but he kept it in session for long periods of time. The Cortes of 1579, 1583, and 1588 averaged over two years in length, while the Cortes of 1592 was still in session when he died in 1598.[45]

The part played by the national assembly in the establishment of the Renaissance Monarchy in England is well known. That country was already sufficiently centralized so that its Parliament did not have to participate in the struggle against provincialism to the degree necessary on the continent. However, Henry VIII made full use of Parliament in his fight against the supranationalism of the papacy.

Sweden furnishes another excellent example of how the Estates Generals served as the tools of the Renaissance Monarchs. There the Riksdag was used

by the nationalistic kings and regents of the fifteenth century in their struggle against the union with Denmark. After that struggle had ended in the emancipation of Sweden and the elevation of Gustav Vasa to the throne in 1523, the Riksdag was co-opted by the monarchy to give weight to attacks upon its enemies. It assisted Gustav Vasa to carry through the Reformation; it strengthened his position by making his throne hereditary; and it countenanced Erik XIV's savage persecution of his opponents among the nobility.[46]

The neighboring kings of Denmark also found a national assembly useful, and in 1536 Christian III summoned the Rigsdag at Copenhagen to accept the Reformation.[47]

The great feudal nobles of France, like their counterparts in the Empire, sometimes created Estates Generals to aid in the unification of their domains. The same Dukes of Burgundy whom we have seen using representative assemblies to unite their provinces in the Low Countries also sought to unite their southern lands by joining the estates of Charolais, Mâconnais, Bar-sur-Seine, and Auxerre with that of the duchy of Burgundy thereby forming the Estates General of Burgundy.[48] Near the close of the fifteenth century the House of Foix-Navarre brought together the estates of Béarn, Marsan, and Gabardan with those of Foix, Bigorre, and Nébouzan to form an Estates General for its French fiefs.[49]

It would have been surprising if the French kings had regarded representative assemblies in a manner different from their fellow monarchs, and they did not. The reign of Charles VII which marked the beginning of the Renaissance Monarchy in France also saw a revival in the use of large representative assemblies. Unfortunately, the French Estates General did not fulfill its original promise and Charles VII abandoned the institution. Louis XI and his successors usually preferred to rely on assemblies of the towns and other consultative groups. The Wars of Religion saw a second revival of the Estates General, but once more the national representative institution failed to become permanent; and the cessation of its meetings during the reign of Louis XIII coincided with the increased use of a new means to control public opinion, the printing press. It is perhaps more than a coincidence that the generation of this monarch saw both the last meeting of the Estates General until the eve of the Revolution and the appearance of a government controlled annual news journal and a newspaper. The modern means of influencing the people replaced that of the Renaissance. This step, along with the separation of the king from his people by the elaborate ritual of the court, the growing power of the administrative nobility, and the creation of a large army under effective royal control, marked the end of the Renaissance Monarchy of France. It had been formed by Charles VII and Louis XI, and in the seventeenth century, it decayed until, with the reforms of Colbert, one can say that few vestiges were left. The monarchy that followed did not rely on popular support; and for that reason, perhaps, it was to die a violent death.

But before we speak further of the decline of representative assemblies in France, we must study the role they played during the great age of the Renaissance. The story begins with Charles VII.

TWO

Charles VII and the Estates

Charles VII

The character of Charles VII is an enigma. As a youth he was weak, indolent, and extravagant. He lacked self-confidence and determination. No one could have been further from being the dynamic leader needed to meet the emergency which confronted the Valois dynasty. As Charles grew older, however, a modest degree of confidence, energy, and wisdom came to him; and it is difficult to decide whether he or his ministers were responsible for the actions of the government. It is not clear whether he was the first and greatest builder of the Renaissance Monarchy in France or whether he was merely the "well-served." [1]

The influence of the young prince, or his advisors, began to be felt in 1417 when, at the age of fourteen, he assumed the title of lieutenant general of the kingdom, his father being too insane to rule. Later, he became regent. When his father died in 1422, he became king. The early years were ones of great trials for France. The old king, Charles VI, was mad. His wife, Isabella of Bavaria, was notoriously immoral. Rival factions of great nobles sought to control the government, which was long damned by an impoverished people for its dishonest and inefficient administration. As if these evils were not enough, a young, ambitious, and capable Henry V of England had already proved his ability by winning a great victory at Agincourt and was seeking to make good his claim to the crown of France. The Hundred Years War had entered its most serious stage and the Valois dynasty seemed near extinction.

By 1418 France was divided into three sections. The first, or western section, including Normandy, Picardy, the Île-de-France, and most of Guyenne, was governed by the English. The second lay along the northern and eastern borders of the country and was governed by the Burgundian dukes who, after the death of Charles VI in 1422, gave a nominal allegiance to the English king. What remained stood by Charles, and with these lands in central and southern France as a base, the monarchy was reconstituted.

Few princes had ever been faced with a more difficult situation. Charles had neither the experience, the prestige, nor the qualities of leadership necessary to rally those who wanted to expel the English. To reconquer the northern and western provinces he needed a large army, and to have an army he had to have money. The remaining crown lands provided little revenue. The aides had to be renounced in 1418 to meet a comparable act by his Burgundian rivals.[2] Only the taille remained, and to increase that tax enough to compensate for the loss of the aides and the revenue normally drawn from the lands held by the English and the Burgundians was a difficult task. To make matters worse, his provincially-minded subjects preferred looking after their own well-being to working for the common good.

At first Charles and his advisors displayed little imagination. With Paris in the hands of the English, they decided to place some of the institutions of the central government in Bourges and the remainder in Poitiers. The former became one of the more frequent residences of the wandering monarch and the usual seat of his council and the *Chambre des comptes;* the latter became the headquarters of his Parlement and *Cour des aides.* Charles was fortunate in having many of his father's officials offer him their services, but even with their experience, he was unable to prevent the decentralization of his already mutilated domain. In 1420 he was forced to create at Toulouse a separate Parlement for Languedoc and Guyenne because of "the great perils" of travel. Although this body was abolished in 1428, it offered an ominous sign that sooner or later other sovereign courts would have to be divided. Another indication of decentralization was the decision to discontinue the regional estates. After a regional assembly at Limoges in May, 1418, for Poitou, Saintonge, Limousin, Périgord, Angoulême, and La Marche, Charles turned for a period of three years to the provincial estates exclusively. One or more separate meetings of the estates of Dauphiné, Languedoc, Auvergne, Limousin, Touraine, and La Marche were held during this period. In each instance, financial aid or military assistance was asked to meet the needs of the newly organized government.[3]

In January, 1421, decentralization was halted; and on the advice of an assembly of princes, prelates, barons, and other notable persons, the dauphin convoked the Estates General to meet at Clermont in Auvergne in May of that year. To understand why Charles turned to an assembly of the estates of his kingdom in 1421, one must review the use that had been made of similar meetings in the past.

The Medieval Estates and Taxation

The late Capetians summoned representative assemblies because both legal theory and practical politics required them to do so. All of them, including Philip IV, were constitutional kings who ruled according to law. Feudal custom had required that the magnates' consent be obtained for important or unusual acts. The Roman Law principle of *quod omnes tangit, debet ab omnibus approbari* not only reinforced this requirement, but actually helped lead its extension to include less important elements of the population when their interests were involved. This could be accomplished only by summoning representative assemblies. The Capetians also found it expedient to use large representative assemblies to rally support for their antipapal policy and for their tax program. Although they were strong kings, neither the Pope at Rome nor the pocketbooks of their subjects could be attacked with impunity. Thus in 1302 Philip IV used the Estates General both to give consent to his antipapal acts and to win support for his policy in this regard.

When it was a question of taxation, the late Capetians sometimes summoned either the deputies from the entire kingdom or those from the provinces in Languedoïl to explain the necessity for a tax, but neither the Estates General nor the estates of Languedoïl supplanted the provincial estates as the ultimate tax consenting institutions. Those who attended the national and regional assemblies often refused to make concessions; and even when they did formally recognize the need of the crown for additional revenue, they could not, or would not, bind their constituents to pay. It was still necessary for the government to negotiate with the provincial estates, the towns, and even the great nobles, in order to get their consent. These negotiations took time. Furthermore, the crown almost always had to reduce the amounts requested of the provincial estates and towns, and to agree to share with the great nobles any tax collected from their domains. Even Philip the Fair concluded that it was easier to gain the Pope's permission to tax the church than to deal directly with the French clergy. In short, in tax matters, large assemblies served as a forum for the king and his principal councilors to explain the need for additional revenue, when propaganda seemed necessary, before summoning the provinces. Probably the Capetians never hoped that their large assemblies could accomplish anything more.[4]

Unfortunately there is no adequate history of taxation and consent under the early Valois; but by the middle of the fourteenth century the estates of Languedoïl had apparently begun to set the amount needed by the king and to specify the nature of the tax, a step forward, if a surprisingly small one, in the light of the numerous requests for money that were made during the English Wars.[5] After consent was given in the Estates General or the estates of Languedoïl, negotiations had to be undertaken with local bodies, for rebates were given by the Valois as by the Capetians. Sometimes the Valois sought preliminary approval in large assemblies; more often they went directly to the provinces for consent, occasionally they felt strong enough to levy a tax on a particular locality without formal approval, on the grounds that it was necessary for the defense of the realm. All depended on the strength of the crown at the moment. For example, after the estates of Languedoïl had voted in December, 1355, a tax on the sale of salt and other commodities, negotiations had to be begun with the estates of Normandy to collect their quota.[6] Or again, when the estates of Languedoïl voted no money in October, 1356, the crown resorted to direct negotiations with the towns and provincial estates with some success.[7] It made no legal difference whether the estates of Languedoïl approved or disapproved a levy, actual consent was given elsewhere.

The reign of Charles V saw little progress towards the formation of a uniform method of gaining consent to taxation. The people did become accustomed to paying. This in itself was an important accomplishment; but when the king died in 1380, the government thought it advisable to assemble the estates of Languedoïl before asking aid from the provincial estates and towns.[8] This revival was short lived. We know of no meetings of the Estates General or of the estates of Languedoïl between 1381 and 1411. Little information has survived concerning the assembly on the last date, but it was followed by a meeting of the estates of Languedoïl in 1413 in which those present refused to vote a subsidy.[9] Thereafter, there was no assembly of a comparable size until that convoked by Charles VII at Clermont in 1421. In a period of over a century, there may have been less than twelve meetings of the three estates of the kingdom or of Languedoïl to discuss taxation, and in no incident has it been proved that the consent granted was regarded as binding by the French people. Always direct negotiations had had to be undertaken with the various localities.

Therefore, when Charles VII summoned the representatives of those provinces that acknowledged him as their king to meet at Clermont in 1421, he reverted to the old practice of asking preliminary approval for a specific tax before going to the provincial estates, towns, and great seigneurs. Probably Charles never dared to hope that the consent of a national or regional assembly would enable him to dispense with local negotiations. There was no historical justification for this expectation, and no evidence has been found to indicate he attempted to bypass the provincial estates on the grounds that consent had already been given. It is more likely that the desperate young prince was persuaded to turn to large assemblies because of their propaganda value, and by this action he inaugurated the most persistent experiment in the use of national and regional representative institutions in France before the Revolution.

Charles VII convoked large assemblies for three purposes: to influence the provincial estates and towns to accept taxation, to consider and ratify treaties, and to advise on domestic matters. Let us first consider the assemblies that were primarily concerned with taxation.

The Estates General and Taxation

Charles made a long and sincere attempt to use large representative institutions in his efforts to get adequate financial support for his government. For nearly two decades he sought some type of assembly through which he might lead, while appearing to follow, public opinion. He tried the Estates General, the estates of Languedoïl, and exclusive reliance on the local and provincial assemblies, but he shifted back and forth as if groping for a solution. Failure to secure the desired results from the large meetings and the growing size of his kingdom eventually caused him to accept the decentralized form of government so characterized by the Renaissance and so desired by his people.

The historian is plagued by a lack of documents on these assemblies. There is no list of the men who attended any of the meetings of the estates during the reign. The brief letters of convocation provide the only knowledge of what provinces and social classes were summoned, and the municipal archives frequently give the only information concerning those who actually attended for the third estate. It is virtually impossible to ascertain the names and status of those who represented the other orders. Frequently, towns and provinces that were summoned sent no representatives.

The letter of convocation in 1421 prescribed that the three estates in all the provinces acknowledging Charles should participate, that is, all save Dauphiné which enjoyed a special status, and evidence shows that deputies were elected in the widely separated towns of Tours, Lyon, Albi, Toulouse, and Narbonne. The two dioceses in Rouergue also sent deputies, but there is no information of who actually attended for the other orders.[10]

Exactly what happened at Clermont is not clear. It is known that the government hoped to get 1,200,000 livres, but only 800,000 were granted, of which 100,000 were to be paid by the clergy and the remainder by the third estate. A large part of the delegation from Languedoc arrived too late to take part in the voting. Those present felt that they were not in sufficient numbers to commit their province, and the south did not agree to contribute until a separate meeting was held at Carcassonne during the summer. The delegates from Rouergue were equally recalcitrant and had less excuse. The vote of the remaining deputies merely set the amount that the crown needed. Approval by the provincial estates, the great towns, and probably the local magnates was still necessary. The estates of Haut- and Bas-Limousin assembled together to approve their share soon after the Clermont assembly. The three estates of Lyonnais rarely met, but the *consulat* of Lyon took the necessary action. Great lords probably consented to the payment of the levy by their towns and peasants, but there is no definite evidence on this particular occasion.[11]

The Clermont experiment must have proved disappointing to the crown. Perhaps, it was because the deputies had voted less than the desired amount, or maybe the individual provincial estates failed to grant their quota of the tax. Perhaps, the whole process had proved too time consuming. Whatever the reason, the government went directly to the estates of Poitou, Limousin, Auvergne, La Marche, and Lyonnais in January, 1422, when money was again needed. In the summer of 1422, similar requests were made to the estates of Auvergne, Haut-Limousin, La Marche, Touraine, and Languedoc and undoubtedly to other provincial assemblies.[12]

In December, 1422, Charles renewed his groping for a more satis-factory means of obtaining financial assistance. He was now king, for his insane father had died, and possibly he hoped that his new title would add weight to his request. He determined to use once more a large preparatory assembly. This time he convoked only the provinces in Languedoïl to meet at Bourges in January. Here 1,000,000 livres were voted; 440,000 were to fall on Languedoïl, 100,000 were to be contributed by the clergy, and the remaining 460,000 were to be furnished by Languedoc, Dauphiné, Quercy, and Rouergue. There is no evidence that deputies from these last four provinces attended the as-sembly or consented to the tax. This strange procedure may be ex-plained by what had happened at the estates of Clermont nearly two years earlier when the delegations from Languedoc and Rouergue had refused to participate even to the extent of establishing the needs of the crown. It was useless to convoke such non-co-operative provinces to a national assembly again, and Charles turned to the estates of Langue-doïl alone to set the total amount of the levy as a preliminary to re-questing all the provinces, both in Languedoïl and in the south, to con-sent to their share.[13]

Armed with the moral claim for 1,000,000 livres, Charles began to negotiate with the provincial estates. In February, 1423, the three estates of Haut- and Bas-Limousin were assembled to approve their share of the tax, the Count of La Marche was given a substantial sum in return for allowing the tax to be collected in his domain, and the town of Lyon won a reduction for itself. The estates of Languedoc met that spring at Carcassonne where the king probably asked for 300,000 livres, but the estates were willing to consent to a tax of only 200,000 livres levied on the third estate and the equivalent of a décime on the clergy. The young king was less fortunate in his dealings with Rouergue. The estates met in May and refused to vote anything because the action taken by the estates of Languedoïl at Bourges seemed to threaten their right of consent. The government capitulated, but in August reconvoked the estates of Rouergue and this time was able to win a grant of all of 4,000 livres. It is not known what action was taken by the estates of Dauphiné or Quercy, but as late as July of the following year the chancellor denied having received any aid from the two provinces.[14]

Charles had to continue his search for an efficient method of getting consent to taxation. In July, 1423, he convoked the estates of Languedoïl, and the session opened at Selles in Berry on the eighteenth of the following month. This time he made no attempt to get the regional assembly to establish the total needs of the government in order to put moral force on the southern provinces. That policy had failed; Charles was content to win from Languedoïl alone a taille of 200,000 livres, and the aides or sales tax on all commodities to be collected for three years. When the provincial estates were later assembled to give their approval, they protested so strongly against the last tax that the government agreed to accept instead an equivalent amount assessed in the manner of the taille.[15]

The amount collected must have proved insufficient, for in February, 1424, Charles VII again ordered an assembly of the estates to meet at Selles. The exact nature of this body is difficult to determine, for the letter of convocation did not specify what provinces were convoked.[16] Two documents refer to a grant voted for "the king our said seigneur by the people of the three estates of his obedience"—a phraseology which suggests that the meeting was a true national assembly, the first since 1421. Two similar statements were made in reference to the payment of deputies.[17] However, the absence of supporting evidence in the archives of the towns in Languedoc raises considerable doubt. It is only certain that those present voted 1,000,000 livres including the aides or equivalents granted for three years at Selles in August, 1423.[18] The provincial estates in Languedoïl gave their consent during the following spring and summer. In May, 1424, the estates of Languedoc and Dauphiné voted a tax, but whether or not their action was related to the grant made at Selles, we are unable to say.[19]

Mystery shrouds the next large assemblies as well. Charles VII ordered the estates to meet at Montluçon in October, 1424; but later the meeting was transferred to Poitiers, and apparently only the provinces from western Languedoïl were represented. A month later a second meeting, this time for the eastern provinces, was held at Riom. Doubtless the separation of the estates was occasioned by the desire of the king to spare the deputies from Lyonnais, Auvergne, etc., the long and dangerous journey to Poitiers insofar as he planned to move eastward shortly himself. Probably both assemblies agreed on setting the total needs of the crown at 1,000,000 livres with the intention that part of this sum would be collected from the unrepresented southern provinces as had been done with the levy voted at Bourges in January, 1423. The estates of Dauphiné and Languedoc were assembled to give consent to their portion.[20]

By the fall of 1425 the financial position of the crown was again desperate. Under the influence of the Constable of Richemont, it was decided to turn once more to the Estates General, and the national assembly was ordered to meet at Poitiers on October 1. The towns of Languedoc did not wish to comply and met elsewhere in November to consent to a levy, and the deputies sent to Poitiers by Rouergue were unwilling to participate in any grant made in so large an assembly so far from home.[21]

Once more the crown had attempted to make use of an Estates General and once more the southern provinces had refused to co-operate. The king had to content himself with getting the representatives from Languedoïl to vote 800,000 francs, of which 100,000 was to be paid by the clergy, 450,000 to be raised by the taille, and the remaining 250,000 by a levy of one-eleventh of the value of all sales of commodities for one year.[22] This last tax aroused so much opposition from the provincial estates when they were asked to give their approval that in April, 1426, the government decided to abolish it in return for an equivalent sum to be collected in the form of a taille.[23]

By the fall of 1426 new funds were needed, but one is not surprised to find that the crown made no effort to assemble the northern and southern provinces together. Indeed, two separate assemblies were ordered for Languedoïl. The first, which consisted of Poitou, Touraine, and other provinces of the center and west, met at Mehun-sur-Yèvre in November; and the second, composed of Auvergne, Berry, Bourbonnais, Forez, Lyonnais, and Beajolais, met at Montluçon the following month. No doubt the king had felt that he could hold two assemblies at no great inconvenience to himself and therefore had decided to spare his subjects as much traveling as possible. The control of the crown over the two meetings is illustrated by the fact that each of them was persuaded to set the needs of the government at the same figure and to agree that the sum should be raised from the entire region by a taille of 120,000 livres and a hearth tax. The crown was less successful when it turned to the provincial estates for approval. At their hands, the hearth tax suffered the same fate as the sales taxes voted in 1423 and 1425, and had to be converted into the taille.[24]

It is highly improbable that a large assembly was held during 1427, but this inactivity was not the fault of the king. In October of that year he decided to make another attempt to bring the deputies of Languedoïl and Languedoc together in a common assembly and ordered representatives from the two regions to meet in the following month at Poitiers. This meeting was postponed several times because of court intrigues and war. Finally, the idea of a national assembly had to be abandoned altogether. The king who needed funds was forced to content himself with smaller assemblies. From the central and western provinces of Languedoïl he won 100,000 livres in a meeting held at Chinon in April, 1428. Presumably there was a similar session for eastern Languedoïl and the estates of Languedoc also met sometime during this period, but there is no evidence that any of these assemblies were used to establish the total needs of the crown.

During the late spring of 1428 another meeting of the Estates General was planned, and the king directed that the three estates of Dauphiné, Languedoc, and Languedoïl meet at Tours in July. This meeting was to have been the largest thus far held during the reign, for it marked the first known instance of the convocation of Dauphiné to meet with the other provinces. Once more the national assembly had to be postponed,[25] but finally, in September, the crown managed to get the deputies together at Chinon.[26]

The inhabitants of southern France had not responded favorably to the demands for a national assembly in 1427 and 1428. Toulouse, for example, had been unwilling to give its delegates full powers to act in the meeting scheduled for Poitiers in 1427, but had instructed them to ask that in the future the estates of Languedoc be held at home. This particularistic attitude was shared by others; for when the national assembly finally did meet at Chinon, the deputies of Languedoc requested the king to respect the promise they claimed that he had made twice before not to order them to assemble outside of their province. Should it be absolutely necessary to break this pledge, the king was asked to abandon the practice of summoning individual ecclesiastics, nobles, and towns. Instead he was requested to have the provincial estates elect "a great and notable embassy from all the estates to go to him together, each at the expense of his estate; for when one is convoked individually, it is impossible to travel together, and furthermore the expense is unbearable, especially for the seigneurs of the church and the nobles." [27] This last statement reflected the deputies' desire to travel in large numbers for security, if travel they must, and especially to avoid the expense of long journeys outside their province. Provincialism was demonstrated at the same time by the request that the Parlement established in the province in 1420 be maintained, a petition that the king did not allow, for the union of the estates of Languedoc and Languedoïl at Chinon was marked by an edict reuniting the Parlements of the two areas. For the first time in eight years Charles had a single sovereign court of justice for his domains.

Rouergue was even less enthusiastic about national assemblies. The deputies from Rouergue refused to take part in the deliberations at Chinon in 1428. They stated in no uncertain terms that if the king wished a subsidy from them, he must convoke their provincial estates. In desperation, Charles did so in December and was rewarded by the paltry sum of 6,000 livres. There is no evidence that Dauphiné participated in the estates of Chinon, but the estates of Dauphiné met in September of that year.[28]

The national assembly at Chinon was not a complete failure. The king won the equivalent of a décime from the clergy and 500,000 livres from the lay estates, two-fifths of which was to come from Languedoc. No special session appears to have been held later in that province to give consent, the vote at Chinon being considered final. It would be easy to exaggerate this apparent triumph over provincialism. The representation from Languedoc at Chinon was complete enough to be considered a true assembly of her estates, albeit meeting outside the province. Some historians have argued that the estates of Languedoc and Languedoïl deliberated separately at Chinon, and there is no doubt that the deputies from the south were careful to defend their privileges. Not only did they ask that in the future they be assembled only in Languedoc, but also they won a promise from the king that no taxes would be levied on them without the consent of their estates.[29]

A period of about two years followed in which our knowledge of the assemblies of Charles VII is grossly insufficient. The towns of Languedoc believed the king intended for the Estates General to meet in March, 1429, and they planned to assemble together to name deputies to save the expense of individual delegations. This meeting of the Estates General was never held, perhaps because of the protest of the estates of Languedoc against sending deputies outside their province. It is more likely, however, that the towns of Languedoc misinterpreted the directives, and that the king had no intention of holding another national assembly so soon.[30] Not until March, 1431, was there another meeting of even the three estates of Languedoïl.

The absence of large assemblies between September, 1428, and March, 1431, may be readily explained. This period saw the first great victories of Charles VII and his triumphant coronation at Reims. He had neither the time nor the need to hold large meetings, for when "the subsidies voted by the estates of Chinon were exhausted, Charles VII, still under the prestige of the marvelous campaign of Reims, thought he could bypass the Estates General and send commissioners to the provinces to treat directly with the provincial estates concerning the levy of a new tax." [31] There is ample evidence that provincial assemblies were held and that the idea of consent to taxation was by no means lost during these years or the three that followed.[32]

Little is known of the assembly of the estates that finally did meet at Poitiers in March and April of 1431 except that an ordonnance was issued at its request and 200,000 livres were voted. This grant was later approved by the provincial estates. A second meeting took place at Amboise the last of November where a levy on merchandise entering and leaving the towns was granted, but later converted into the taille as a result of the strong protests of the municipalities.[33]

Near the end of 1432, Charles VII decided to make still another attempt to use the Estates General, but the meeting which was to have taken place at Poitiers on February 20, 1433, had to be postponed for unknown reasons.[34] The three estates of Languedoïl did meet in September and October of that year at Tours. A taille of 40,000 francs and a hearth tax of five sous to be collected for six months were levied. This last assessment proved unpopular, and at the request of the provincial estates was changed into the taille.[35] In August, 1434, the king again held a meeting of the three estates of Languedoïl at Tours where a subsidy of 40,000 livres was voted.[36]

Two months later, Charles VII returned once more to the idea of holding the Estates General, and he ordered the people of the three estates of Languedoc and Languedoïl to meet him at Montferrand in Auvergne in December. This meeting was postponed until January and finally abandoned altogether.[37] Probably the change in plans was occasioned near the end of January by the necessity of the king to move to Poitiers where a hasty attempt was made to bring the three estates of western Languedoïl together. The eastern portion of the region was ordered to appear before the king at Issoudun in April, 1435, but the assembly was almost certainly not held. At Poitiers a poorly attended meeting voted a taille of 120,000 livres and consented to the aides for four years, but the protests of the provincial estates caused this second tax to be changed to the taille.[38]

In February, 1436, the king returned to the problem of financing his government. The estates of Languedoïl met at Poitiers, agreed to a taille of 200,000 livres, and repeated the performance of the preceding year of voting the aides. There is some doubt, but the estates probably intended to let the king have the aides for three years. In May, Charles followed up this success by winning a similar grant at Paris from the region north of the Seine and the Yonne.[39]

This time Charles was in a stronger position than on the previous occasions when he had obtained the consent of the regional estates for the aides. He had recently made peace with the Duke of Burgundy; eventual victory over the English was now assured. He must have hoped that his new prestige would help his negotiations with the provincial estates. It may have, but he was only partly successful. Some of the provincial estates were prevailed upon to accept the aides, but others changed the tax to the equivalent. Where the aides were established, however, they were often collected without the consent of the provincial estates; nor did Charles ever bother to appeal to the estates of Langue-doïl for a renewal of the grant.[40] To the revenue from the domain and the *gabelle,* he had added the aides as a source of income he could levy at will, except in those provinces where the provincial estates had emerged victorious.

Great as was the victory of the young king, he had by no means freed himself from the problem of getting consent for taxation. He derived only 3 per cent of his income from the domain and 9 per cent from the *gabelle* in 1461, the last year of his reign. This revenue he had always controlled, and now he had added the aides which, including the equivalents, amounted to 30 per cent of the royal income. The remaining 58 per cent came from the taille.[41] As long as the estates controlled this tax, the crown could not become financially independent.

The progress made toward financial independence in the north and center of the kingdom in 1436 was not fully duplicated in the south. A subsidy which did not include the hated aides was won from Dauphiné in August, and early the following year the king presided over an assembly of the estates of Languedoc at Béziers in which the aides were voted for a definite period of three years.[42]

No more large assemblies of the estates appear to have taken place until August, 1439, when the king ordered the prelates, barons, and representatives of the towns of his kingdom to meet at Paris. Because a plague broke out in that city, the meeting was transferred to Orléans where the sessions were held from about October 20 to November 2. This assembly has often been considered the most important that took place during the reign of Charles VII. A completely erroneous theory has developed that the estates at this time consented to the creation of a permanent standing army and voted a permanent taille for its support, that the king was thereby freed from the necessity of getting consent for taxation, and that national representative institutions ceased to be convoked except in rare emergencies. Simple and convenient as is this explanation of the decline of national representative assemblies in France, it contains scarcely a word of truth, as Antoine Thomas pointed out as early as 1878.[43]

The letter of Charles VII convoking the estates did not even mention the need for a subsidy or a standing army. The towns were only asked to give their deputies powers to discuss the proposed peace with England, almost certain proof that the crown had no intention of asking for any radical change in financial policy.[44] Strong peace parties existed in both the warring kingdoms, and negotiations had been intermittently carried on near Calais during 1439. By late summer it had become apparent that France could have peace only if Normandy, Guyenne, Calais, and Guines were surrendered in full sovereignty to the Lancastrians. Before making such a momentous decision, Charles VII had decided to assemble the three estates to get their opinion, and more important, to rally support for whatever policy he had resolved to follow.[45]

It was for this purpose that the princes, lords, prelates, and deputies of the towns assembled at Orléans near the end of October, 1439. There has been some controversy as to what regions were represented. The letters of convocation specifically stated that it was the notables of the kingdom who were convoked, not just those of Languedoïl. The Ordonnance of Orléans refers to the presence of the three estates of the kingdom, and Charles VII later reproached the town of Lunel in Languedoc for not having sent deputies. But no evidence has yet been found to show that the bourgeoisie of Languedoc or Rouergue even assembled to choose representatives, though some ecclesiastics and nobles from these provinces may have come to Orléans. The newly freed towns to the north of the Loire were more obedient and the Dukes of Orléans, Burgundy, and Brittany and the Count of Armagnac sent ambassadors, but there was no other representation from their domains.[46]

At the opening assembly the chancellor explained the nature and progress of the peace negotiations and copies of the articles of the treaty were given to those present so that everyone would be fully informed. For more than a week the estates debated the question of peace or war without arriving at a decision. During the course of the debate, the sufferings of the people from marauding soldiers came under discussion, and out of this emerged those portions of the Ordonnance of 1439 which dealt with the army. The purpose of these articles was to restore discipline, not to create a permanent army. Discussion of the sufferings of the people led to the question of taxation; articles in the ordonnance forbade the nobility to interfere in the collection of royal subsidies, to take part of what was collected, or to levy the taille or aides on their own subjects without the consent of the king. Nothing whatsoever was said about a permanent taille, and only 100,000 livres were voted.[47]

The three estates at Orléans failed to come to a decision on the proposed peace, and Charles ordered the representatives of his kingdom to meet again in February, 1440, at Bourges to make a second attempt to reach an agreement. He evidently anticipated a revolt by certain powerful seigneurs if he failed to rally popular support behind the course of action he had determined upon. This fear was realized when, early in February, some of the great feudal magnates reached an accord at Blois, and the dauphin, Louis, lent his adherence. This revolt, known as the Praguery, prevented the king from keeping his appointment with the estates. The deputies waited and waited. Their number was great. We know that there were twenty-seven from the third estate of Languedoc alone; doubtless there were many from Languedoïl and the newly liberated territory north of the Loire as well. Finally, early in August the king gave most of them permission to go home. The deputies of the clergy may have remained another month to consent to a tax, and the deputies from Languedoc who had come so far were especially invited to meet the king at Saint-Pourçain. On their way, they were brutally attacked and robbed. This dismal event marked the final episode of the last known meeting of the Estates General until 1468.[48]

We are thus brought face to face with one of the most critical problems in the constitutional history of France. Why did Charles VII, after nineteen years of continual use, abandon the large representative assemblies? His motive could hardly have been fear. The assemblies had made no effort to control the government, and he could not have foreseen the long-range threat of the meetings to the crown, a threat that the Tudor monarchs failed to realize a century later. He had convoked the Estates General and the estates of Languedoïl during his early years of weakness; why should he drop these institutions when he became strong?

Charles VII did offer an explanation. Early in 1442 a group of rebellious great nobles met at Nevers where, in the hope of winning popular support, they criticized the king for levying the taille without convoking "the princes, prelates, barons, and people of the three estates of the kingdom." [49] The king replied that he had sought consent whenever possible, but that he had the right to levy the taille on his own authority because of the emergency in which the kingdom found itself. Then he added significantly, "it is not necessary to assemble the three estates to levy the tailles because it is only a burden and an expense to the poor common people who have to pay the cost of those who attend. Several seigneurs have requested that we cease to make such convocations and are content for these reasons that we send commissioners to the *élus* in accordance with the good pleasure of the king." [50]

Was this the real reason that led Charles to abandon the Estates General and the estates of Languedoïl? In part, yes; he must have been particularly embarrassed to have kept the deputies waiting at Bourges for six months in 1440. His concern led him to transfer the burden of the payment of the delegation from Languedoc to their provincial estates who could bear it better than the individuals or the towns. [51]

Nevertheless, one cannot say that the large assemblies were unpopular with all the people. Rather it seems that in some areas they were favored, in some areas they were not. The inhabitants of the outlying provinces tended to dislike them. Charles VII had convoked the Estates General on at least nine occasions, but in several instances the towns of Languedoc had been unwilling to name deputies, the record of Rouergue was no more impressive, and Dauphiné may never have answered the summons. [52]

The provincial attitude of the deputies from Languedoc and Rouergue was still more apparent in the very limited number of occasions they did attend the Estates General. The former pleaded not to be convoked outside of their province, and only in 1428 did they agree to a tax while in the national assembly. Rouergue was even less co-operative and proudly refused to participate in the discussions. Indeed, the crown could not even get Rouergue to hold joint assemblies with the estates of Languedoc in 1424 and 1433. [53] The mystery is not so much why Charles VII eventually abandoned the idea of summoning these provinces to the Estates General, but rather why he persisted so long in calling them.

The inhabitants of the various provinces of Languedoïl had proved much more co-operative. They had usually come when summoned, although it must be confessed that their record was far from perfect. Charles VII felt it necessary to threaten those who failed to attend the estates at Selles in 1424, and the deputies of Tours waited at Loches in 1432 nine days after the appointed date for the estates before leaving because "the seigneurs and good towns had not come." [54] But on the other hand, when once assembled, the estates of Languedoïl had always voted at least part of the financial assistance requested. Many persons may have regretted the necessity to pay their own or a deputy's expenses, but there is no proof of strong opposition by the people of this region to these assemblies.

There is even evidence that failure to hold large assemblies of the estates to give initial approval to taxation caused some criticism in

Languedoïl. In 1435 the deputies of Tours arrived at Poitiers after the termination of a meeting of the estates of western Languedoïl in which a grant had been made. Before the king and his council, they were asked to give their adherence. After a night of reflection, the deputies refused, saying that if the king needed money, he should assemble the estates "of all his obedience." [55]

In November, 1441, the estates of Auvergne complained that their share of the levy on Languedoïl had been increased in spite of the desolation of their province. They petitioned that no more than their former quota be asked of them in the future. Implied, at least, was the desire to return to the earlier procedure of having the estates of Languedoïl give initial consent to taxation, a desire which the king recognized and promised to respect, though without result.[56]

The French people then were so divided that there was no overwhelming opinion for or against the institution, and the king may well have been persuaded that a majority of his subjects were actually opposed. It is not unlikely that some royal officials sought to bring him to this view. The estates could hardly have been popular with many of this class, for the deputies never failed to call the attention of the king to the administrative abuses in the kingdom. There was no way officials could prevent individual complaints from reaching royal ears, but they could, at least, stop a collective attack by the three estates by advising against their convocation and advocating that it was the king's privilege to levy what taxes he pleased, especially in time of emergency. Commynes later reported that there was such talk among officials, but he was careful to add that he had never heard a king voice a like opinion.[57] Thus the complaints of many of his subjects about having to send deputies to the Estates General, added to the advice of some officials, may have influenced Charles to change his policy, but circumstantial evidence points to an additional factor. Charles VII decided to abandon the Estates General and the estates of Languedoïl because they were no longer necessary.

During the early years of the reign, the war had placed a heavy burden on the treasury at a time when the income from the royal domain was almost nil. Money was needed, but the prestige of the crown was too low for Charles to go directly to the provincial estates as often as necessary without first carefully preparing public opinion. This could best be done by bringing together local leaders and deputies from as large an area as possible to give the royal councilors a chance to explain the financial needs of the government and to ask for aid. The estates fixed the amount to be levied and each province was assessed its share. The provincial estates were thus placed on the defensive because the clergymen, noblemen, and burghers who attended the national and regional assemblies also participated in the smaller meetings. They and their constituents whom they had bound by their action were morally obligated to vote something.

Unfortunately for the crown, this obligation was only partially fulfilled. The provincial estates and towns were rarely willing to grant all the money asked of them, and the great seigneurs were apt to demand a share of any royal levy collected from their domain. The estates of both Haut- and Bas-Limousin did not hesitate to insist on a reduction of their share of a tax levied with the consent of the estates of Languedoïl meeting at Bourges in 1423. The estates of La Marche won a reduction of 2,500 livres from a total of 12,000 levied on them by the estates of Languedoïl meeting in Poitiers in October, 1425. The three estates of Auvergne voted only 30,000 of the 45,000 livres required of them by the grant made to the king by the estates of Languedoïl in April, 1431. The estates of La Marche got a 20 per cent reduction of its share of the grant accorded in 1433 by the estates of Languedoïl and other examples could be given.[58]

In a few parts of France the provincial estates did not have the right of consenting to taxation, but here the crown found it necessary to negotiate directly with great towns of the region before collecting a tax. Lyon provides a good example of this situation. The three estates of Lyonnais were rarely summoned, and the crown simply divided the levy on that province between the town and the *plat pays*. The former almost invariably protested during the first two decades of Charles's reign and, usually alone, but occasionally in conjunction with the *plat pays*, negotiated with the crown for a reduction in the size of the levy. Rarely during this period did Charles fail to give at least partial satisfaction.[59]

The king also had to contend with the great seigneurs, who had to be recompensed when they consented to the collection of a royal tax in their domain. La Marche was assessed 13,000 livres as its share of the tax voted by the estates of Languedoïl in January, 1423, but in return for 8,000 livres, the king surrendered to the Count of La Marche this entire sum and also that due from his seigneuries in Languedoc.[60]

The Estates General and the estates of Languedoïl had proved to be but partially satisfactory instruments to influence public opinion during the early years of the reign, and after the coronation at Reims in 1429 and the reconciliation with Burgundy in 1435, Charles felt strong enough to proceed without their questionable assistance. Between 1436 and his death in 1461, he went directly to the provincial estates and towns for financial aid except for the small grant he won from the estates at Orléans in 1439.

The ease with which Charles was able to abandon the large representative assemblies should by no means be considered a victory for the crown. He would undoubtedly have preferred to win approval for taxation in one large assembly as did his English rival, who was thus able to make negotiations with so many small assemblies unnecessary. Indeed, it was far more difficult for Charles to control the deliberations of the provincial estates and the towns than those of the Estates General. When the representatives of the kingdom met, they were in his power. Persuaded by the royal councilors, impressed by the royal majesty, surrounded by the palace guard, and far from their homes, they rarely mustered sufficient courage to resist the king's desires. In the provincial estates and municipal assemblies, on the other hand, the reverse was true. The king was not present. In his place stood one or more royal commissioners who inspired little awe among the local leaders. There was no council to guide the deliberations and the initiative was seized by the members of the assembly who treated and bargained with their monarch instead of following his lead. Secure in a fortified town or castle, surrounded by their friends, and far from the royal army, they did not hesitate to change the form of a tax, reduce the amount of the levy, or even refuse to vote anything at all. If they granted money, they were likely to request concessions in the same breath. Thus it was the provincial estates and the privileged towns that were the true checks on royal taxation; and if we except the deputies from the southern provinces, the members of the Estates General were reasonably pliable. Charles VII had often persuaded the Estates General to vote higher taxes than he had been able to get the provincial estates to accept, and time and again the national assembly agreed to the hated aides only to have the provincial estates refuse to pay this form of tax. Unsatisfactory as the Estates General and the estates of Languedoïl must have been, they would have been preferred to the provincial estates if they could have given final consent to taxation.

Charles VII, like the monarchs of the late Middle Ages, sought unified institutions for his multitude of sovereignties, and the assemblies of the estates were by no means an exception to this rule. His decision to abandon the large representative institutions in favor of the provincial estates was but one aspect of the policy adopted around 1440 of giving into the particularistic desires of his subjects. Each new province conquered by his armies brought new demands for local autonomy. The system of centralization proved unworkable or at least cumbersome. "The kingdom was so large that in most areas, such as justice, finance, and accountancy, it was impossible to deal with everything simultaneously at Paris. It was necessary to create elsewhere other sovereign courts and other departments which would bring the subjects nearer to the royal administration." [61] This movement was hindered by the egotistic opposition of the officials in power, and it took shape only as the necessity became overwhelmingly apparent. Even before 1435, steps had been taken to subdivide the administration of the aides, and the domain was soon to be treated in a like manner. A *Cour des aides* was established at Montpellier in 1437 and a Parlement at Toulouse in 1443 for Languedoc. A similar division of the two courts was later made to satisfy the demands of other historic provinces, and the *Chambre des comptes* suffered a similar fate. Indeed, it was the simultaneous decentralization of the royal administration, the sovereign courts, and the representative institutions that marked the dividing line between the Medieval and the Renaissance Monarchy in France.

The Provincial Estates and Taxation

The decision of Charles VII to abandon his attempt to use the Estates General and the estates of Languedoïl to give preliminary consent to taxation only meant that he went directly to each province and town for help without preliminary fanfare or publicity to prepare public opinion. Occasionally the government had bypassed the larger assemblies before 1440 because of an urgent need for money, an obviously justifiable request, or a feeling that the propaganda effect of the larger assemblies could safely be dispensed with, as a result of the temporary enhancement of the crown by military and diplomatic victories. In 1422, between 1429 and 1433, and between 1437 and 1439 the king had gone directly to many of the provincial estates in Languedoïl for aid; this was his habitual method of getting grants from Languedoc, Dauphiné, and Rouergue. On three occasions Charles asked the town of Lyon for assistance before 1436 without the prior consent of the estates of Languedoïl. Two requests were for funds to ransom important soldiers, and the third was to provision Orléans in 1429.[62]

The failure of the crown to get the preliminary consent of the Estates General or the estates of Languedoïl was of no great concern to the provincial estates. The only change was that the prelates, nobles, and deputies of the towns were spared the expense of a journey to the national or regional assembly, and the king and his council decided royal needs without formally asking their advice. Only the three estates of Auvergne are known to have offered any objection to the new procedure. The provincial estates were still asked to give their consent to the taille. If the amount levied on them seemed too large, they could and did protest. Even little Franc-Alleu, a territory of only twenty parishes, managed to get its share of the taille of 1437 reduced from 700 to 500 livres. The latter figure was almost always requested of her estates from that time. The estates were also free to submit their grievances for royal redress.[63]

Two developments did forebode little good for the provincial estates. The first grew out of the aides voted the king in 1436, and the second resulted from the reduced financial needs of the victorious monarch at the end of the Hundred Years War.

The aides in 1436 were taxes on the sale of food, merchandise, and wine. These taxes by their very nature were generally unpopular, but the method of collecting them was especially disliked. The ordonnance establishing the aides provided that they were to be turned over to tax farmers, and it was widely believed that only a fraction of what these men collected found its way into the hands of the king. This situation troubled the people, for if the royal needs were not satisfied, requests for additional taxation could be expected.[64]

In consequence, there was a strong tendency for the provincial estates to offer the king an equivalent in lieu of the aides. This equivalent usually took the form of a direct tax assessed and collected after the manner of the taille. One is apt to think of the taille as being the most hated of all taxes, but during the fifteenth century it was usually regarded as the least objectionable form of levy. It was collected by the provincial estates or, in the *pays d'élections*, by the *élus*, royal officials whose accounts were carefully audited by their superiors, or by the representatives of the provincial estates. It was presumed that the substitution of the equivalent meant lower taxes because the loss in collection was less.[65]

In 1435 and in his earlier attempts to impose the aides, Charles VII had suffered ignominious defeat, but in 1436 he could add the prestige won from a treaty with Burgundy to the consent of the estates of Languedoïl when he began to negotiate with the provincial assemblies. One by one the provincial estates were cajoled into paying the aides or offering an equivalent in their stead. Basse-Auvergne won a year of grace before accepting the aides. Limousin, La Marche, and Périgord escaped until 1451 when they finally agreed to pay an equivalent. Other provinces in Languedoïl came into line, and when once the aides or the equivalent was agreed upon, they were often collected without further consultation with the estates.[66]

The most famous battle concerning the aides took place in Languedoc. In January, 1437, the provincial estates consented to the hated tax for three years. By 1439, they were already petitioning the king to remove the levy at the appointed date, a request that he failed to grant because of his great financial needs. Probably the estates repeated the petition each time they assembled thereafter, but only for their meeting in October, 1442, is there much information. In that year they once more protested against the aides, and the king, who was then in the south, replied that the assemblies of the estates were harmful and he didn't intend to use those of Languedoïl any more. This statement must certainly have frightened the estates with its faintly concealed hint that their existence was also in jeopardy, but it soon became apparent that they had no cause for fear. A few months later the king bowed to the particularistic desires of his subjects by creating a Parlement at Toulouse, and at the same time he offered to change the aides to an equivalent. The three estates of Languedoc were not again threatened for two centuries; but future kings permitted no reduction in the amount of the equivalent, in spite of many protests.[67]

By judicious concessions, the crown had won a partial victory, and between 1461 and 1493 it got about 65,000 livres annually from the equivalent in Languedoc alone.[68] A small, fixed income had been won that was difficult for the provincial estates to challenge because it was at their request that it had been established. The king had found a welcome substitute for the aides which had been voted under protest for limited periods of time. Perhaps he had insisted on the aides to make the provincial estates happy to accept a less objectionable substitute. Then too, where there were no provincial estates or privileged towns, the aides were collected without consent.

But the total income derived from the royal domain, aides, equivalent, and *gabelle* was insufficient to cover the needs of the government. The taille was still essential. As long as the provincial estates maintained their right to consent to this tax, their life was assured.

At first there seemed to be little possibility that Charles could reduce the taille enough to make the provincial estates willing to disregard their right of consent. In 1445 he actually moved in the opposite direction by placing an additional burden on the realm. To restore order and to protect his subjects against bandits, marauders, and the English, he issued ordonnances establishing 2,000 *lances* of six men each to be garrisoned in and supported by the various provinces. At first the assessment to support the troops was in money and in kind, but after a few years the provincial estates, whose consent, of course, had been requested, won the right to meet the entire burden by a money payment that became known as the *taille des gens de guerre*. The tax was heavy. Auvergne supported 160 *lances* at an annual cost of 59,520 francs in 1449. In addition, the province paid the regular taille of 35,500 francs and aides and *gabelles* amounting to at least 20,000 more. The total figure came to 115,020 francs of which over half went to support the local garrison.[69]

The expense of the army was so great that the provincial estates often sought a reduction in the number of troops allotted to their defense, and by 1451 the favorable progress of the war and the restoration of order enabled the king to grant their request. The number of *lances* in Auvergne was cut by twenty making possible a reduction in the tax of about 7,500 livres. Of far greater importance, Charles abandoned the regular taille altogether. With the approach of peace, the royal domain, aides, and *gabelle* provided sufficient revenue for the government, and the *taille des gens de guerre* supported the army.[70]

The effect of this reform on the people was immense, the total tax burden on Auvergne being reduced by over a third. Small wonder little protest was raised when, in the same breath, the king ordered the *élus* to impose the necessary taxes to support the *lances* without convoking the provincial estates to give consent.[71] The taille to support the army, like the aides some years earlier, had come to be levied by royal command alone.

The relative complaisance with which the inhabitants of Auvergne and other provinces in Languedoïl and the généralité of the Outre-Seine surrendered their right of consent is also explained by the fact that petitions submitted by individuals, towns, and other corporate groups were as apt, or more apt, to be heard favorably by the crown than requests forwarded by the provincial estates. This was brought out clearly by a tax investigation conducted under Charles VIII. It was revealed that in the généralités of Languedoïl and Outre-Seine, where there were no provincial estates, the inhabitants paid the taille at per hearth rates of 19 sous and 27 sous respectively. In Normandy and Languedoc, where the provincial estates had continued to give consent, the taille was collected at a rate of 60 sous, 8 deniers, and 67 sous per hearth.[72] The preference for individual petitions is also illustrated by the attitude of Lyon. When the town was told to elect deputies to go to the estates at Poitiers in November, 1427, some of the other communities in Lyonnais suggested that they choose a delegation in conjunction with the town, but the *consuls* refused—even though one of their number was sufficiently farsighted to point out that they would be stronger if they acted as a unit. The majority thought that they would more likely win special favors if they went separately to the king.[73] It was true that when they had acted with the countryside the year before, the communities had not co-operated fully, but the fact remains that it was easier for the king to make reductions for a single town than for an entire province. Lyon refused to co-operate because she hoped for bigger concessions if she acted alone.

In Limousin and La Marche where there had been no *élus,* the office was created and the newly appointed officials were told to collect the taxes in the same manner as in Auvergne. The estates of central France were not officially disbanded. With royal permission the feudal seigneurs of Auvergne and La Marche occasionally convoked the three estates to vote taxes for their own use. Sometimes the king summoned them to approve a treaty, to elect deputies to the Estates General, or to codify or revise the customary law of the province; but these convocations were exceptional and the last decade of Charles's reign saw a decay in the representative institutions of this region. Unfortunately little is known of the provincial estates in other parts of Languedoïl. We can only assume that they suffered a similar fate. Certainly sessions of the provincial estates of Poitou, Berry, Forez, Touraine, etc. were rarer after 1451.[74]

The right of the great towns to give consent was less jeopardized by the changes during these years. When Lyon received its assessment of the taille from the king during the 1440's, an assembly of the town levied a tax on its citizens to meet the royal demands just as had been done earlier when the three estates of Languedoïl had first given approval. A special taille was instigated in 1445 to support the eight *lances* assigned to the town, but in 1451 the regular taille was virtually abandoned leaving only the tax for the garrison. As a result, the total taille dropped from 6,228 to 3,381 livres. Even so the municipal leaders did not hesitate to try to get further reductions soon thereafter. Thus the municipal governments benefited from these changes without suffering an eclipse like the provincial estates.[75]

The provincial estates outside of Languedoïl that had acknowledged Charles VII fared much better. Languedoc and the other areas to the south did not seem to have had their estates threatened in any way by these changes. Here *élections* had never been established, and the crown generally lacked the fiscal organization to assume the role of tax collector, especially when faced with the opposition of strong provincial estates.

The fate of the provinces reconquered from the English varied. The towns of Champagne had been assembled in 1431 shortly after their liberation from the English, and in 1436, 1437, and 1445–46 there were meetings of the deputies of the towns or the three estates of all or part of the reconquered territory to the north of the Loire. Thereafter, there were no known assemblies of the estates of this region during the reign.[76]

The crown may have considered doing away with the estates of Normandy. Scarcely had the province been reconquered than the king summoned the estates to meet at Rouen and vote 290,000 livres to support the *lances*. Since those who assembled in November, 1450, had voted much smaller sums when the English were their masters, they did not hesitate to grant the crown a mere 75,000 livres. A little later, the *procureur* and several *échevins* of Rouen met the king at Tours where they appear to have accepted an additional levy of 125,000 livres in the hope of getting confirmation of the privileges of the province. For seven years the matter hung in balance. There are no records of any meetings of the estates, but it is known that the taille and the aides were levied and collected. Then, in the spring of 1458, the crown decided to come to terms and the privileges of Normandy were confirmed. Indeed, they were more than confirmed, for in the Charter of 1315 the king had merely promised to levy taxes only in case of necessity, but in 1458 he committed himself to first winning the approval of the three estates of the duchy. That December the estates voted the king over 270,000 livres to support 580 *lances,* repair certain fortresses, and meet various other expenses. For the few remaining years of the reign, the estates met each November or December and at no time voted less than 250,-000 livres for a year. The Normans had learned how to pay for their privileges and their estates were convoked periodically for nearly two centuries.[77]

Nowhere is our ignorance concerning the estates greater than for southwestern France. During the period of English rule, local assemblies of the three estates appear to have come into existence in Bordelais, Bazadois, and Lannes; and they sometimes joined together in common meetings known as the estates of Guyenne. The estates of Armagnac, Agenais, and Comminges do not appear to have participated in these gatherings at this date.[78]

The French reconquest of the region was gradual, but important victories in the early 1440's enabled the government to hold separate assemblies for Armagnac and Agenais in 1443 and 1444 to ask for subsidies to support the *lances*. The crown was met by refusal, but the imprisonment of several *consuls* and the quartering of troops in some of the recalcitrant towns produced a more reasonable attitude. The estates of Armagnac and presumably of Agenais met frequently thereafter to vote the tax for the *lances*.[79] The three estates of Lannes were only asked to defend themselves against the English, and while they balked at even this relatively inexpensive request, there was no armed resistance and the estates continued to be convoked throughout the reign. In 1455 the crown added the request that the local inhabitants agree to pay for the repair of the principal forts in the area. By this time the estates had become accustomed to voting taxes and there is no record of any difficulties arising.[80]

During the campaign to reconquer Bordelais in 1451 Charles promised to respect the privileges of the area, privileges that to the inhabitants at least included freedom from paying the taille and freedom from garrisons, but after the French had been victorious, the king ruled that both the troops and the taille were necessary. A revolt broke out, the English sent assistance, but once more the French armies emerged as victors. This time fewer privileges were promised to the inhabitants, and no mention was made of the role of the estates. There may not have been any more assemblies during the reign.[81]

Charles's policy in regard to the provincial estates had not been consistent. He had reduced their role in central and northern France, but in Languedoc, Normandy, and perhaps Dauphiné and Burgundy, the estates were more firmly entrenched at the end of his reign than ever before. Local circumstances governed his attitude in each case, but as a general rule where the provincial estates were strong and co-operative, they were permitted to survive. Where they were not, they were in jeopardy.

The Estates and Foreign Policy

The Estates General was not only convoked to give preliminary approval of taxation, it was also summoned to advise on foreign affairs and to ratify treaties. This connection between the preparation and ratification of treaties and representative institutions was rooted in both theory and practice. Treaties often involved the cessation of land, but according to feudal law the lord-vassal relation was one of mutual obligation. The king could no more surrender the fief of a vassal to another king without the vassal's consent than the vassal could abandon his lord. Therefore, the transfer of territory—whether fief, town, or province—involved getting the consent of those directly concerned. The plebiscite was by no means a twentieth century innovation. Under the influence of Roman law this limited approach was expanded into the concept of the inalienability of any fundamental aspect of sovereignty, whether fiefs, parts of the royal domain, or prerogatives, because any alienation affecting the public welfare was the concern of all. Should such an alienation seem advisable, it was necessary in accordance to the Roman Law principle of *quod omnes tangit* for the crown to get permission from the estates of the realm.[82]

The concept of the inalienability of sovereignty was clearly enunciated at the assembly of Vincennes in 1329 and was included by Charles V in his coronation oath in 1364. Gradually the principle came to be considered one of the fundamental laws of the French monarchy, although it was by no means universally honored by the French kings who invoked or forgot it as their needs dictated. Nevertheless, a sovereign who desired French territory, was wise to insist that the French king gain the consent of the three estates, in order to prevent him from using the inalienability of the domain as an excuse to revoke the treaty at an opportune moment. By the same token, if a French king found it necessary to make a choice between surrendering part of the kingdom to a foreign prince or continuing a costly war, it was to his advantage to associate his subjects with his decision in order to escape blame if his choice proved to be the less popular one. Wars caused many hardships on the subjects of a prince, but a reduction in the size of the kingdom meant an increase in taxes on what remained. The choice could be a difficult one on which the sovereign could and should demand council.

Another factor that probably led to many demands for the three estates to give approval to treaties grew out of the idea that a king could not bind his successors. Towns and provinces invariably requested a new king to confirm the privileges granted them by his predecessors. Even royal debts might be called into question by a new succession. If treaties were to be perpetual, therefore, they ought to be approved by the three estates and registered by the Parlement of Paris. These precautions were not always taken, but they appeared frequently enough to become a characteristic of the diplomacy of the various Renaissance Monarchies of Europe.

The Treaty of Troyes of May, 1420, provides an example. By its terms Henry V of England and his descendants were promised the succession to the French throne. This agreement was obviously subject to challenge by the excluded dauphin, Charles, and his supporters. The treaty sought to meet this objection by insisting that the consent of the three estates of the two kingdoms be given in order to insure that "concord, peace, and tranquility . . . be perpetually observed in the future. . . ." [83] The treaty further stipulated that neither the mad Charles VI of France, the English king, nor the Duke of Burgundy would make any peace or other agreement with the dauphin without the advice and consent of the other two rulers "and the three estates of the two kingdoms. . . ." [84] About six months after the treaty was signed, the three estates of that part of the country controlled by the English and Burgundians met at Paris and gave their consent.[85] This situation made it necessary for Charles to consult the estates at important junctions in his political and diplomatic maneuvering. The three estates at Paris had denied his right to succeed his father. Would it not be advisable for him to convoke still larger assemblies in which his title and position was tacitly acknowledged? Peace with the English without total victory involved territorial concessions. Again the consent of the estates was advisable because of the concept of the inalienability of the domain. Finally, there was the question of practical politics. Charles VII needed the full support of those who acknowledged his suzerainty, and their support could best be achieved if he consulted them frequently to explain his policies.

Undoubtedly, diplomatic questions often came up during the assemblies of the estates that were convoked primarily to discuss the financial needs of the crown, but sometimes the estates were assembled to give advice on purely political and diplomatic matters. The first such occasion arose early in 1425. Charles VII had determined on a change in policy which looked towards a rapprochement with the Dukes of Brittany and Burgundy and involved the appointment of Richemont as constable. To publicize and explain this change, which was designed to bring about the return to peace and the eventual unity of the kingdom, he held a large assembly at Chinon in March, 1425, and still another one at Montleul in May. The exact composition of these meetings is unknown, but mention is made of the presence of the princes of the blood, members of the nobility, the clergy, the Parlements, and deputies of the "good towns." [86]

A reconciliation with Brittany was effected at Chinon, but Burgundy proved more difficult. The king summoned the three estates to Amboise in June, 1432, to advise him on this question.[87] As matters drew to a close in 1435, another assembly of the three estates was held at Tours and was followed in September by the Peace of Arras with the Duke of Burgundy.[88]

The assembly of the Estates General at Orléans in 1439 and the meeting scheduled for Bourges in 1440 were intended to deal with the question of peace with England, but in the former a relatively small tax was also voted. Renewed negotiations with England led Charles to order another large assembly to meet at Tours in April, 1444. Two chroniclers report the presence of all three estates, but another document merely refers to the "great seigneurs, barons, and clergymen in very large numbers." The omission of the "good towns" receives negative support by the absence of documents in the communal archives on the election of deputies.[89] Thereafter, there were assemblies to give advice, but for none of them has sufficient evidence been found to prove that the municipalities participated. Indeed, with the conclusion of the war, there was less need to consult the estates on diplomatic matters and there were probably no further convocations of the Estates General during the reign.[90]

The Estates and Domestic Policy

The third reason that Charles summoned large assemblies was to give advice on domestic affairs. When only one or two of the estates were concerned with a particular matter, they alone were summoned. The Pragmatic Sanction of Bourges in 1438, for example, was prepared by an assembly of twenty-nine archbishops and bishops, several abbots, and a great number of deputies from the universities and chapters of the kingdom, in conjunction with leading nobles and members of the king's council. Many other large assemblies of the French clergy were held during the reign. There were meetings at Bourges in 1440 and again in 1444, at Rouen in 1449, at Chartres in 1450, and at Bourges once more in 1452.[91] The great ordonnance of Montils-les-Tours of April, 1454, for the reformation of justice resulted from the deliberation of "several seigneurs of our blood and line, several prelates, archbishops, bishops, barons, and seigneurs of our kingdom, and the people of our grand council, and some of the presidents and other people of our court of Parlement, and other judges and experienced men of our kingdom. . . ."[92] The treason trial of the Duke of Alençon in October, 1458, made necessary an equally great assembly of peers, prelates, nobles, councilors, and judges.[93] These and other assemblies were large enough and frequent enough to preserve the popular, consultative nature of the monarchy in spite of the decline in the use of the Estates General for financial and diplomatic purposes after 1440.

When Charles VII died in 1461, he left to his son a people accustomed, though not yet fully reconciled, to paying enough taxes to support a frugal government in time of peace. National and regional assemblies were no longer necessary for propaganda to prepare the provincial estates and towns for these demands. Indeed, some of the provincial estates had ceased to be consulted on revenue matters, although others were more firmly entrenched than ever before. The privileged towns in the areas without estates had maintained their right of consent, and the nobility and royal officeholders had made good their claim to exemption from nearly all contributions. Only the inhabitants of the countryside paid without consent, and these people had rarely participated in the provincial estates in the days when the estates had been regularly convoked. The achievement of an adequate income by the crown had been far less of a victory than has been imagined. Those who paid without consultation had had little or no voice before, and those who formerly had been asked to give their consent often escaped altogether.

Charles had been forced to give up any idea he may have had of establishing a unified kingdom on the English model. Not only had it been necessary to recognize the privileges of provinces, duchies, counties, and towns, of nobles, ecclesiastics, officeholders, and burghers, but he had been forced to decentralize the royal administration. Even the sovereign courts had lost their unity with the creation of comparable provincial institutions. A standing army and a militia had been created that was equal to the task of repelling most foreign invasions and of suppressing robbers and brigands, but it was clearly inadequate to hold an unwilling population in subjection. Thus Charles VII bequeathed to his son a monarchy dependent upon popular support, and to secure this support, consultations with the vocal elements of the population were necessary whenever any important changes were desired. Of this son, Louis XI, it may be said, no king of France ever had a more original mind or was more willing to introduce innovations, and no king of France consulted his subjects more often.

THREE

Louis XI and the Estates

Louis XI and Taxation

Louis XI began his reign with an attempt to increase the popularity of the monarchy. He dismissed many of his predecessor's advisors, abolished a number of offices, suppressed the *Cour des aides,* made concessions to the great nobles, and confirmed the privileges of provinces, monasteries, towns, and other corporate entities.[1] He even determined to reform the existing tax structure. Where there were provincial estates, he planned to replace the old taille and aides by a single tax designed to yield an equal amount, but levied as the estates desired and collected by officials they named. The *élus* and other royal tax officers were to be abandoned. The wily king further hoped to force the privileged to pay their share of the contributions. The plan reflected the original mind of the new monarch and his willingness to flaunt traditional practices; but had it succeeded, royal power would have suffered grievously from the loss of tax-collecting machinery.

The Normans entered into the new arrangement with enthusiasm. They believed that honest tax collection under the supervision of their provincial estates would make possible the reduction of the amount each individual would have to pay, but their optimism proved unjustified. The new tax officials were less efficient or less trustworthy than those of the crown, and in 1464 the old system of taxation with the *élus* was restored at the request of the Normans themselves. Somewhat similar experiments were tried by the estates of Languedoc and Dauphiné with no better success.[2]

Where there were no provincial estates, Louis directed his officials to make an extensive poll of the town councils to determine the least objectionable form of taxation; but before these interviews were completed, he replaced the aides in the countryside with an additional imposition levied in the form of the taille. He exempted a large number of towns from the taille; to encourage trade, he relieved them from part

50

of the aides as well. The revenue possibilities of the towns were not neglected, however, for Louis XI did not hesitate to demand gifts and forced loans, a practice which forfeited part of the goodwill he had won.[3]

Louis even revived many of the provincial and regional estates to give consent to taxation. In the fall of 1463 when he needed money to repay the mortgage the duke of Burgundy held on the towns in Picardy, he summoned the three estates of the provinces of eastern Languedoïl to meet at Montferrand; of western Languedoïl, to meet at Tours; and of Champagne and the surrounding region, to meet at Troyes. Other assemblies were held in Périgord, Lannes, the Somme region, and probably elsewhere.[4]

The restoration of these and perhaps other provincial estates for taxing purposes was short lived, and Louis returned to the policies of his father. Existing provincial estates were allowed to function, but those that had been deprived of the right of consent were left moribund. Only in southwestern France were the assemblies abandoned by Charles VII definitely re-established. Here the three estates of Guyenne probably met in 1461. A little later they were called into session by Louis' brother, the Duke of Guyenne, and when the huge province reverted once more to the crown, they were summoned on many occasions.[5]

It is impossible to say why Louis abandoned the other provincial estates. Certainly it was not because he made no further financial demands on the people, for during his reign taxes became excessive. At first the rise in the taille was slow and fluctuating, but beginning in 1469 it increased steadily from 1,200,000 to 4,600,000 livres in 1481. The income from the aides and *gabelle* remained about the same, but under Louis the total amount collected in taxes increased well over two and a half times. Small wonder that by his death in 1483, many had begun to long for the days of Charles VII.

Higher taxes were caused by increased expenditures and the necessity to make generous concessions to the nobility. Pensions and court costs became greater, the number of *lances* nearly doubled, and other elements in the army were expanded. Part of the additional cost should have come from the aides, *gabelle,* and royal domain, but the first two levies were alienated with reckless abandon and the last brought in far less money than one might have supposed considering the extinction of many great feudal houses. Actually, Louis found it advisable to turn escheated lands over to the nobility keeping little more than the titles of Duke of Burgundy or Count of Provence for himself. The holdings of the Count of Armagnac, for example, were granted to over twenty-four people who, with three exceptions, were nobles of the sword in Louis' service. These men were not content with the normal income from their new seigneuries, but attempted, with considerable success, to appropriate royal taxes from them as well. As a result, Louis increased the annual revenue from the royal domain from 50,000 livres to only 100,000 livres in spite of the numerous fiefs that escheated or were confiscated. Matters were made worse by the failure of his plan to tax the nobility and the exemptions he granted to merchants and officials.[6]

The Consultative Assemblies

Louis' willingness to ignore public opinion by increasing taxes and his failure to continue to use some of the provincial estates should not be interpreted as meaning that he was opposed to assemblies. Indeed, he "loved to consult, and one of the characteristics of his administration was the frequency of the convocations of intelligent and experienced people."[7] He had scarcely been crowned before he held at Paris on September 9, 1461, a meeting of "the seigneurs of our blood, prelates, nobles, and others of our kingdom."[8] At this assembly he revoked his father's alienations of the royal domain. Similar meetings were held at Tours in December, 1464, at Paris in July, 1466, and no doubt on many other occasions.[9] When the advice of the army was needed, the prelates were dropped and in their place the "captains and chiefs of war" were assembled with the council.[10] To rally support against Burgundy, he brought together at Tours in November, 1470, twenty great nobles, five bishops, some bailiffs, members of the Parlement, and financial officials.[11] When only the clergy was concerned, he might summon to Lyon the "archbishops, bishops, abbots, prelates, and other notable clerics of our kingdom," as he did in January, 1476.[12] The universities and chapters were specifically included in another meeting of the clergy of the kingdom in September, 1478, at Orléans.[13] When a judicial matter was involved, he might hold an assembly consisting of the *Grand Conseil* and the presidents and councilors of the Parlement of Paris, as at Tours in March and April of 1479. If the matter was in part judicial and in part religious, he might summon with the Parlement of Paris, some notables from the University at Paris, the *requêtes de l'hôtel et du palais,* and the *Chambre des comptes,* as he did in Paris in May, 1463.[14]

When important matters of administration, trade, commerce, or currency were under consideration, Louis XI did not hesitate to turn to the towns for advice. In 1461 he required certain municipalities to send deputies to a national assembly; in 1463 he commissioned royal officials to consult the municipal leaders; in 1464 the deputies of the towns met at Paris to advise on monetary problems; in 1466 the towns were told to send their opinions on certain matters to be considered in a meeting of the more important royal advisors; and in 1468 the deputies of the towns met with members of the other orders in an assembly of the three estates.[15] The fact that Louis XI repeatedly sought the advice of his subjects does not mean that he put himself in their tutelage. For example, he ordered the towns to send deputies to Tours on October 20, 1470, to discuss means to weaken the fairs of Flanders and to prevent trade with the states of the Duke of Burgundy, but just before the deputies met he issued an ordonnance forbidding this commerce. Furthermore, over half of the recommendations of the deputies were rejected and in November a second ordonnance was issued in accordance with the royal desires.[16] The following September the deputies of the towns assembled at Tours to discuss the same subjects.[17] In the spring of 1479, the towns sent deputies to Paris to advise royal officials on how to prevent the circulation of foreign currency in France and the export of French currency abroad. Other assemblies of the deputies of the towns were held in May, 1480, and June, 1481, to deal with this matter.[18] The number and variety of the meetings were great, and they dispel any idea that Louis XI was opposed to assemblies.

Sometimes Louis preferred to summon the deputies of the towns to large regional assemblies. He used this form of consultation especially in connection with his efforts to repopulate the town of Arras after he had driven out some disloyal inhabitants. Early in June, 1479, Louis issued orders for the deputies of the towns to meet at Paris, Lyon, Tours, Rouen, or Saint-Jean-d'Angély. Regional assemblies were held on the same subject in September, 1480, and again in July and August, 1481.[19] The reunion of Provence and Marseille to the crown led the king to order an assembly of the towns to meet in January, 1482, to advise on the development of trade made possible by the acquisition of new ports in this area.[20]

Occasionally, the towns were directed to name representatives to meetings that at first seemed to have little to do with trade or commerce. In June, 1483, they were told to send deputies to Amboise to witness the celebration of the marriage of the dauphin to Marguerite of Austria. After the ceremony, the chancellor told the deputies of the twenty-one towns present that the king wanted to improve the administration of justice, increase trade, and, if possible, establish a common law and a single system of weights and measures for the kingdom. A few days later at Tours, the deputies were further informed that the king would also like to have the nobility engage in trade without loss of privilege and the tolls removed except at the frontiers of the kingdom. A meeting was set for September 6 to discuss these matters, but this assembly was never held. The proposed reforms were delayed for more than three centuries; for, on August 30, 1483, Louis XI died.[21]

The Estates General of 1468

The obvious preference of Louis XI for small advisory assemblies did not prevent him from holding the Estates General when it suited his purpose. During the spring and summer of 1465 a coalition of rebellious nobles made several proposals for a meeting, but they coupled their request with the demand that the aides be suppressed and the taille reduced. Louis had no intention of holding a large assembly to discuss such proposals. The Estates General would be assembled only to support his cause, and not to serve as a weapon in the hands of the disloyal nobles. He preferred to buy temporary peace at the price of giving his dissatisfied brother, Charles of France, the duchy of Normandy as an appanage. Soon Louis was seeking means to revoke the gift. War ensued and he drove his brother from Normandy. Charles won the aid of the Duke of Brittany and managed to recapture some Norman towns. Burgundy and Savoy promised him assistance, and negotiations were begun with England. Louis recognized the seriousness of the situation.[22] He determined to rally public opinion to the royal cause by means of an Estates General. On February 26, 1468, during a brief truce, the letters of convocation were issued.[23]

The letters to the towns were addressed to "the clergymen, bourgeois, men, and inhabitants." They directed that deputies be named to attend a meeting of the three estates of Tours on April 1. The king did not ask each locality to elect the same number of deputies. Lyon and Poitiers were to send one clergyman and three laymen;[24] Tours, Troyes, Chartres, Rodez, Châlons-sur-Marne, Agen, and probably Évreux and Périgueux, one clergyman and two laymen;[25] and Blois, and probably Senlis and Millau, two laymen only.[26] Otherwise, the various letters were virtually identical: the king expressed his concern over sufferings occasioned by the civil war; he apologized for setting the date for the meeting so soon after the letters of convocation were sent; he insisted that the assembly arrive at its conclusions before the termination of the truce on May 1.

The towns held their election at different times during the month of March. Except for Lyon and Périgueux, where the municipal councils dominated the proceedings, the deputies were named in general assemblies of the inhabitants. In Tours, Troyes, Chartres, Laon, Châlons-sur-Marne, and Poitiers, the clergy and lay population elected their deputies together. In Orléans and Lyon, they acted separately. Only in the latter city did any difficulty develop. A long standing quarrel with the clergy led the municipality to name the entire delegation, including the deputy for the first estate.[27] It is impossible to ascertain the desires of the electors concerning the civil war. The cahier of Lyon was given over to local issues and to the problem of foreign currency, and the deputies of Rodez and Millau were content to turn in a joint petition protesting against heavy taxation in Rouergue.[28]

There is no real proof that either Louis XI or the rebellious nobles tampered with the elections in the towns, or that the king convoked only those great prelates and nobles who would do as he said. The oft-quoted statement of Commynes that Louis summoned whom he wished does not apply to the estates of 1468. Commynes himself associated his remark with a meeting which he said took place at Tours in March and April of 1470. Since the king was at Tours at that time, there could conceivably have been an assembly. However, the events he described fit the meeting held at Tours in November, 1470, and it is likely that he referred to this assembly.[29] That Louis summoned in 1468 those who had a right and a duty to attend, and not just those who would do as he wished, is indicated by his letter ordering the Duke of Bourbon, who was something less than pliable, to be at the estates.[30]

The estates failed to open at the appointed date. Louis himself did not enter Tours until the afternoon of April 5. He came in great magnificence, accompanied by a large number of princes and seigneurs who were also richly dressed. The usually carelessly attired monarch was clearly doing his best to impress those present.[31]

The meeting opened the following morning at eight o'clock in the great hall of the archepiscopal hotel. Present, in addition to the king's council, were five of the six peers of the church, the Bishop of Noyon being too sick to attend, and nineteen other archbishops and bishops. For the second estate, over twenty-four nobles are named as attending, and we are told that others were present in great numbers. The largest single group was the clerical and lay deputies from sixty-four towns; they must have numbered close to two hundred.[32] Many came from far-off places in Languedoc and Guyenne, but conspicuously absent were deputies from the towns of Burgundy and Brittany. Provence and Dauphiné sent no deputations, but the count of the former and the Bishop of Valence from the latter attended. It was a large assembly even though some provinces did not participate.

The king opened the estates about 10 o'clock with a brief speech. He left the explanation of the purpose of the assembly to the chancellor, Guillaume Jouvenel des Ursins, an experienced man who had served Charles VII in this capacity. He spoke for two hours on the rights, dignities, and prerogatives of the king and of the dangers in separating Normandy from the crown. In the course of his oration, he suggested that there were three points on which the king wished advice. Should Charles of France have Normandy as an appanage? How should the Breton troops be removed from the Norman towns? And finally, what should be done about the threat of an English invasion in alliance with the Duke of Brittany.[33]

During the week that followed, the three estates deliberated under the careful direction of the crown. For the first three days the king's councilors and a few of his loyal friends held the floor almost continuously.[34] Speaking for Louis were men like Guillaume Cousinot, Seigneur of Montreuil and royal chamberlain; Guy Bernard, Bishop of Langres, onetime *maître des requêtes de l'hôtel du roy* and future chancellor of the Order of Saint-Michel; Pierre Doriole, a faithful official who was to be elevated to the post of chancellor in 1472; and Jean d'Estouteville, Seigneur of Torcy, grandmaster of the crossbowmen.[35]

The only speech which survives in full was given by Jean Jouvenel des Ursins, Archbishop of Reims and brother of the chancellor. For more than a generation Jean Jouvenel had played a prominent role in the affairs of the kingdom. He was addicted to writing long letters and delivering long speeches whenever the opportunity offered. Several of his epistles dealt with the assemblies of the estates during the reign of Charles VII. In one of his interminable orations, Louis had interrupted him three times with orders to be brief; on April 8, 1468, the impatient monarch was not present and the learned bishop talked endlessly.[36]

He began by pointing out—with the aid of numerous biblical references—that it was the duty of a subject to obey his king, a king that he, Jean Jouvenel, had annointed. He harped on the civil war, arguing that the princes were trying to break the body politic by separating the head from its members. The duchy of Normandy must not be given to Charles of France as an appanage. He pointed out that when Charles V had been faced with the problem of providing for his brothers, he had assembled the three estates and it had been decided that each brother should have 12,000 livres revenue from a duchy, but no appanage. To provide such a jurisdiction was to weaken the crown and bring hardship on the people. Then the old man wandered. He talked of the sufferings of the people, the burden of taxation, the exactions of the Papacy, until finally he came to an end with one of his innumerable Latin quotations.

The other councilors stuck more to the point. They agreed that the rich province of Normandy, which yielded 600,000 livres in revenue per year, must not be alienated from the crown, and that the practice of giving appanages to members of the royal family was dangerous. Not until April 9 did the towns, led by the Paris delegates, finally manage to be heard. They held the floor most of the time during the two days that followed and the opinions they voiced were almost identical to those of the royal advisors.[37]

The groundwork was thus prepared for the king to return to the assembly. During the morning of the twelfth he appeared accompanied by the princes of the blood and the members of the council. He spoke in a low voice for half an hour. When he had finished, several of those who had come with him urged the assembly to ask for a statement concerning the appanage for Charles. Louis signaled for the deputies to gather around him and in a familiar manner explained that Charles was young and powerless; to give him Normandy was to surrender that province to his allies—the Duke of Brittany and the English.

The remainder of that day and the day which followed were devoted to speeches by the nobility and the clergy. Meanwhile, the estates prepared their recommendations and when they had finished, the king returned to the assembly to hear them read. The chancellor thanked those present, and the estates came to an end.[38]

The recommendations of the estates were all that Louis could have wished. They praised his actions and intentions, they stated that he could not separate the duchy of Normandy from the crown without violating "the solemn oath that he had made at his coronation to protect the rights of his crown"; and they recalled an ordonnance of Charles V which limited a male member of the royal family to a county worth 12,000 livres, but announced their willingness for him to give his brother an additional 48,000 livres, and to create a duchy for him. Concerning the activities of the other malcontents, the three estates expressed the hope that the Duke of Burgundy, as a peer of France, would try to safeguard the rights of the crown and persuade Charles of France to accept the royal offer, they condemned the Duke of Brittany for seizing towns in Normandy and for making an alliance with the English, and they promised their full support in case the rebellious lords failed to comply with the will of the king on these matters. Truly Louis XI had managed the assembly well. He had in its pronouncement a valuable propaganda weapon to use against his enemies and in the deputies, who attended, sympathetic interpreters of his policy when they returned to their homes.[39]

It is true the estates named a committee to give advice on matters of justice and order, but this was done at the king's suggestion and many of those elected were his loyal advisors. There was nothing to fear here. Indeed, the committee appears to have been intended to serve as an additional propaganda weapon against the dukes. Its only specifically assigned task was to meet Charles of France and the Duke of Brittany in order to persuade them to adhere to the will of the three estates of the kingdom.

It is not known what happened to this committee. Probably Louis decided that it was not immediately needed and let it lie unused. The royal cause was progressing satisfactorily, peace was made with Charles and the Duke of Brittany in September. The decisions of the estates in favor of Louis were useful to him when it came to providing a duchy for Charles in lieu of Normandy. When Charles demanded Guyenne with all the royal rights and the homage of the Counts of Albret, Foix, and Armagnac, Louis XI was able to refuse, saying that such a concession would be contrary to all the laws of the kingdom and the decision of the estates. But when Louis thought it to his own interest to insure peace by granting his brother 20,000 livres more than the estates had suggested, he did not hesitate to do so.[40]

The Estates and Treaties

The estates were again used to implement royal policy near the close of the reign when the long struggle for the Burgundian succession was brought to an end. The Treaty of Arras provided for the cession of Burgundy and Artois to France and the marriage of the dauphin to Marguerite of Austria. It was further agreed in Article 89 that the treaty would be ratified by the three estates of the kingdom of France and by the three estates of the provinces of the Low Countries. The article stated that the French king would dispatch letters to the three estates of his kingdom telling them

to undertake to support the treaty and all the points and articles contained therein; and if it should happen . . . that the King, the Dauphin, or their successors . . . break the agreement, . . . they will not aid, assist, or favor them, but on the contrary will give all aid, favor, and assistance to my said lord the Duke, to his son, and to his country in order to support the said treaty. . . .

In addition, the princess of the blood, peers of France, the deputies of the University of Paris and of twenty-seven towns, and the prelates and nobles of the counties of Artois and Burgundy were to promise to support the treaty. The subjects of Maximilian were to give like guarantees.[41]

It is noted that the treaty did not stipulate that Louis XI would have the three estates of his kingdom assemble together, but that he would dispatch the necessary instructions to them. From the beginning, therefore, he intended to get the required approval in assemblies of the estates of the bailiwicks, probably to save the time and the expense of having deputations sent to some central locality. The necessary letters were dispatched to the bailiffs and seneschals on December 3. They were told to assemble the three estates of their jurisdictions to elect proctors with ample powers to accede both to the treaty and the marriage. These proctors were then to swear to uphold the agreement, a copy of which was included with the letters of convocation.[42] In this manner Dauphiné, Provence, Burgundy, and the estates of forty-five bailiwicks and seneschalsies ratified the agreement.[43] In addition, twenty-one towns took separate oaths to uphold the treaty, as did the University of Paris, the ecclesiastical and lay peers of France, and a few other prelates and nobles. Thus all the elements ordinarily present at the Estates General were contacted, and the use of bailiwick estates brought the treaty before many who normally would not have been consulted.[44] This method of getting the consent of the three estates to treaties was to be used again in later reigns.

The assemblies to ratify the treaty with Maximilian were followed by a meeting of the deputies of the towns and other notables to witness the marriage of the dauphin with Marguerite of Austria in June, 1483. On this occasion, as we have seen, Louis revealed far-reaching plans for the administrative and economic reorganization of the kingdom, plans which would have necessitated many assemblies in the future, but on August 30, just a week before the first of the scheduled meetings of the deputies of the towns was to take place, he died. He had continued the consultative traditions of the Renaissance Monarchy; but his arbitrary actions and occasional disregard of privilege, coupled with heavy taxation, had forfeited popular support. It was doubtful whether the crown could withstand the onslaught of the prince, noble, and town during the years that followed.

FOUR

The Estates General of 1484

Preliminary Moves

The task of withstanding the tide of reaction against the policies of Louis XI was made doubly difficult by the fact that he left as his successor a child who had celebrated his thirteenth birthday only two months before. A regency was technically necessary, for in accordance with an ordonnance made in 1474, a king had to be at least fourteen years of age before he could govern in his own name.[1] The interim of ten months before Charles VIII reached the appointed age was sure to be followed by a much longer period in which real power would reside with those who controlled his person or his council. The strongest individual claims for these privileges could be established by the queen mother, Charlotte of Savoy; Louis, Duke of Orléans; and Pierre and Anne of Beaujeu. The queen mother could point as a precedent to the regency of Blanche of Castile during the minority of Louis IX, but more recently Charles V had left the government of the kingdom to his brother and the council when he tried to provide for the administration of the kingdom. Moreover, Charlotte of Savoy was a meek, mild woman who had been relegated to a very minor role by her late husband. She was a threat only if she fell under the influence of one of the clever schemers of which the French court was never lacking, but this possibility passed with her death in December, 1483. The Duke of Orléans was equally inexperienced. He had just begun his twenty-second year when Louis XI died, and had achieved a reputation at that date only for his athletic prowess and his frivolity. The finer points of his character were not to become apparent until he himself became king. Nevertheless, unpromising as the young prince might appear, as heir to the throne he could not be ignored.

Pierre and Anne of Beaujeu offered a third possibility. Anne was the oldest surviving daughter of Louis XI and had just turned twenty-two when her father died. She inherited his original qualities of mind, but not his meanness of character. She was calm, dignified, and even regal in her bearing. Her father had possessed none of these kingly qualities. She knew when to temporize and negotiate, and when to strike boldly. Her father had often been devious and timid when opportunities lay before him, and yet rash when caution ought to have been his guide. She was a good judge of men and those whom she chose were both able and loyal, whereas her father's appointments were bad more often than not, and few monarchs were more frequently betrayed.

As a husband for his daughter, Louis XI had selected Pierre de Bourbon, Seigneur of Beaujeu, and for once his judgment of character had not been faulty. Pierre was twenty-two years older than his wife, and though a relatively poor nobleman at the time of his betrothal, he was heir to the extensive domains in central and eastern France of his older brother, Jean II, Duke of Bourbon. He had been a member of the League of Public Good, but Louis XI detached him from the feudal coalition and entrusted him with more and more authority during the years that followed. His marriage to Anne early in 1474 led to an ever increasing role in the government and during a grave illness in 1481, Louis XI had instructed the dauphin to obey him in all things. The following year the king dictated instructions to this effect and had them signed by the dauphin and other seigneurs. The Duke of Orléans was forced to swear never to ask for the person or the government of the dauphin, and as a further precaution Beaujeu was named lieutenant general of the kingdom. On his deathbed Louis XI directed his son-in-law to go to Amboise to take charge of the young prince to make triply certain that the following reign would commence with the chosen mentor in control of the new king.[2]

Pierre had one thing that his wife had not—experience. Less intelligent, but equally steadfast and conscientious, he brought a background of long service in important governmental posts to the family coalition that was to compensate for the handicap under which his wife labored because of her age and sex. They were a devoted couple; the historian is unable to detect any difference between their ideas and policies. It is useless to speculate on who was dominant, so harmoniously did they work together.[3]

A fourth possibility lay in turning the upbringing of the king over to his mother, the Beaujeus, or Orléans, and the government of the kingdom over to a coalition, including representatives of these three factions and the principle nobles headed by the Duke of Bourbon. Bourbon had had a long, distinguished, and relatively faithful career in the service of the crown, but he was not one to minimize his contributions. When ignored or slighted, however unintentionally, he was apt to retire sullenly to his estates to nurse his wounded feelings and his gout until those in authority stooped to cajole him back into a better humor. One might have expected the old noble to have thrown the immense weight of his power and prestige behind the Beaujeus, but he was jealous of his younger brother and clearly of the opinion that as the most experienced statesman among the king's relatives, he ought to have the direction of the government.

The Beaujeus possessed two advantages over their rivals; they had the custody of Charles VIII at the death of the old king and the support of most of the bureaucracy who could look only to them for protection against the revengeful forces of the reaction. Yet these very advantages pointed to the weaknesses of their position. The support of the bureaucracy and the close association of Pierre with the former government attached them to the old regime in a far closer degree than was comfortable. To achieve popular support, the Beaujeus had to separate themselves from the policies of the late king, but to attack Louis XI was to deny their own claim to authority and to forfeit the loyalty of the officials on whom the administrative control of the government largely depended. Furthermore, the military forces lay in the hands of the nobility and the bulk of this class was not favorably inclined towards them. Clearly, their only possible course was to temporize, even to retreat, until they could find the necessary allies to make possible a bid for power.

The first problem was to associate the great nobles and the towns with the government, for these two groups, with the local royal officials, controlled the provinces. Louis XI had hardly breathed his last before the Beaujeus summoned "the princes and seigneurs of the blood in order to have their advice." [4] They also informed the towns of the king's death and asked them to give their loyal support to the new ruler.[5] Several weeks probably elapsed before the magnates began to arrive,[6] but once they gathered, their number was so great that the château at Amboise became crowded. By the time the Duke of Orléans got there, lodging could be had only at an inn, and there he was joined by his cousin, the Count of Angoulême.[7]

Little specific information survives on the events of the first few weeks, or for that matter, for the first year of the new reign. An unusual lack of chronicles and ambassadorial reports has led historians to interpret this period in the light of later developments. They have generally seen the Beaujeus as keeping a tenuous hold on the government until the flight of Orléans from court in 1485. Actually, the Beaujeus appear to have been quickly supplanted in the control of the government by a council composed of the great nobles and their protégés, and it was only with difficulty that they were able to maintain custody of the king. This council was established soon after the death of Louis XI at the instigation of the king, the queen mother, the Dukes of Bourbon and Orléans, and nineteen other persons. It represented not the victory of a single magnate but rather a coalition of various factions. Bourbon and Orléans attended its meetings as the heads of princely families. The fifteen nobles and prelates who comprised the remainder of the council were chosen because of their governmental experience or their power in this or that locality. Some like Louis d'Amboise, Bishop of Albi; Jean de Beaudricourt, Governor of Burgundy; Aymar de Poitiers, Seigneur of Saint-Vallier; and Philippe de Commynes, Seigneur of Argenton; and Pierre de Beaujeu himself had been intimately connected with the government of the preceding kings and owed much of their position to them. Others like Odet d'Aydie, Count of Comminges; Jacques de Saint-Pol, Count of Richebourg; Alain le Grand, Sire of Albret; Pierre de Rohan, Marshal of Gié; and Francis d'Orléans, Count of Dunois were powerful noblemen in their own right and in some cases could regard the past with bitterness only.[8]

It is virtually impossible to assign these councilors or the other nobles at court to any particular party. Most of them shifted their position from time to time, or at least flirted with rival factions as they sought to divine whether the queen mother, Orléans, Bourbon, or the Beaujeus would eventually triumph. Making the proper choice would decide whether they would hold the lands granted them by Louis XI or regain those that he had confiscated. It has too often been assumed that those who had profited in the preceding reign automatically supported the Beaujeus, and that those who had suffered turned to their rivals. This was by no means the case. Philippe de Commynes had been awarded part of the lands of Seigneurs of La Trémoille and of the Duke of Nemours, but he associated more with the Sire of Albret and the Duke of Bourbon during the early days than with the Beaujeus. On the other hand, La Trémoille became a devoted adherent of the Beaujeus, and the Duke of Lorraine, after some hesitation, came to believe that it would be more fruitful to court their friendship than to ally himself with the Orleanists. Likewise, Jacques de Brézé, who had suffered severely at the hands of Louis XI, soon joined his daughter. Sometimes families sought to insure themselves against a possible miscalculation by placing one brother in the Orleanist camp and another at the side of the Beaujeus. Thus Georges d'Amboise, then Bishop of Montauban and later the great friend and advisor of Louis XII, chose his future king, and Louis d'Amboise, Bishop of Albi, leaned more towards the daughter of his former master.[9]

This much appears certain: the Beaujeus and their followers were a minority in the council, a fact that was clearly brought to light by the early actions of the government. The Duke of Bourbon took the title of lieutenant general of the kingdom from his brother as well as the governorship of Languedoc. To these positions he added that of constable of France, a post he felt that he had long deserved. Orléans was made governor of Vermandois, the Île-de-France, and Champagne. To these honors he added the *gabelles* and fines collected from his lands, a company of 100 *lances,* and a pension of 24,000 livres per year.[10] Lesser figures had to be content with lesser prizes. The Count of Dunois took the governorship of Dauphiné; Marshal des Querdes, another councilor, received the capitancy of Meulan; and Jean de Beaudricourt was authorized to collect the revenue from three castellanies given him by Louis XI. Only the Beaujeus received nothing.[11]

It is impossible to believe that they took nothing because they were unusually altruistic. Pierre had already earned an unsavory reputation as a land-hungry noble in an age when this characteristic was commonplace.[12] Nor is the presumption justified that the Beaujeus made concessions to their rivals to keep them from demanding more tangible evidence of power. They must have known that in five or six years Charles VIII would begin to assert his independence. The control of his person for this brief period would hardly compensate for the loss of important offices to Bourbon or for the failure to gain new governorships and lands as others were doing. No, the Beaujeus took nothing because they were too weak to do otherwise. This fact is not surprising when one remembers that the couple had no extensive estates upon which to base their power as did Bourbon, Orléans, and Albret. They could only bide their time until their rivals fell to quarreling among themselves, or at least until they could find additional support for their cause.

Surprisingly enough the council provided France with a relatively stable government and a genuine program of reform. The taille was cut by one-fourth, an action which necessitated the reduction of the army and the dismissal of the six thousand Swiss troops in the pay of Louis XI at the time of his death. The alienations of the domain by the late king were revoked, and a few of his most hated officials were punished. Several great nobles who had been imprisoned or exiled were released or allowed to return to France, a reprieve hardly to the advantage of the Beaujeus, for among those freed was Charles d'Armagnac, part of whose estates had been given Pierre by Louis XI.[13] By December the new administration was sufficiently well established to debate an ordonnance for the reformation of justice and to consider the strengthening of the liberties of the Gallican Church, both measures were calculated to receive considerable popular support.[14]

It was during this period of compromise between the various factions and of the conciliation of the people that the Estates General was convoked. The decision to assemble the deputies of the three estates had been taken soon after the death of Louis XI, but it was not until October 24 that the letters of convocation were issued. Historians have not reached an agreement as to who was primarily responsible for this action. Much of the difficulty has arisen from the presumption that the Beaujeus were in control of the government. Pélicier argued that at first the princes thought they could control the youthful Anne of Beaujeu and that when they realized their error, they accepted the advice of Commynes and asked the council to convoke the Estates General in order to win popular support for their cause. His evidence consisted of the claim made by the Duke of Orléans more than a year later that he had asked that the estates be summoned. Additional proof, Pélicier believed, was found in the initial choice of the town of Orléans for the meeting.[15]

There are difficulties that prevent ready agreement with these arguments. The order establishing the council soon after the death of Louis XI had stipulated that that body should administer the kingdom *until the estates could meet.*[16] Thus, the decision to assemble the estates had been taken before the rivals of Anne of Beaujeu could possibly have learned whether or not they could control her actions. There is no valid reason for associating Commynes with the summoning of the estates beyond that, like millions of others, he was favorably inclined towards representative assemblies; nor is there evidence that he had shifted to the Orleanist camp. His attendance record at the meetings of the king's council was poor and he was not one of the signatories of the letter convoking the estates.[17] It is true that in January, 1485, Orléans claimed that he had been partly responsible for the convocation of the Estates General, but at that time he was trying to win popular support at the expense of the Beaujeus. His statement, therefore, cannot be taken as proof that he actually took this stand in September, and October, 1483.

The initial choice of Orléans for the estates does not necessarily indicate that the young duke dictated the letters of convocation. Indeed, one historian has argued that the selection of Orléans resulted from the desire to accentuate royal supremacy.[18] From where else could the activities of the discontented prince be better watched? Furthermore, the letter convoking the estates was signed by Pierre de Beaujeu and the Bishops of Albi, Coutances, and Périgueux who generally associated with the Beaujeu faction, by the Duke of Bourbon, the Marshal of Gié, and the Count of Comminges of the independents, and by the Count of Dunois who was then intriguing with the queen mother.[19] Conspicuously absent were the names of the young duke and his avowed followers.

There is then no valid reason for attributing the idea of convoking the Estates General to Orléans and his advisers, but it is certain that the Beaujeus supported the convocation. In all probability they were dissatisfied with the substitution of conciliar government for their own rule and looked to the deputies of the estates to restore them to the position that Louis XI had intended. No doubt Bourbon and the other great nobles agreed to the meeting in part because they believed that the deputies would prefer them to the Beaujeus or Orléans and in part to avoid putting themselves in an unpopular position.

The letters issued at Blois on October 24 directing the three estates to meet at Orléans on January 1 indicated that the decision to hold the Estates General had been made by the magnates when they had met soon after the death of Louis XI, but no mention was made of the necessity to constitute a more permanent council. The letters merely directed that the electors prepare remonstrances for their deputies and give them "sufficient power in writing to conclude, consent, and agree to all that will be done, ordered, and concluded in the said assembly." [20]

The one unusual feature of the letters of convocation was the directive on the way in which the delegates were to be selected. In the past, the nobles and prelates had been individually summoned by the king or his subordinates, and the monasteries, chapters, and towns had elected deputies. This time the letters were sent to the bailiffs and seneschals, and they were instructed to assemble "the churchmen, nobles, bourgeois, and inhabitants" of their jurisdictions to elect one deputy from each order, or two in the case of the large bailiwick of Vermandois and the provostship of Paris. It is highly improbable that any Machiavellian intentions were behind this change in procedure. [21]

The various factions within and without the council adhered to the new plan without making any known protests, a fact which clearly indicated that the procedure directed was not regarded as favoring anyone. Indeed, the introduction of bailiwick elections greatly reduced the possibility of interference, for under the old system many participants had been chosen by the government. The most likely explanation for the change lies in the desire of the crown to reduce the costs of holding the assembly. Indeed, the new system was less of a breach with the past than a comparison of the letters of convocation would indicate, for royal directives or no, provincial and bailiwick estates had served occasionally as electoral assemblies for more than a century.

As early as 1312 the cost of the delegations of the episcopal cities to the estates at Vienne was borne in part by towns in the dioceses that were not summoned. Several years later twelve nobles of the Toulouse area gave a composite procuration to someone to attend an assembly of barons for them, and in 1351 the three estates of the bailiwick of

Amiens sent deputies to Paris to an assembly.[22] In 1421 some councilors of Albi considered consulting the principal towns of the diocese concerning the representatives they had been required to send to the estates at Clermont. In return, they expected assistance in paying the cost of the deputation. The same year the three estates of the dioceses of Rouergue either directly or indirectly named and financed the delegation from that province, and in 1425 and 1428 the procedure was repeated.

A nobleman was recompensed by the estates of Limousin for attending the assembly at Bourges in January, 1423, and the Bishop of Limoges was paid by the estates of Haut-Limousin in 1435, a strong indication that they represented the areas as a whole and were not merely attending in their own name. Lyon joined with the communities of the *plat pays* to depute to the estates of Poitiers in October, 1425.[23] The three estates of the duchy of Burgundy and the counties of Mâcon and Charolais named deputies to join the embassy of their duke to a meeting of the estates of France scheduled for February, 1440.[24] The loss of the archives of most of the provincial and bailiwick estates prevents the evidence from being more complete, but enough is known to indicate that there was a strong preference in many places for local elections in lieu of direct summons.

The reason for this desire to have group elections in lieu of individual attendance and deputation by towns and chapters was clearly brought out by the representatives of Languedoc at the estates of Chinon in 1428. They petitioned the crown to assemble the three estates of their province "to elect a great and notable embassy from all the estates to go to the king together . . ." should it be necessary for them to meet again so far from home. They pointed out that when they were convoked individually, it was difficult for them to get together to travel in a group, presumably for protection, and that the expense entailed by those so summoned was unbearable. In his reply to the request, the king mentioned a proposed national assembly scheduled for March 1, 1429, and this statement led the towns to take steps to send a joint delegation, but the meeting was never held.[25] The restoration of order at the close of the Hundred Years War made it unnecessary for a large number of deputies to travel together for protection, but the expense that fell on those individually summoned, and even on the towns, chapters, and monasteries, was immense and the demand for provincial and bailiwick elections continued.

Two other factors made desirable the convocation of the Estates General by province or bailiwick rather than by the individual. Throughout the century, provincial, bailiwick, and local estates had sent deputies to the court with their petitions when they saw fit, and it was natural to use the same technique to carry their grievances to the national assembly. The use of the estates of the bailiwicks and seneschalsies a year earlier to approve the Treaty of Arras in the name of the three estates of France could not but have had its effect. As was so often the case in the Renaissance Monarchy, the change, seemingly so abruptly introduced by the letters of convocation in the fall of 1483, in reality only gave official sanction to a practice that had been slowly developing over a long period of years.

The days between the convocation of the Estates General and the opening of the assembly were ones of almost ceaseless activity for the Beaujeus. Pierre participated in the deliberations of the council where, it has been argued, his position was strengthened by the necessity to introduce specialists from the various sovereign courts to help the original fifteen, many of whom had no judicial or financial experience. However, even if it is correct to assume that most of the legal and financial experts were pro-Beaujeu, their admission to the council did not alter the basic fact that the preponderance of military power still lay with the great nobles. Until the Beaujeus could draw part of this class into their camp, they could not hope to govern the kingdom.[26] Meanwhile, they profited from their control of the king's person to win popularity with the leaders of provincial society. They were present when their young charge received the flood of deputations that came from towns, provinces, and other groups to congratulate him on his succession to the throne and to obtain confirmation for their privileges. They must have contrasted favorably with the libertine Duke of Or- léans whose name appears more frequently on the list of those who attended the meetings of the royal council than one might expect, but who nevertheless had his heart more set on pleasure and his mind more occupied with intrigue than with the routine of government. Even before Orléans had learned of the death of Louis XI he had established relations with Francis II, Duke of Brittany, in the hope of winning the hand of his eldest daughter and heiress. Before any arrangement could reach fulfillment, it was necessary for Orléans to obtain an annulment of his marriage with Jeanne, the crippled daughter of Louis XI. He was balked in this design not only by the Beaujeus, but also by the queen mother, who was determined to protect her daughter. To keep her friendship and to prevent a premature disclosure of his intentions, the youthful duke openly accepted his wife, but at the same time continued his negotiations with Brittany.[27]

Other great nobles were added to form a web of feudal alliances not unlike those that had plagued the preceding reign. The Beaujeus were not totally unaware of these developments, but they could only wait for the Estates General to meet. It was on this body that they pinned their hopes, for they believed that the deputies could not only be persuaded to recognize their custody of the king, but also to reconstitute the council as they directed. Thus the power of the vocal elements of the population would be turned against their rivals. Endorsement by the deputies of the bailiwicks would do much to offset the advantage held by the magnates because of their extensive estates.

The elections in the bailiwicks were held in late November and in December. On the whole, the new procedure functioned smoothly, though many of the great towns continued to send individual delegations along with those elected by the community of the bailiwick. Tours went so far as to try to act alone for Touraine, but a second assembly was ordered which the lesser towns attended. The three orders usually voted together, but there were some exceptions. Disputes were quite rare, and where they did occur, local not national issues were at stake.[28]

There is insufficient evidence to evaluate the degree in which the various factions influenced the elections. The great nobles had a natural advantage in their domains for they assembled the estates. Thus, it was the Duke of Bourbon who issued the directives to his subordinates for the elections in Bourbonnais and Forez, and it was an ardent supporter of their duke who was chosen by the nobility of Orléans.[29] The Count of Comminges did not hesitate to modify the election rules by informing the voters in his seneschalsy of Lannes that if they felt that the three deputies prescribed by the royal orders of convocation were too few, additional ones could be named.[30] But when all is said, there is no direct evidence that the great nobility tried to influence the elections, and the generally favorable results in their lands could well have come from a tendency on the part of the inhabitants to vote for the avowed followers of their natural leaders.

There is reason to believe that the Beaujeus were more active. Certainly they were not above taking full advantage of the numerous deputations sent to court during the fall of 1483 by towns, provinces, and other groups to congratulate the king on his succession to the throne and to ask for a confirmation of their privileges.

A detailed account of the Burgundian delegation for this purpose has come down to us. Led by Jean de Cirey, Abbot of Cîteaux, they arrived at Blois on October 25, the day after the letters convoking the Estates General were issued. There was a public audience in which the abbot delivered an ornate speech full of classical allusions, but negotiations behind the scene were of greater importance.[31] Philippe Pot, Seigneur de la Roche, onetime advisor of Philip the Good and Charles the Bold, later loyal servant of Louis XI, and at that time one of the principal Burgundian representatives, was permitted by a decree of November 4 to keep the office of grand seneschal of Burgundy, the lands of

Saint-Romans granted him by the late king, the palace of the former dukes at Dijon, and the castellany of Rouvres, in spite of the recent ordonnance revoking the alienations of the domain and other estates given away by Louis XI.[32] We know of no immediate reward granted to the Abbot of Cîteaux, but his abbey had a case pending before the Parlement of Paris against the Abbot of Clairvaux, and on March 10, 1484, while the Estates General was still in session, he succeeded in having the dispute transferred to the *Grand Conseil* where the influence of the court could be more readily felt.[33] Then on November 13, less than ten days after Philippe Pot had been confirmed in the gains he had received from Louis XI, Charles VIII wrote a letter to the members of the three estates of Burgundy asking that both Pot and the Abbot of Cîteaux be named deputies of the Estates General.[34] The Beaujeus had first won their loyalty, and then they used their control over the young king to secure their election.

It cannot be proved that the Beaujeus established equally friendly relations with members of other delegations to court during the fall of 1483 or that they tampered successfully with the elections elsewhere. Only one of the six members of the deputation from Dauphiné was elected to the Estates General, and chance would have led to that much repetition.[35] Two of the six members of the Parlement of Paris sent by that body to court in September were later elected to attend the Estates General, but as the crown did not even think to order that sovereign court to nominate representatives until January and made no protest when those chosen did not actually come to Tours, it appears clear that there was no conscious interference here.[36]

A large percentage of the deputies to the Estates General held public office, but again there is no proof that the Beaujeus or the other members of the council threatened to have the king withhold confirmation of their positions until assurance of co-operation was given. This is not to say that the deputies were motivated by no considerations save duty to those who elected them. Many wanted public office, and those who loyally supported the victorious faction were likely to receive fitting rewards.[37] The difficulty was to guess who was going to be victorious, and as well-informed a man as Philippe de Commynes made the mistake of not betting on the Beaujeus. Surely there must have been many deputies who fell into the same error. When all is said, neither side made a concerted effort to influence all the elections or to bribe all the deputies when once they were chosen. Rather they were content to ensure that they had a few friends in the estates. The bulk of those elected were almost certainly unattached to any faction.

Too few cahiers survive to give a clear idea of the temper of the country in regard to the struggle between the various parties. Indeed, the provincial and local assemblies preferred to ignore this fundamental question and to concentrate on winning further guarantees for their privileges and rectifying their grievances. The right of provincial estates to give consent to taxation was generally insisted upon as was the demand that financial levies be more equally distributed among the various jurisdictions. The costs of justice, the ignorance and brutality of judges and lesser officials, and illegal tolls on the transportation of goods were inveighed against. There was a frequent demand that royal officials be native-born residents of the province in which they served. Burgundy protested against the confusion in the currency, Dauphiné on the limitations placed on hunting and fishing, Languedoc on the cost of the military service rendered by the nobility without pay, and Lannes on the irresponsible attitude of the upper clergy.[38]

While the deputies were being elected, the court moved from Blois to Cléry where on December 10 the king issued letters changing the meeting place of the estates from Orléans to Tours because of the pestilence that was raging in the former city.[39] He then returned to Amboise where his reign had begun a few months earlier and where it was to end in 1498. From Amboise, Charles moved to Montils-les-Tours between December 28 and January 3 to establish his headquarters for the Estates General.[40]

The assembly that met at Tours was no more important than many of those which had gone before, and it exercised relatively little influence on the future development of France. Its significance is derived mainly from the long and detailed journal of the session left by Jean Masselin, deputy of the clergy of the bailiwick of Rouen. Earlier meetings of the three estates are often known only by an ordonnance, a brief report in some communal archives, or at best the short, uninspired, official account of a royal clerk. Masselin, on the other hand, provides us with a journal unmatched in its clarity and detail by any other account of an assembly in France or elsewhere prior to the last quarter of the sixteenth century. Yet the very excellence of Masselin's journal has often led historians to accept blindly his opinions and prejudices, for there are no documents to check the accuracy of his statements except in regard to basic facts. When one deals with personalities and motives, it is necessary to remember that Masselin was an able but proud man who interpreted events through Norman eyes. Indeed, when it came to apportioning the tax levied on Normandy among the various bailiwicks of that province, his sight grew dimmer and he wrote only as a native of Rouen.

Jean Masselin was born about 1433 of good bourgeois parents. He became a doctor of both civil and canon law, and by 1468 had been named a canon in the cathedral chapter of his native city. His knowledge of law made him the frequent representative of the chapter in its legal and financial affairs; thus the role of proctor he assumed on his election to the Estates General was far from new to him. In the years that followed his service at Tours, he received ever increasing recognition both as an administrator of genuine ability and as a leader of his chapter. He became dean, and finally vicar-general for the archbishop and councilor in the Norman *échiquier*. Success added to his pride and made him more susceptible to the desires of the great. He supported a royal levy on the clergy in 1491; in his will he boldly asked to be buried in the choir of the cathedral at Rouen, an area usually reserved for those of royal blood.[41]

Masselin does not say when he reached Tours, nor does he explain why the formal opening of the Estates General did not take place until January 15. Perhaps this tardiness was caused by the late arrival of many deputies. Perhaps the government was not ready or some of the princes were delayed. In any event, the intervening two weeks were not entirely wasted. The deputies verified their powers, and on January 7 Beaujeu took advantage of the lull in activity to invite them to Montils where he introduced them to the young king. This and perhaps other attempts to influence the deputies before the opening of the estates was later to arouse the ire of a staunch follower of Orléans.[42] The young duke, however, evidenced little concern at either the machinations of the Beaujeus or at the need to court the favor of the deputies. Rather he established himself in Tours away from the king where he led a life of gay frivolity hardly calculated to win support for his claims to govern the kingdom.[43]

The Opening of the Estates and the Preparation of the Cahier

On the fourteenth the king entered Tours with pomp to attend the opening of the estates. The ceremony was held in the great hall of the archepiscopal palace the following day. The walls had been draped with tapestry and a platform constructed to hold a throne draped with the blue robes on which the king sat when he held a *lit de justice* in the Parlement of Paris. On either side of the throne, the princes, dukes, counts, and prelates were placed. Before them were the bailiffs, seneschals, councilors, secretaries, and finally the deputies themselves. The meeting was opened by a clerk calling the roll of the deputies and a speech by the chancellor.[44]

The chancellor was William de Rochefort, a member of the old Burgundian nobility. He had studied law, had been councilor of Duke Philip the Good, but had found it expedient to leave the Burgundian service. Like the more famous Commynes, he had been given employment by Louis XI who had named him chancellor a few months before his death. Rochefort was new at his post when the Estates General opened, but he had enough experience as a soldier, jurist, and diplomat to play a clever game during the two months that followed.[45]

It was expedient, Rochefort thought, to remain in the Beaujeu camp, but he acted with care because the strong reaction against the old regime could easily be turned by the discontented princes into an attack on himself and the faction he represented. His role was to flatter the deputies, to give them hope, whether justified or not, of reforms to come, and above all to channel their efforts towards preparing a list of grievances to be righted. He did not specifically mention the establishment of a new council for the youthful king. To have done so would have roused the ire of those magnates who were content with the existing situation. Clearly it was better to wait for the deputies to raise the question as they were sure to do sooner or later. To achieve his purpose, he took as the theme of his address an explanation of why the Estates General had been convoked.

The assembly was to provide an opportunity for the deputies of the nation to meet their king and to express their loyalty to him. The French people, Rochefort argued, had always been devoted to their rulers, and here he drew a sharp contrast with the English who had just transferred the crown to the assassin of the young sons of Edward IV. The assembly likewise provided the king with an opportunity to become acquainted with his subjects, to assure the union and concord of the head and members of the body politic. Rochefort sought to calm any fears that the deputies might harbor because of the age of the king. Had not David and Solomon been minors when they assumed the reins of government? Turning to more specific matters, the chancellor said that Charles had such great confidence in the deputies that he was going to ask them to participate in the government. In the first months of his reign economies had been introduced, the alienations of the domain since the death of Charles VII had been revoked, the church and the administration of justice had been partly reformed, and friendly relations had been established abroad, but still the chancellor remarked pointedly, the crown needed money for the defense of the realm and other important affairs. It was for the people to inform the king of their grievances, to report any oppression by public officials, to advise on how peace, justice, and good government could be achieved. The king, in turn, would execute their desires. Thus union and sympathetic understanding would be achieved. He invited the deputies to deal first with matters concerning the general good of the kingdom and the person of the king and then with those pertaining to individual provinces and towns. The king, Rochefort promised as he ended his address, would give an audience whenever they desired.[46]

It was not until January 17 that the real work of organizing the assembly began. The initiative was taken by the Paris section, one of whose number, Jean Henri, chanter of Paris and *maître des requêtes de l'hôtel,* suggested that the deputies divide themselves into four or six sections in order to facilitate discussion. It would take too long, he argued, for everyone to give his opinion in a general assembly. As Henri had been admitted to the king's council on several occasions shortly after the death of Louis XI, his proposal may have reflected the desires of one of the factions in the government, but there is no real evidence.[47] After a long debate, the proposition was accepted and the assembly was subdivided into six nations or sections following the six généralités for finance. The first included Picardy, Champagne, Paris, and most of the bailiwicks north of the Loire River; the second was Burgundy; the third, Normandy; the fourth, Aquitaine; the fifth, Languedoc, Dauphiné, Provence, and Roussillon; and the sixth, Languedoïl.[48]

This done, the deputies turned their attention to the election of a president; after various opinions had been expressed, their choice fell on Jean de Bilhères-Lagraulas, Abbot of Saint-Denis and Bishop of Lombez. The nomination of Lombez was dictated by his position as senior member of the Paris delegation. He had been a councilor under Louis XI, an ambassador to Spain, and had recently been appointed president of the *Cour des aides.* His past, of necessity, ought to have made him a defender of the old regime, but his avarice and ambition led him to desert the party of his former benefactor in return for more rapid advancement. Throughout the Estates General he was attacked by Masselin for his allegiance to the princes, but as a reward they readmitted him to the royal council near the close of the assembly and soon thereafter named him president of the *échiquier* of Normandy. The triumph of the Beaujeus near the end of 1484 temporarily prevented his further advancement, but in 1489 Charles VIII returned him to the government as he did so many other enemies of his sister. In that year Lombez participated in the trial of the Dukes of Orléans and Brittany and concluded the Peace of Frankfort with the Habsburg, Maximilian. He was later made an envoy to Rome where his immorality was said to have shocked the Borgia court of Pope Alexander VI, but if this be true, it did not prevent his elevation to Cardinal in 1493, six years before his death.[49]

The deputies refused an offer made by the crown to loan them clerks, and instead chose two of their own number to serve in that capacity. This decision was calculated to insure greater independence from the royal council. But as one of the clerks, Jean of Reims, was a protégé of the Bishop of Lombez, troubles were to follow. For a time, however, peace reigned and the deputies united in sending a delegation to the Archbishop of Tours to request that a general procession and a sermon be held every Sunday to insure the success of the assembly.[50]

On the next day which was Sunday the religious services were held as requested. From Monday through Thursday of the following week the sections met in separate rooms. Little is known of their procedure except that each had its own president, Jean de Rély serving for Paris, the Abbot of Cîteaux for Burgundy, and Jean Masselin for Normandy. The last named section had already prepared a cahier, and the deputies spent their time in repressing certain articles that did not appear necessary and in separating those of special interest to the province from those pertaining to the whole kingdom. On Friday the deputies held a general assembly to hear each section read its articles on the church and the nobility. Other parts of the cahier were read on Saturday, but progress was slow because many of the articles had not been carefully prepared.[51]

This situation caused the deputies to reconsider the question of procedure on the following Monday, and it was decided to name a committee composed of two members from each order in each section to prepare the general cahier to be presented to the king. Those selected were to take an oath to work for the common good and not to divulge any of their activities. Already, Masselin informs us, some deputies had leaked information to the princes and the general public. Here we have the first indication of ill-feeling among those present, an undercurrent which Masselin frequently alluded to, but never fully explained. The estates also decided that all the articles in the cahier should be read before the king, but hope was held out that the three- or four-hour task so well calculated to bore the thirteen-year-old monarch could be divided into a two-day ceremony. This done, Jean de Rély, canon of Paris, was elected speaker.

Once more the prestige of the capital city was indicated. Rély was a native of Arras and had become rector of the University of Paris in 1471. He was a leader in the pre-Reformation Catholic reform movement and a scholar of some note having helped translate the first Bible into French. Lefèvre d'Étaples dedicated a work on Aristotle to him and Pico della Mirandola numbered him among his correspondents. By 1485 he had become the confessor of Charles VIII and later he was granted the important and lucrative posts of Bishop of Angers and Dean of Saint-Martin of Tours.[52] At this time, however, it is impossible to tell with certainty whether he was allied to any faction.

The day on which Rély was elected was also marked by an unknown deputy's recommendation that the estates provide for the upbringing of the king and the composition of his council. One wishes that Masselin had given his name, but whoever he was, his proposal had no immediate effect, for the deputies refused to consider such a controversial and dangerous matter until the cahier had been prepared. It did remind the princes and the deputies of the conflict that lay ahead.

This brief reprieve was utilized by the Orleanists to try to win the support of the wavering and neutral deputies. As their spokesman before the estates, they chose Philippe de Luxembourg, Bishop of Le Mans, deputy of Maine, and nephew of the famous Louis de Luxembourg, Count of Saint-Pol and Constable of France, who had been decapitated by Louis XI. Here was a man who had little cause to love the royal family or the advisors held over from the preceding reign. His speech to the deputies was not fully recorded, but in general, he pointed to the sufferings of the French people and the necessity of avoiding the prodigalities so characteristic of the era of Louis XI. Pensions especially should be guarded against, and in a grand gesture he reported that the leaders of the Orleanist party were willing to surrender all of theirs. Turning to the question of the council, the bishop recommended that only honest and experienced men be admitted. Members who, in the past, had oppressed the people or had received excessive pensions should be removed.

This effort to drive the former advisors of Louis XI out of the council was made only in the name of the Dukes of Orléans and Alençon, the Counts of Angoulême, Foix, and Dunois, and several other seigneurs. Conspicuously absent were such magnates as Lorraine, Albret, Comminges, and above all, Bourbon. A powerful independent block still existed among the great as well as among the deputies. It is not surprising that the generous, if sincere, offer of the Orleanists had no immediate effect on the actions of the deputies, and they had to content themselves with the thanks of the assembly.[53]

It was rather a combination of the apparent good will of the Orleanist princes and a constant stream of evidence revealing the harsh, incompetent, extravagant nature of the government of the late king that slowly roused the anger of the deputies against the royal bureaucracy and those, like the Beaujeus, who found themselves in a position of having in any way to defend it. The attack on Louis XI began innocently enough on Monday, February 2, with the reading of the general cahier that had been prepared by the committee chosen by the six sections. It was certainly not the purpose of the committee to side with the Orleanists, nor did the duke anticipate his good fortune. Rather the source of this new development was the nature of a cahier itself.

The cahier was a petition of grievances coupled with recommendations on how the listed wrongs could be righted. Since Louis XI had reigned during the preceding twenty-two years, few of the deputies had been heads of families under any other king. The difficulties they faced were naturally enough charged against his rule, and the reign of Charles VII was but a remote memory of their youth. Sufferings they had then been subjected to had been mitigated by the lapse of time or else were blamed on the English wars. Thus in article after article, the cahier attacked this or that action of the late king, or pleaded for a return to the days of Charles VII. The greatest accomplishment of Louis XI was to make his father a popular king, a feat that the poor dauphin of Joan of Arc could never have accomplished for himself.

The cahier's chapter on the church shed glory on Charles VII by asking that the Pragmatic Sanction of Bourges be enforced. The election of bishops and abbots was requested, and reservations, provisions, annates, and appeals to Rome in judicial cases were attacked. Fortunately for the Beaujeus, they were able to avoid criticism for the multiple changes in ecclesiastical policy introduced by Louis XI because they had participated in recent actions of the royal council designed to lead, in part at least, toward a return to the practices of the earlier regime. The innovations of Louis XI found stalwart defenders only among some of the bishops who pointed out that the new proposals would weaken the authority of the Holy See. Their arguments were to no avail, and they were shouted down by the opposition which included an overwhelming majority of the lay deputies and the lower clergy as well.[54]

The chapter on the nobility likewise reminded the deputies of the differences between the policies of Louis XI and his father. The committee recommended that the privileges, prerogatives, and jurisdictions of the second estate be respected as in the time of Charles VII and his predecessors. The pointed failure to mention Louis XI was followed by complaints against the frequent convocation of the *ban* and *arrière-ban* which had impoverished the nobility and by the request that foreigners be excluded from military commands and service in the royal household. Charges were made that hunting rights had been infringed upon by the crown officials, and once more a nostalgic request was made to return to the good old days of Charles VII.[55]

In the chapter on the third or common estate, the same theme was stressed. The articles emphasized the poverty of the people and attributed it to the scarcity of currency brought about by wars and the export of precious metals to Rome. Heavy taxation, especially without the consent of the estates, was attacked and a strong plea was made for the abolition of the taille. To remove the necessity for this tax, the king was asked to revoke all alienations of the royal domain made by Louis XI and to curtail expenses. The last was to be accomplished by reducing the size of the army, stopping pensions, or at least greatly reducing them, and decreasing the number and pay of royal officials.[56]

Neither these articles nor the ones on the nobility had occasioned much debate, but those on justice struck too near home for some to remain silent. This chapter was the longest in the cahier and included a request that the appointee who had won his position by special favor be replaced by the official who had formerly held the office. This ill-concealed move to supplant the bureaucracy of Louis XI provoked a strong reply by the Bishop of Lombez, a former royal official, who knew well the difficulties of far-reaching reform in this direction. He argued that the idea of removing the desired officials was bad because it would open to litigation almost all the offices in the kingdom. This situation would anger king and princes alike. The bishop's effort to protect the bureaucracy of Louis XI was challenged by those who held that this was no problem because nearly all offices were automatically vacated by the death of the late king. No decision could be reached and on the following day, it was decided to appoint a committee of six to revise the chapter. This was done and a rewritten cahier was submitted to the deputies on February 9, when the articles were approved after some debate on three or four of the more controversial ones. Even at this late date, the Bishop of Lombez may not have been above resorting to trickery to avoid the long and detailed articles desired by the majority. The clerk, Jean of Reims, a favorite of that prelate, failed to include several resolutions. Masselin admitted the possibility that it may have been a case of forgetfulness, but he was clearly suspicious. In the end nothing was said about removing the officials, but the very long chapter on justice spoke out strongly against the sale of offices, an innovation which was blamed on Louis XI. The deputies stood for election of officials and their tenure for life or during good behavior. They complained about the costs of justice, from the clerical fees charged by the chancellery to the commissions claimed by the councilors of the Parlement. They petitioned that the provincial and local customs be put in writing as ordered by Charles VII and that justice be done to the seigneurs dispossessed by Louis XI.[57]

The chapter on commerce was brief but important. The deputies asked for freer circulation of goods within the kingdom and permission to export abroad by land and sea. They expressed concern over the departure of native currency from France and attacked the fairs at Lyon for the role they played in this outward flow. Other articles requested that toll roads and bridges be kept in a decent state of repair and that financial and judicial officials be forbidden to engage in trade as in the time of Charles VII.[58]

The constant repetition in the cahier of the theme that Louis XI had introduced every form of political, economic, social, and administrative evil into France was reinforced by the tales of the deputies from Maine,

Anjou, and Chartres of the cruelties inflicted by his agents who collected fines and *gabelles,* and by visits of representatives of several nobles seeking the support of the estates in their quest for justice against wrongs done them by the late king.

The first of these representatives was Philippe, Seigneur of Croy, who appeared with his advocate before the deputies to request that they petition the king to return Porcein, Croy, Renti, and other properties to him. He admitted that he had fought with Maximilian and the Flemings in the late war, a fact not surprising since his father had been an important official of the Burgundian dukes, but he argued that he had been forced to do so because of the threats of the late king. Certainly he must have been in a difficult position during the last years of Louis' reign because his wife was none other than Jacqueline de Saint-Pol, daughter of the constable who had been executed for treason. The legal basis for his request was that by the terms of the Treaty of Arras the confiscated lands of rebellious nobles were to be returned. He indicated, quite correctly, that the subjects of the princes had sworn to make sure that the treaty was observed, a pertinent reminder, for the year before many of the deputies at Tours had been assembled in their respective bailiwicks to promise to uphold the agreement.[59]

The plea of the Seigneur of Croy was followed by one on behalf of Charles, Count of Armagnac, who had just been released after a long term of imprisonment and wanted the restitution of his confiscated domains. Count Charles owed his difficulties to his own and his family's rebellious activities during the reign of Louis XI, but his house was an ancient one that had often served the crown well, and this fact was stressed by his spokesman. The introduction of the Armagnac issue was hardly calculated to help the Beaujeu cause, for Pierre had participated in the destruction of that family and had received part of their confiscated lands as his reward.[60]

Also harmful to the Beaujeu cause was the appearance of representatives of the three sons and two daughters of the Duke of Nemours. The late duke was a member of the House of Armagnac and his wife was the daughter of Isabella of Luxembourg. With these family connections it is not surprising that Nemours had on three occasions rebelled against Louis XI, the last time in alliance with England and Burgundy. On this occasion Pierre de Beaujeu had forced him to capitulate, but Louis, his father-in-law, had refused to honor the terms of surrender he had granted and Nemours was brought to trial. When the Parlement appeared inclined towards leniency, Louis had appointed an extraordinary commission presided over by Beaujeu. The unhappy duke was condemned to death and his lands confiscated, the bulk of them going to the members of the commission that had tried him. Beaujeu himself got the lion's share, and Philippe de Commynes was one of those who was indulged at Nemour's expense. The representatives of the landless children had no hesitation in alluding to the unsavory role Beaujeu had played, although he was not mentioned by name, and they reduced the deputies to tears when they pictured the pleadings of the wife and the unfortunate position of the children.[61]

More serious still to the cause of the Beaujeus was the appearance of representatives of René II, Duke of Lorraine, before the Estates General on the following day. The duke was a courageous, able leader who had won renown for his victory over Charles the Bold near Nancy less than a decade before. It was he and not Louis XI who had overthrown the House of Burgundy, but in return for his services the late king had refused to recognize his claims to Bar and Provence. If these territories were surrendered, it would undo much of King Louis' work, but if the Beaujeus refused to support Lorraine's claims, they might drive him into the arms of Orléans. It was a delicate situation which the royal council sought to solve by arguing that the king was a minor and could not undertake to make such a concession until he was of legal age. Dissatisfied with this reply, the duke now placed his cause before the estates for mediation.

The deputies could not have failed to be impressed by these reminders of the severity of the late king, or by the fact that there were those high in the council of Charles VIII who had profited by the wholesale confiscations. Half-forgotten were the manifold acts of treason that these great nobles had committed before Louis had struck with severity. Indeed, public opinion of the day seemed content to see magnates forgiven again and again for their rebellions, regardless of the sufferings they caused. Only men of lesser estate could be executed by kings without arousing protests of sympathy. The deputies refrained from discussing the affairs of these lords at the time because of more pressing business, but embassies continued to be sent to them; and, at last, they included an article in their cahier asking that the nobles be heard and justice done them.[62] It was in the face of these reminders of the brutal acts of the late king that the deputies of the three estates turned their attention to the fundamental question of the governance of the king and the composition of his council.

The Question of the Council

Three factions then vied for control of the king and his government. One, headed by Pierre and Anne of Beaujeu, had advocated the calling of the Estates General in the hope that the deputies would consent to the arrangements that Louis XI had made for the upbringing of the king and the government of the kingdom. During the debates that followed, they clearly advocated the popular cause by insisting that it was both the right and the duty of the deputies to name the members of the king's council. By such tactics, they hoped to free themselves from their rivals.

The second party had played little or no role in the convocation of the Estates General. Headed by the young Duke of Orléans and composed largely of his relatives, this group first showed a deep interest in the estates near the end of January when their spokesman, the Bishop of Le Mans, presented to the deputies an offer to surrender their pensions, coupled with the suggestion that oppressive and dishonest royal councilors be replaced by honest and experienced men.[63] In February, when it had become obvious that this move to win popular support had failed, Orléans reverted to his earlier position that it was his right as heir to the throne and as first prince of the blood to have the custody of the king and control of the government.

The third party was the largest and most powerful. It was composed of the great feudal nobles, men like the Dukes of Bourbon and Lorraine, the Counts of Albret, Comminges, and Richebourg, the Marshals des Querdes and de Gié, and their followers in and out of the royal council. Their strength lay in their numbers, their weakness in lack of internal agreement. At first some, or all of them, had favored the convocation of the Estates General, but by the time the meeting was held, they had recognized their dominant position in the council and they were loathe to accept any effort on the part of the deputies to tamper with that body. They were not wholly selfish in their desires to remain in power. Orléans appeared to be an irresponsible, inexperienced playboy, and Beaujeu had earned an unsavory reputation for the greedy way in which he had devoured the confiscated domains of the rebellious nobles during the preceding reign. The retrenchments and the reforms of the past four months had been largely their work, and it is worthy of note that these policies were partly abandoned when the Beaujeus became firmly entrenched a year later.

The first specific proposal to deal with the upbringing of the king and the composition of his council had been made on January 26 by an unknown deputy, but it had been decided to postpone debate until after the cahier had been completed because of the complicated nature of the subject and the danger involved in considering the rights of those who then held power.[64] Shortly thereafter, the Bishop of Le Mans, in the name of the Orleanists, had recommended that the dishonest and oppressive councilors be dismissed by the estates; but even the Orleanists additional offer to abandon their pensions brought from the assembly only a deputation to thank them for their generosity.[65]

On February 3 the Orleanists made another attempt to disrupt the proceedings by dispatching Mathurin Brachet, Seigneur of Montagu Le Blanc, to speak to the assembly. Le Blanc held the official post of chamberlain to the duke, but he was more often employed as ambassador and master intriguer. He had been sent to Nantes a little more than a year before to make an alliance between his master and the Duke of Brittany. Now he was back at court with the mission of stirring up animosity among the deputies against the great nobles who stood for the status quo. His discourse was brief and to the point. The activities of the estates were being noised abroad in spite of the rule for secrecy. Le Blanc departed without having named anyone as being responsible, but Masselin placed the blame on the Bishop of Lombez who was president of the assembly and several others who frequented the houses of the great.[66] He was probably correct, as events were to prove, but none of the three parties suffered from lack of informants among the deputies. The Bishop of Le Mans, Robert de Foville, Guillaume de Montmorency, and Guillaume Le Fuzelier acted in this capacity for Orléans. The Beaujeus could count on Philippe Pot and the Abbot of Cîteaux from the Burgundian delegation and doubtless many others, and the magnates had in addition to Lombez, Jean of Reims, one of the clerks of the estates, and a host of friends and vassals. Indeed, two members of the council of fifteen, the Bishop of Périgueux and the Marshal des Querdes, were deputies and had unquestioned access to the assembly.[67] Masselin on one occasion charged that both the Beaujeus and the Orleanists had informers in the Norman section.[68] Under such circumstances one can readily imagine how the deputies flocked to this or that prince after the daily session of the estates to report on new developments in the assembly and to plan the activities of the morrow. In vain did Masselin and other unattached delegates inveigh against this practice. Throughout the meeting each of the three factions at court was well aware of the events that were transpiring in the archepiscopal palace at Tours.

It was the Bishop of Lombez who suggested on February 4 that the deputies begin to study in earnest the problem of providing for the king's education and the government of the kingdom. On neither this nor any other occasions is it likely that he was voicing his own ideas; he had almost certainly been closeted with the magnates the preceding evening, and was prepared to carry the fight against the Beaujeus. But, Lombez suggested, before any voting took place the assembly ought either to be reorganized by bailiwick or else balloting should be done by the individual deputies. The old system of voting by sections was unjust because both Paris and Languedoïl were larger than any two or three of the other sections put together. There was some justice in this observation, but the small Burgundian and Norman sections, whose votes had until now equaled those of Paris and Languedoïl, were not apt to surrender their rights willingly. After a long debate, the plan was dropped.[69]

Undaunted by the failure to improve their voting power, the Parisians returned to the arena with a list of the fifteen councilors that had been named by the magnates after the death of Louis XI, and recommended that they be kept in office as a reward for having convoked the estates. In addition, they suggested that the princes choose nine more councilors from a list of twelve or sixteen prepared by the estates, to bring the total to twenty-four. The true origin of this proposal was indicated by an added proviso giving the Dukes of Orléans and Bourbon the right to veto the choice of any councilor whether of the original fifteen or of the ones to be selected. An alliance had been born that was fraught with danger for the Beaujeus. Orléans had at first believed that a majority of the deputies would support his pretensions because of his exalted birth, but his proposal to change the council that had been presented by the Bishop of Le Mans had occasioned little response. Clearly Orléans needed additional support in the Estates General, and this could be had only by joining Bourbon and the independents. The alliance was both costly and embarrassing to him. It meant the acceptance of many councilors who had played prominent roles in the preceding reign, but who were in accord with Bourbon, and it necessitated the abandonment of the Bishop of Le Mans. That prelate bitterly assailed the Bishop of Lombez for his misfortune. Lombez was of the party of the independents, being very likely attached most closely to Albret and Comminges, for he came from southern France and was definitely a supporter of the Armagnacs. It is not improbable that he had served as the go-between in the negotiations for the new alliance and had persuaded the Orleanists that the removal of any councilors was certain to cause trouble. Fortunately, Orléans and Bourbon had already taken the precaution of assuring the deputies that there was no longer any enmity between them, and Le Mans' bitterness had little effect on future developments.[70]

The members of the new coalition had chosen Paris to voice their plan because that section held precedence over the others. They exercised enough influence in this region to persuade a majority of the deputies to accept their proposals, although admittedly there was a strong pro-Beaujeu minority. Orléans ought to have been able to bring considerable pressure to bear. He was governor of the Île-de-France and Champagne, and most of his lands, including the duchy of Orléans, lay within this section. Many from the Paris region were anxious to accept the council of fifteen anyway because six of their number came from the area. Since it was to the council that the inhabitants would have to appeal for special concessions in taxation and other matters, the more members of that body who were interested in the area the better.

The Parisian proposal threw the deputies into a quandary. To acquiesce was to perpetuate in office several councilors who were regarded as bad administrators and dangerous men. To ask for their removal from office was to incur the anger of the magnates who had appointed them. After many protestations of their respect for the prerogatives of the princes and their unwillingness to judge anyone unworthy of being in the council, the Normans proposed that each section choose three persons to participate in an electoral college, along with eight of the fifteen existing councilors who were to be selected by the estates as a whole. This electoral college would in turn appoint twenty-four or thirty-six permanent councilors after taking an oath to choose only able and virtuous men. The elected councilors would be asked to take an oath before the estates. This proposal, which had the merit of preserving, or perhaps more accurately, of usurping authority for the estates, was also supported by the deputies from Aquitaine and Languedoïl. The Burgundians, aided by the deputies from Languedoc, sought a compromise between the Paris and Norman positions. They recommended that the princes choose twelve councilors from the fifteen already named and that the estates also name twelve, two from each section.[71]

At this point, Masselin thought, an able president could have brought the deputies to a common accord if he had so desired, but Lombez had no such intentions. Only the Paris section supported the proposal to keep the original fifteen councilors and to leave to the magnates the final choice of the additional members of the council. Any agreement reached at that moment was sure to be to the disadvantage of the princes. To gain time, Lombez adjourned the meeting until 2 o'clock the following afternoon.[72]

The brief respite was used by the various factions to recoup their forces. Jacques de Brézé, Seneschal of Normandy and devoted adherent of the Beaujeus, had been attending the morning session, although nowhere is he listed as being a deputy. After the adjournment, he had galloped to the château of Montils where he had a conference with Pierre de Beaujeu. By 2 P.M. he was back at Tours with the recommendation that the Norman deputies put their fears aside and elect all the councilors. To leave to the princes the right to name the council, Beaujeu had told him, would only offer them an object of discord. For the first time the Beaujeus had clearly shown their desire to have the deputies select the royal council in order to escape from those named by the other magnates the preceding September.[73]

Several royal councilors of the Beaujeu faction who were present offered the Normans the same advice. There was no way, they felt, to remove those who were inexperienced or dishonest without doing away with everyone named by the magnates. To select some to stay and some to be removed would incur the anger of the princes who had been responsible for the appointment of the latter. The Norman deputies were far from convinced by these arguments. They knew that their debate was being reported to the undesired councilors and to the princes, and they were fearful of the consequences. At length it was decided to recommend a compromise. Twelve of the original fifteen councilors would be accepted by the estates in concurrence with the princes, and twenty-four would be elected by the deputies, four by each section. If the representative from Paris and Languedoïl claimed the privilege of naming more than the smaller sections, the Normans agreed to limit their nominations to three.[74]

We do not know what transpired on the afternoon of February 5 in the other sections, but when the deputies met in full assembly the next day, they were confronted by a deputation of five led by the Seigneur of Boissy. He stated that he had been sent by the king and that his four companions came as the representatives of the Dukes of Orléans and Bourbon. The latter half of this avowal seems true enough, but it is doubtful whether Boissy was speaking for the king or Bourbon because it had been the duke who introduced him into the royal council.[75] His message was brief. The king and the princes had been surprised to learn that on the preceding day a roll of the councilors had been presented to the deputies as if it had come from them. In order that the deputies would not in the future rely on a third party, they were sending the approved list of the councilors. With this brief and obscure speech, Boissy handed the list to the president and departed leaving the deputies thoroughly confused as to what he had meant.[76]

It is difficult to arrive at an explanation for this episode. It might be argued that the two dukes thought that the Parisians had furnished the deputies with an incorrect list of councilors, but there was no reason to suspect them for they clearly favored the princes in all other matters. More likely, the purpose of the deputation was only to underscore the fact that this was the list of councilors that the princes had approved, with the none too subtle hint that the deputies would do well to leave it alone. The actions of Lombez at this point are not easy to explain. When he received the document from Boissy, he examined both sides of it, and amid the demands of the deputies for a public reading, he at first sought to turn it over to the Paris section. Whether Lombez was fearful that the princes had suddenly altered their policy without notifying him and had changed the list of the councilors, or whether he affected surprise in order to remove the growing suspicion that he was in league with the magnates, we do not know. It is only certain that Masselin was so angered by the episode that he introduced into his journal at this point a bitter attack against Lombez for his corruption, blind ambition, willingness to support evil royal councilors, and eagerness to curry favor with the princes.[77]

The scroll submitted by Boissy was in fact the original document signed shortly after the death of Louis XI by the king, the queen mother, the Dukes of Orléans and Bourbon, and nineteen other magnates. The names of the councilors were the same as those submitted by the Paris section, but the imposing scroll did give an air of finality to the whole affair that was by no means lost on the deputies. To remove any remaining doubt, the estates named a delegation to go to the king and the princes to ask if the purpose of their embassy had been to forbid any changes in the composition of the council.[78]

That same afternoon a twelve-man deputation headed by Masselin was granted an audience by Charles. The clergyman thanked the king for the confidence he had shown in the estates and remarked that they were at present having difficulty preparing the articles on the council, but hoped to be finished in several days. The Bishop of Albi replied for the king that all diligence should be used to complete the task and asked if the cahier could be submitted on Monday, February 9. Masselin pleaded for an extra day or two, and the assembly before the king was set for Tuesday. The deputies had won the tacit approval of the king, controlled as he was by his sister and brother-in-law, to consider the question of the council. There remained the necessity to negotiate with the Dukes of Bourbon and Orléans.[79]

Masselin had been more outspoken when he and his fellow deputies were ushered into Bourbon's presence. He specifically asked whether the duke intended that the list of councilors submitted by Boissy should be final, without additions or subtractions. Bourbon was too experienced a statesman to put himself in direct opposition to the aspirations of the estates and he gave the deputies his permission to constitute the council as they saw fit. There were equally effective ways to secure his ends without courting unpopularity, as events were to prove.[80]

The Duke of Orléans was lodged in the town near the church of Saint-Julien. He had been present at the royal audience and knew what the deputation from the estates wanted when it arrived at his door. Nevertheless, he had no ready answer for their questions, but rather sought to escape by excusing himself to keep a dinner engagement. By the following Monday, however, he had learned enough of the trend of the deliberations of the estates to take a strong stand. He completely abandoned any pretense of recognizing the right of the deputies to select the councilors. Once more he dispatched Le Blanc to the archepiscopal palace with a message that he preferred that the question of the council be passed over in silence because of the deputies' failure to maintain his pre-eminent rank and dignity.[81]

Saturday the ninth and Monday the eleventh were devoted to hearing the reports of various delegations, approving of the speech that Rély was to deliver before the king on Tuesday, and making a desperate effort to complete the cahier that was to be presented on the same day. The question of the council continued to give the most trouble. In practice it was to be resolved on the basis of the relative power of the contending factions, but the theory that each side developed to defend its position is nonetheless of interest. There were those who argued that when a king was a minor or incapable of acting for himself, it devolved upon the estates to constitute a council and that the estates should not supplicate but rather command until the council had received from it the sovereign power. This argument was advocated by supporters of the Beaujeus such as Philippe Pot and by those deputies who were not in the party of any prince, but were anxious to claim all possible privileges for the estates. Of this number one must count Jean Masselin. Others argued that at such times the government of the kingdom devolved upon the princes of the blood and that consultation with the estates was unnecessary. This position was taken by the supporters of Orléans, Bourbon, and most of the members of the council that had been established soon after the death of Louis XI.[82]

The debate was long and exciting, but unfortunately only the eloquent speech of Philippe Pot, deputy from Burgundy, has been preserved for us in detail.

"The desire which most of you entertain," he said,

to comprehend the true status of our assembly emboldens me to convey to you as briefly as I can the lessons of wisdom and experience concerning the authority and liberty of the estates, and I hope to convert to more rational views those of you who are so alarmed by this duty of selecting councillors that you would flee from it as from a conflagration or other imminent peril. Before expounding my own views, however, I must refute the opinions of my opponents, and I will deal first with those who consider that the care of the king and the kingdom belongs to the princes of the blood. To which princes would they give it? To the heir-presumptive to the throne? No, they say, for that would be an obvious inducement to the guardian to conspire against his ward, and it has been expressly prohibited by the law. Their conclusion, therefore, is that the government should be entrusted to the nearest relative, and to the next nearest should be assigned the guardianship of the king's person. But no arrangement of that kind can protect the king from conspiracies; and even if it did in some feeble degree contribute to his safety, it would find no sanction in the law, no support in present facts, and no countenance in earlier precedents.

Having thus disposed of the pretensions of the Duke of Orléans and the Count of Angoulême, Pot assailed the Duke of Bourbon and the other magnates:

I turn to the equally futile and still more dangerous arguments of my other opponents, who assign the regency and protectorship to the whole body of royal princes. Who are these princes? Do they include those descended from the royal house in the female line? Truly, a goodly company! Even if they be limited to the male line, could any unity of action be expected of them, or any guarantees for the maintenance of justice and equity? A vague partition of power among a group of princes could lead only to contentions and armed affrays, and nothing would come of it but illegal tyranny. The throne is an office of dignity, and not an hereditary possession, and as such it does not pass to the nearest relatives in the way in which a patrimony passes to its natural guardians. If, then, the commonwealth is not to be bereft of government, the care of it must devolve upon the Estates General of the realm, whose duty it is, not to administer it themselves, but to entrust its administration to worthy hands.

History and tradition tell us the kings were originally created by the votes of the sovereign people, and the prince is placed where he is, not that he may pursue his own advantage, but that he may strive unselfishly for the welfare of the nation. The ruler who falls short of this ideal is a tyrant and a wolf, and is no true shepherd of his flock. Have you not often read that the commonwealth is the people's common concern? Now if it be their concern, how should they neglect it and not care for it? Or how should flatterers attribute sovereign power to the prince, seeing that he exists merely by the people's will? And so I come to the question under discussion, namely, to the problem which arises when a king by infancy or otherwise is incapable of personal rule. Now we are agreed that the commonwealth is the people's; that our king cannot himself govern it; and that it must be entrusted to the care and ministry of others. If then, as I maintain, this care devolves neither upon any one prince, nor upon several princes, nor upon all of them together, it must of necessity return to the people from whom it came, and the people must resume a power which is their own, the more so since it is they alone who suffer from the evils of a long interregnum or a bad regency. I do not suggest that the right of government is taken from the sovereign. I argue only that government and guardianship, not rights and property, are for the time being transferred by law to the people and their representatives; and by the people I mean all subjects of the crown, of what rank soever they be. If, then, you will regard yourselves as the deputies of all the estates of the realm and the depositaries of the aspirations of them all, you cannot avoid the conclusion that the main object of your convocation is to direct the government by your counsels in the vacancy which has arisen through the minority of our sovereign. To this were you bidden by the letters which convened the estates and by the speech which the chancellor delivered in the presence, and with the approval, of king and princes. Nothing could more clearly refute the opinions of those who hold that we have been summoned here merely to vote taxation, and are not concerned with other objects—opinions contradicted by the traditions of the constitution as well as by the course of events.

Some one will object, perhaps, that since the beginning of the reign the princes have constituted a council, carried on the government, and managed state affairs without having been obliged to consult the estates. The answer is that the estates could not be called together at a moments notice, and that some provisional arrangements had to be made. So the princes ruled until the estates met; but today the estates are assembled, and to them the supreme power now belongs. It is for us to confirm the acts of the past and to provide for the future. In my view, that which has been done can have no authority until the estates have sanctioned it; nor can any institution rest upon a safe and pure foundation, if established against their wishes or without their express or tacit consent.

The Estates General is no new thing, and there is no novelty about a delegation of government to a council selected from their midst. When the succession was in dispute between Philip of Valois and Edward of England, the estates adjudicated upon the controversy, and their decision was our true answer to the English claims. During the misfortunes of John's captivity the estates assumed the whole burden of government, although the king's son, Charles, was twenty years of age. Or you may pass from these earlier precedents to facts within living memory, and recall how the country was governed and administered through the estates when Charles VI succeeded to the throne at the age of twelve. The authority of the estates is, then, based both upon precedent and upon reason, and there is no cause to be afraid of putting our hands to the nomination of a council. It is a task upon the accomplishment of which the future of the country—its welfare or ruin—depends. You are here to declare freely what God and your consciences tell you is for the country's good; and if you shirk the fundamental question, your whole edifice will be reared upon the sand. For who then will hear your petitions or receive your remonstrances, or cure your ills, or supply a remedy?

The powers of the estates being established, Pot turned to the question of the composition of the council, and here he offered what was, in effect, a compromise between the various factions:

I shall be asked—But what of the council appointed on the king's accession? Are we to declare these councillors unworthy of the office? Are we to run counter to the sovereign's will and the princes' orders? It is true, of course, that councillors have actually been appointed: well, you can reappoint them; their appointment is provisional and in expectation of your meeting. Now that you have met, are you going to reject as beyond your powers a prerogative which your predecessors enjoyed, and by their steadfastness preserved? There is nothing to hinder you but your own weakness and pusillanimity. Let not any weakness of yours prejudice a liberty which your fathers so jealously guarded. Let it not lead to the ruin of your country, so that you incur the condemnation of posterity, and suffer the glory which should be the reward of your labors to be turned into an eternal shame.[83]

This eloquent speech may have been received with favor and attention by the assembly as Masselin said, but it had no effect on the voting of the sections.[84] Indeed, it was soon apparent that the Beaujeus had lost considerable ground over the weekend.

Paris was the first to report; as was expected, the deputies from this section advocated leaving the number and the personnel of the council up to the princes. Gone was their earlier proposal that the magnates should add nine new councilors from a list of twelve or sixteen selected by the estates.

The Burgundians maintained their earlier position that the council should consist of twelve men named by the princes and twelve elected by the estates, two from each section. A proviso was added that princes of the blood in the masculine line should have the right of entrance in the order and degree of their kinship to the king, but this was hardly a serious concession as the right of the princes to attend was presumed anyway. All letters and ordonnances ought to be issued in the king's name, but nothing should be concluded without the consent of the majority of the council.

The Normans were nearly in accord with the Burgundians. They advocated keeping only eight instead of twelve of the original councilors and taking eighteen deputies from the estates. Thus they shifted the preponderance of power into the hands of those named by the estates. The differences between the two sections could be compromised, and so confident were they of victory that they had already selected their candidates for the council.[85]

It must have come as a rude shock to the Normans and Burgundians to discover at this point that the princes and their allies had been busy over the weekend. The deputies from Aquitaine had formerly stood beside the Normans, but now, as a result of pressure from the Counts of Albret and Comminges, they swung behind the Paris section. The two nobles were influential members of the original council of fifteen, and the deputies from that region had high hopes of receiving special favors through their good offices, or at least so Masselin charged.

The deputies from Languedoc and Languedoïl were so divided that they could reach no decision. Formerly they had stood with the Normans and Burgundians, but the subtle work of the princes had so divided them that they could take no decided stand. One can make a good guess who these princes were. Languedoc had no great nobility, but its governor for many years had been none other than the Duke of Bourbon, and Dauphiné, which was also a part of this section, had as its royal governor the Count of Dunois, near relative and close advisor of the Duke of Orléans. Bourbon was equally powerful in Languedoïl where he held extensive lands in Bourbonnais, Forez, and Auvergne, was governor of Lyonnais, and had just placed his protégé, the Seigneur of Culant, in the post of bailiff of Berry.

By Monday night the deputies had despaired of reaching an agreement before the royal audience on the morrow, but they voted to tell the king that they would terminate the affair as soon as possible.[86]

In the early afternoon of the following day, Charles appeared before the deputies. The meeting was long, although neither Charles nor his chancellor delayed proceedings by making speeches. Rély was given the floor almost immediately, but his oration was so full of biblical and classical allusions, of historical anecdotes, and unmitigated flattery, that he had to postpone a large section of his address to another day in order to avoid boring the young king. His speech was organized into six sections, each intended as a reply to one of the six reasons the chancellor had given in the opening assembly for the convocation in the estates. In no part was there much that was not common to the thought of the time. The mutual duties of the king and his subjects were stressed and the fact that both were to be judged by God was pointedly made. The difficulties which beset the various estates and the disorders to be found in the administration of justice were exposed. When Rély finally stopped without having touched on the question of the council, the clerk of the estates read the first three chapters of the cahier and the meeting came to an end, having been endured for at least three hours.[87]

On Wednesday morning the deputies assembled by sections to attempt once more to solve the problem of the council. The difficulties that had plagued them on this matter by no means abated. Paris and Languedoïl continued to complain about the injustice of voting by sections. A Norman offer to permit the two large sections to name three or four councilors to their two was rejected as being an insufficient concession. Within the individual sections there was considerable debate. The Parisian, the Champenois, the Picard, the Orléanais, and the Chartrain could not agree on who from the Paris section should serve on the council. The princes and great nobles continued their intrigues and Masselin specifically charged them with intimidating the deputies of Aquitaine and Languedoc. The fear of offending the magnates and the desire of some deputies for rewards from those in high places added to the difficulties in reaching an agreement. If no agreement was made, the status quo would be maintained, a situation not unpleasant for the Paris section which Masselin charged with having six men on the council already, or with Languedoïl that had more than three. These two sections and the followers of the princes made little effort to compromise, for they had nothing to lose by continued intransigence.[88]

In a desperate effort to bridge the gap, a Norman, Jacques de Croismare, drew up a series of articles on the council which differed by a single clause from those demanded by Paris, but this clause was all-important; it provided for the election of two councilors by each section to serve with those on the original list. The Parisians weakened to the extent of recognizing the possibility that twelve might be chosen from among the deputies; but they continued to insist that the right of election belonged to the king, or to his original council, and not to the sections. Still no agreement could be reached.

The question of the royal guardianship also caused contentions. A messenger from the Duke of Orléans, after pointedly reminding the Norman deputies that his master drew large revenues from their province and regarded himself as their friend and protector, complained about their articles on the royal council and their desire to surrender the government of the king to the Beaujeus. If the king was to have a guardian, that office by right belonged to the duke, and no one else. Should the deputies persist in dealing with the matter, they were directed to say that the Beaujeus should be "near the person of the king" and nothing more.[89]

An envoy from the Beaujeus recommended that the phrase *custodia atque regimine,* which had been in the original Norman proposal, be omitted so as not to offend the duke, and that the article should only say that the Beaujeus were to be "near the person of the king as they had been until the present and as it had been ordered by the late king and queen." Left to decide between these two alternatives, the deputies from Normandy compromised by stating that the Beaujeus should be "near the person of the king as they had been until the present." [90]

It had been hoped to hold a second full assembly of the estates for the presentation of the cahier on that day and the deputies, the chancellor, and some great nobles and prelates assembled for this purpose, but a message was received from the king postponing his appearance until the morrow in order to give the deputies an opportunity to complete the cahier. Masselin suggested that the true cause of the delay was a quarrel between the princes over the guardianship of the king. The failure of the princes to assemble with the other magnates for the scheduled audience and a reminder sent by the Duke of Alençon that his dignity and rank must not be overlooked gives added credence to this view.[91]

The deputies determined to make the most of this brief reprieve, and after new failures to reach an accord on the council, they elected two deputies from each section to meet at the domicile of the president in the evening to resolve the issue. The debate of this committee was long and bitter with the Normans and Burgundians holding out against the desires of the other four sections who were near agreement. Some suggested that each section submit a separate petition relative to the council, a proposal that was readily acceptable to the princes for it would leave to them the privilege of choosing the one they preferred. For this very reason many deputies objected. At length a compromise was drafted to be submitted to the assembly the next day.[92]

On February 12 the assembly approved, with minor changes, the recommendations submitted by the committee. The Beaujeus were defeated on the question of the council, for the right of the original councilors to seats was tacitly recognized. The king and the council were given the privilege of naming twelve new councilors, two from each section. To this council was entrusted the government of the kingdom and all acts, ordonnances, and letters issued in the king's name were to have its approval.[93] The result was to confirm the dominant position of the independents in the government. The Burgundians and Normans did have enough influence to win acceptance for the idea that the deputies ought to name delegates to meet with the council and discuss the cahier that the estates presented, but no mention was made of this proposal in the cahier and events were to prove it unacceptable to the princes.[94]

The Beaujeus won a minor victory when Pierre was given the right to preside over the council in the absence of the king and the Dukes of Orléans and Bourbon, this in spite of the remonstrances of an envoy of the Duke of Alençon. On the other hand, the Beaujeus thought it expedient to have Philippe Pot ask the deputies to refrain from accepting the Norman proposal concerning the guardianship of the king because it would lead to quarrels between the great.[95]

That afternoon the king and his suite met with the deputies to hear the remainder of the Rély speech. The scholarly clergyman took every opportunity to display his knowledge, but he was briefer than on the earlier occasion and once he brought the deputies to tears when he pleaded the cause of the children of the Duke of Nemours, the eldest of whom appeared before the king during a brief interruption in the oration. When Rély had finished, Jean of Reims read the rest of the cahier. It took him more than an hour, an interminable time, because he spoke as though his mouth were full and he stammered as well. Perhaps it was for this reason that the chancellor made his reply brief. After consulting the princes, he thanked the deputies for their advice. The king and the princes were particularly pleased, he repeated, with the articles on the council, and the request that some deputies be added to that body was also acceptable.[96]

Most of those present undoubtedly thought that the reply of the chancellor would terminate the audience. They were mistaken. The dull afternoon was suddenly turned into one of intense excitement when Charles d'Armagnac threw himself on his knees before the throne and begged to be heard. When the king consented, he signaled his lawyer who began a long oration. He told how the elder brother of the present count had been driven into rebellion, how he had been captured and treacherously slain before his wife and relatives. That virtuous woman of royal blood had been attacked and later killed when her captors forced her to take a potion designed to abort her expected child. The present count had played no part in the rebellion of his brother, but he had nevertheless been seized, imprisoned, and tortured for fourteen years. The Parlement had moved his acquittal, but powerful enemies prevented the execution of the decree. Now free, he demanded the return of his lands and the punishment of his enemies. It was a violent, bloody speech devoid of the scholarly ornaments and pious platitudes that had characterized the earlier part of the assembly. The advocate had not dared to charge the late king with responsibility for the sufferings of the noble house, nor to mention Pierre de Beaujeu, who had been given part of the county of Armagnac; but he had not hesitated to single out henchmen of Louis XI such as the Count of Dammartin for their roles in the terrible crimes. Many of these nobles were present and by their gestures sought to show the scorn in which they held the orator. The chancellor promised that the case would be heard before the council, and the assembly quickly disbanded. The rumor spread among the deputies that the quarrel had been continued in the king's chamber. Dammartin had argued that all that had been done was on the order of the late king and that Armagnac was a traitor. The Count of Comminges, a member of the Armagnac party, called him a liar, and swords were drawn; only respect for the king and the princes prevented a battle.[97]

On this note of violence the second phase of the assembly of the estates came to an end. It must have been a bitter experience for Pierre de Beaujeu. He had had to hear the advocates of the cause of Nemours and Armagnac speak—an embarrassing experience—for he held a large part of the lands of both houses. Within two months the royal council over which he had failed to win control ordered the return of the Armagnac estates to their hereditary owners.[98] Small wonder the despoiled Beaujeus displayed little desire in the future to convoke the Estates General.

Financial Negotiations

The deputies must have been reasonably content. Their work seemed nearly completed. They had provided for the royal council without incurring the anger of the princes. They had submitted a long list of grievances to be corrected by a committee of deputies and the councilors. It is true that they had been quite cautious on the question of the composition of the council, but only a majority in the small Norman and Burgundian sections felt that they had erred on this score. Little did they suspect what activities occupied the princes on the day following the royal audience, a Friday the thirteenth in which the plans were probably laid that were to dash their fondest hopes.

On the morning of the fourteenth the news fell. A group of deputies came upon the Bishop of Lombez in front of the cathedral, and he presented them a scroll that had been given him the evening before. It contained a list of sixteen deputies who were summoned to appear at Montils that afternoon to confer with the royal council concerning the cahier. Those selected were drawn in equal numbers from four classes: the clergy, the nobility, the bureaucracy, and the bourgeoisie. No effort had been made to achieve a sectional balance. Six came from Paris, only two from Normandy, and one from Burgundy. Omitted were men like Philippe Pot, the Bishop of Châlon, and Jean Masselin, who had enjoyed leading positions among the Beaujeu supporters; but included were men like Lombez, who had sided with the princes. The weak position of the Beaujeus in the council was clearly shown, and it is difficult to assign to their faction any of the sixteen that were chosen except the Abbot of Cîteaux, and he had not played a prominent enough role in the estates to have offended the princes. Masselin was clearly perturbed. He charged that most of those named were weak and poorly informed, and that they were servants of the great. Perhaps his harshness came in part from the spirit of faction and in part because his own name had been omitted, though earlier the Norman section had recommended him for the council. The other deputies present were evidently less concerned, although Masselin reports the contrary, for they decided that they would not even assemble to debate the new development until they learned from the sixteen what happened at Montils.[99]

Two days elapsed without any news. Then the chancellor took Masselin to Montils because of his experience in financial matters. Masselin found that six of the original sixteen deputies were conferring with tax officials, and the remainder were dealing with other matters. Apparently Masselin did not actually take part in the deliberations, but he learned enough to sense that the desire of a few for big pensions was making the reduction of the taille a difficult task.[100]

Masselin probably returned to Tours that evening, for he attended a meeting of the estates the next day to hear a speech by the chancellor. That official had been dispatched to Tours to silence complaints over the council's naming the sixteen deputies to discuss the cahier. He began by pointing to the generous concessions the king had already made. The youthful monarch had consented to the use of deputies as clerks of the session, rather than royal appointees, so that no outsider needed to attend the discussions, and he had held two audiences in which the deputies had been permitted to say what they pleased. The chancellor then argued that the king was free to act on the cahier without consulting the estates, but that he would permit them to choose six more delegates, one from each section, to join the sixteen who were then meeting with the council at Montils.

The deputies replied that they had asked the king to select twelve of their number to sit in his council, but they had hoped to name those who were to treat with the council concerning the cahier. They refused to accept the royal offer to elect an additional deputy from each section, because to do so would be to recognize the sixteen chosen by the government. Two sections, probably Paris and Languedoïl, demurred, but without success. No doubt the recalcitrant attitude of the deputies was partially provoked by the stripping of their assembly hall of the tapestries and other decorations after the last royal audience. This action indicated that there were those who thought that it was time for the assembly to disband.[101]

Meanwhile, the sixteen continued to meet with the council. Those who opposed the princes could take some comfort in the promise of the Abbot of Cîteaux that nothing would be agreed upon without the consent of the estates. He reported that there was dissent on a great many questions, not only between the council and the sixteen, but also among the magnates themselves as to the size of the army and the contingent financial levies. On February 19 the deputies were assembled to hear the Duke of Bourbon speak in his capacity of constable. He reported that the council and the sixteen had first debated that part of the cahier which dealt with the needs of the people, but that now they had turned to the question of the army. Here, after consultation with the military authorities, it had been decided that the limit of 2,000 *lances* set by the estates was insufficient for the defense of the kingdom. The conquests of the late king had made necessary a larger army than that possessed by Charles VII because of the proximity to enemies. For province after province, a clerk read the military's analysis of its needs. The total came to 2,500 *lances* and about 6,000 infantry, some 21,000 men in all if the *lances* were kept up to strength.

When the clerk had finished reading the report, Lombez asked permission for the deputies to deliberate before replying. Bourbon agreed provided the military took part to explain its needs. This the deputies refused to consider, although they did offer to hear further from the army. Bourbon, ever inclined to consider the wishes of the estates, acquiesced.[102]

The next day the magnates again appeared before the deputies to hear the reply to the army proposals. Masselin had been elected their spokesman, and the Norman cleric came quickly to the point. The size of the army could not be dissociated from other demands on the treasury. If the army was to be increased, economies must be effected elsewhere in order not to place an additional burden on the people. Therefore, four matters ought to be considered together: the expenses of the king and his household, the number and pay of the royal officials, the size of the army, and the number of pensions. In addition, he asked that they be given figures on the income from the domain and taxes. The intent of the deputies was clear. They wished to show that with careful economies the king could live, or nearly live, on the revenue from his domain and that taxes could be greatly reduced or abolished.[103]

That afternoon the chancellor returned with the princes' answer. He repeated the argument that the troops were needed for the defense of the kingdom and added meaningfully that unpaid soldiers had a habit of living on the people. He stressed the necessity of heavy royal expenses to maintain the dignity of the crown and pointed out that officials were necessary for the administration of the kingdom and had a right to be paid. Pensions were just rewards for long and notable services to the state. Nevertheless, the king would accede to their requests and his financial officials would show them their books the next day except that the amount of the individual pensions would not be given.[104]

Masselin expressed the assembly's appreciation of the king's action and then turned to the less important but more controversial question of the disputed fiefs. He asked that the confiscated lands of the Constable of Saint-Pol be returned to his heirs, and that the Seigneur of Croy regain his estates as promised in the Treaty of Arras. He pleaded that justice be done to the Count of Armagnac and to the children of the Duke of Nemours. The chancellor replied that these matters were being studied and that no one ought to despair of obtaining justice. Certainly they need not if the estates could have their way, for the deputies were ever sympathetic with the problems of the fallen great. Already the Bishop of Lombez had sponsored an article to be added to the cahier asking that the king, or at least his lieutenant, hold a public audience one day each week to hear the complaints of any who wished to speak. The plight of the dispossessed barons had clearly aroused the sympathies of the assembly, and Lombez had been quick to exploit the situation, for was not Pierre de Beaujeu one of the chief profiteers from their misfortunes? [105]

The financial question occupied the deputies for the next ten days. As promised, twelve royal financial officials appeared the following morning loaded with papers giving the income from the domain and various taxes. The deputies pounced on these figures with glee and quickly came to the conclusion that they had been falsified. The income from the royal domain had been set at a little more than 100,000 livres. This sum added to the aides came to only 755,000 livres. Many deputies felt that the amount reported coming from their province was underestimated, but the findings of modern scholars have tended to support the royal claims.[106] The expenses of the king were shown divided into six categories, the last of which consisted of a list of nine hundred persons receiving pensions. It was this that most angered the deputies, although the amount given was not revealed.

Lombez sensed a growing revolt and sought to speed the deliberations, but his suggestion that a committee be named on the spot to discuss budgetary problems with the financial officials was rejected.

The deputies retired into the seclusion of their respective sections to discuss what action they should take.

The assembly was indeed in a quandary. The royal revenue seemed lessened and the drains on the treasury excessive, but it was dangerous to suggest that the princes had ordered that the former be falsified and hardly diplomatic to disapprove of royal extravagances and pensions to specific individuals. The solution was at length offered by Jacques de Viry, judge of Forez, who spoke for Languedoïl. He began by praising Charles VII for regulating the number and wages of his officers and creating very few pensioners. After his death, however, misgovernment had set in, and the three orders had fallen from their flourishing estate. For these reasons the deputies had asked that the crown revert to the policies of Charles VII in every section of their cahier save in the matter of subsidies. Here it had been felt that the people were no longer able to pay as much as they had in their earlier, more prosperous years, and that the peace following the expulsion of the English had removed the necessity for heavy taxation to support an army. Thus Viry revealed the determination of the deputies to pay less than under Charles VII. It is only with this prospectus in view that one can correctly assess the import of the remainder of his speech.

He pointed out that when an individual was quite sick a severe remedy might prove fatal, but the frequent application of mild remedies would bring recovery. So it was with the government which had become dangerously ill during the past reign. To remove all bad officials and to abolish all pensions would provoke serious trouble. A milder cure was needed. In the name of the deputies of Languedoïl, Viry offered the sum paid under Charles VII, on condition that the tax be divided equally between all the provinces, including those recently reunited to the crown, and that this grant be for two years only, after which the Estates General would be assembled again.[107]

The proposal of the judge of Forez has too often been considered from the standpoint of popular rights. In fact, as an official of Bourbon, who was also Count of Forez, and as the spokesman of the Languedoïl section, which of late had followed the policy of the princes, he reflected in his address the desires of the old duke. The deputies had intended to pay little or no taille; now they were asked to vote the same sum as under Charles VII. The proposal to hold another meeting of the Estates General in two years was hardly a move to frighten Bourbon. He had been largely responsible for the convocation of the present assembly and had displayed considerable patience in dealing with the deputies. The proposal of Viry had the unique virtue of being of service to the princes and at the same time cognizant of the welfare of the people. It meant a substantial reduction in taxation and this, in turn, necessitated economy by the government. But it also meant recognition by the deputies that some taxation was necessary.

To Masselin fell the task of presenting the reply of the deputies to the princes. He sought to justify the low financial offer of the estates by arguing that governmental economies were possible. He struck out at the growth of the bureaucracy and gave figures to show that it now cost nearly ten times as much to collect the revenues of Burgundy as under Duke Philip the Good. He attacked the idea of having a mercenary army and insisted on the capacity of the French nobility to defend the country. A wise government and a loyal people were the best protection. He denied that the estates had limited the army to 2,000 *lances* in their cahier; rather they had asked that the army's size be reduced to that at the time of Charles VII, and clearly they thought that there had then been fewer than 2,000 *lances*. There was no need for a large garrison in Picardy or for troops in the interior as if the English had the wings of angels to fly there. Pensions should be given only to those who had rendered conspicuous service to the state. The financial officials had falsified the figures on the income from the domain, he charged, and had exaggerated the expenses of the government. As an example of the latter, he pointed to the statement that it had taken 1,100 livres to furnish the hall for the estates. Anyone could see that it could have cost no more than 300 livres. This observation later brought forth the comment from someone present that he had been charged to decorate the hall at Orléans where the estates had first been ordered to meet and then at Tours, and that the total cost had been only 560 livres, part of which had not been paid him.

It was only after this lengthy justification that Masselin revealed that the estates were willing to pay a taille of only 1,200,000 livres, a figure which they thought represented that tax during the reign of Charles VII. The increased private sources of revenue the crown was presumed to have acquired by the acquisition of Burgundy, Franche Comté, Anjou, Maine, Dauphiné, Provence, Roussillon, Cerdagne, and most of Picardy made this offer seem very generous to the deputies. The request for another meeting of the Estates General in two years pointed to their hope that administrative reforms would make possible further reductions by that time.[108]

When Masselin finished, the chancellor conferred briefly with the princes and then announced that the king would seek advice concerning their offer. The next four days saw a lively debate among the princes and councilors. Agreement was difficult, Masselin reported, because some of the councilors were pensioners and wanted to continue to enjoy their large emoluments. The needs of the army aroused more bitter debate. Finally, the council decided to summon two deputies from each

section to hear Beaujeu and others explain the necessity of offering a
larger sum, but to no avail. When the chancellor brought a formal reply
to the estates on the following day, he was faced with a hostile audience.[109]

His speech was relatively brief. He pointed to the dangers which beset the kingdom because of the minority and the foreign threat, dangers
which made necessary a larger army and more taxes than there had
been under Charles VII. Nevertheless, the king acceded in spirit to
their request and would accept an offer of 1,500,000 livres, a sum
which, the chancellor argued, had the same purchasing power as the
1,200,000 livres collected by Charles VII. The newly acquired territories
were not to be included in the assessment; they were to make separate
payments. The position of the council was not unreasonable. The additional 300,000 livres to be levied on the older provinces could be
justified by the greater prosperity of the kingdom and perhaps by a
rise in prices. The central fact was that the princes had been willing to
go to considerable lengths to explain the need for taxation, they had
showed the deputies the financial records of the crown, and now they
were willing to cut the taille from 4,400,000 livres levied by Louis XI
during the preceding year to 1,500,000 livres. Perhaps no French
government ever went further to meet the desires of the people. It was
with justification that the chancellor concluded by directing the deputies
to retire, not to deliberate, but to thank the king for his good favor.[110]

The deputies were in no mood to express their gratitude. While the
chancellor was talking, many of them became restless and murmurs
filled the room. The president sensed the unfavorable reaction of the
assembly and asked permission to deliberate. The chancellor, after
consulting the princes, agreed, but ordered them to take counsel now
in order to give their answer that afternoon. This the assembly refused
to do, and the following day was set for their reply.[111]

Left alone, the deputies began to debate by sections. There was widespread indignation at the proposition of the chancellor. Many repented
the offer they had made. If they had suggested a lower figure in the
beginning, the council might have been willing to compromise for the
amount levied under Charles VII. By naming the maximum figure at
the start, they had weakened their bargaining position. A growing desire
to return home made protracted negotiations difficult. Some suggested
that each province take as a farm all the revenue collected within its
boundaries, including that from the domain. They argued that the royal
income from all sources other than the taille could be more than
doubled if honestly and efficiently collected. Others felt that to do so
would be usurping royal authority. No one seemed to realize that the
estates had no power to back up its demands save that derived from

public opinion, a fickle force that was difficult to arouse before the widespread use of printing. The deputies ought to have co-operated completely with the government except for insisting that the grant be limited to two years. In this manner they might hope to be convoked again, and with frequent meetings they could keep relatively low taxes.

Only the deputies of the Paris section showed any inclination to make further concessions. They recommended that an additional 300,-000 livres be voted for one year because of the needs of the kingdom and in honor of the new accession to the throne. The Burgundians argued that they had never participated in a tax levied under Charles VII and that they were willing to contribute only what they had under Duke Philip the Good. The remaining sections refused to make any further concessions. Masselin was elected to explain once more the position of the assembly, a duty he sought to avoid because he had learned that his previous speech had incurred the anger of the princes who had come to regard the Normans as their principal opponents in the estates.[112]

As usual the activities that took place in the archepiscopal palace were quickly reported to the great who found themselves in a quandary. They wished to avoid making an arbitrary assessment for fear it would lead to unrest. On the other hand, they felt that the amount they asked was the minimum on which the government could operate. At length they decided to make one final effort at persuasion, and the leading deputies from each section were summoned to meet with those princes and councilors who were regarded as being particularly influential in their region. Eight or nine Norman delegates were confronted by five councilors headed by the Count of Dunois, and a lively debate ensued. The councilors threatened the deputies by saying that the king would remember the way they acted; they cajoled them by arguing that the people would be very happy to see the taille reduced to one-third of its former rate; they sought to divide them by advising that they would win special favors if they were the first section to accede to the royal will. The deputies justified their defiance by saying that no one ought to be surprised at their defending the people's interests with all their strength. Once the domain had sufficed to support the king, then the aides had been established, and next had come the taille. To consent now might be to continue the taille forever.[113]

The debate waxed bitter. One councilor stated that the king had the right to take the goods of his subjects to provide for the defense of the realm. Another shocked those present by saying of the people: "I know these rogues. Treat them to anything but severe taxation, and forthwith they grow insolent. If you spare them in the matter of this *taille,* they will become unbearable. They are unfit for liberty; therefore you must keep them in subjection; and you cannot accomplish it better than by the retention of this tax." [114] "Strange words," reported Masselin, "to come from the mouth of a man so eminent! But in his soul, as in that of all old men, covetousness had increased with age, and he seemed to fear the reduction of his pension." [115]

The deputies now changed the subject to the division of the taille among the provinces. The duchy of Normandy, they said, had always been made to contribute a fourth, although it formed only an eighth of the kingdom. The councilors offered no hope for an immediate reapportionment, and justified this attitude on the grounds that Normandy was richer than the other provinces. When asked what part of the proposed taille of 1,500,000 livres they would consent to pay, the Normans suggested 250,000 livres. The councilors recommended 350,-000 livres as the minimum figure since they had customarily paid one-fourth. The deputies hinted that 300,000 livres might be acceptable, but that they could conclude nothing without their colleagues, and the audience came to an end.[116]

This last exchange revealed an ominous wedge that could be driven between the sections. They might agree on what the kingdom should pay, but they could not apportion the tax to anyone's satisfaction. Burgundy had already shown signs of relying on its traditional privileges, now Normandy pleaded for a more favorable division. A policy of divide and rule, or separate negotiation was opened, and no deputy had the fortitude to withstand this approach.

When the deputies from the six sections returned to the archepiscopal palace, they found that some of their number had been persuaded to comply with the royal desires, but that the majority remained steadfast. It was decided to stick to the offer of 1,200,000 livres for two years, but to add an additional 300,000 for one year to pay for the coronation and the entrance into Paris. It had been noted with some concern that the councilors had talked as though the tax would be of unlimited duration, and this upset the deputies as much as the quantity that was asked.[117]

At ten o'clock the next morning, the Dukes of Orléans and Bourbon arrived to hear the reply of the estates. Masselin's address was longer and more filled with biblical and classical allusions than was his wont. Evidently he wished to do full honor to the occasion, for the king had been expected. A storm prevented the young sovereign from attending, but Masselin obviously had not learned of this development in time to change his speech. Much of it was directed towards the head of the state, with the thesis being developed that the people were the masters of their own property and that "what is good for subjects is good for the king." [118]

When Masselin finished, a clerk read the terms of the grant. The king was first asked to approve the various recommendations made in the cahier, then he was offered 1,200,000 livres for two years and 300,-000 livres for one year to pay for his coronation. The estates expressed the desire to name a deputation to assist in the division of the tax which they wanted to take place before their departure, and they requested that the exact time and place be set for the meeting of the Estates General that was to take place in about two years. No new taxes should be levied without their consent.[119]

The chancellor departed, but returned later in the day with instructions that to speed the proceedings, the assembly was to choose three delegations to treat simultaneously with the council on taxation, justice, and the church. The deputies reacted favorably except on the government's suggestion that only one man from each of the four most heavily taxed sections be elected to the committee on taxation. No one section would trust another on this score, nor had bailiwicks any faith in their neighbors. Each and every jurisdiction wanted to be represented, and in the end the six sections each sent three or more deputies to meet the committee of the council headed by Beaujeu and Dunois.[120]

The next day was Sunday, but so anxious was the council to bring matters to an end that Beaujeu summoned the committee chosen by the estates to Montils. Here a financial official proposed that the tax be divided between the provinces in the same ratio as in the past. The suppression of nearly two-thirds of the taille meant that there would be a substantial reduction for all. The assessment on the Île-de-France, for example, would be reduced from 604,975 livres, 14 sous to 208,800 livres, and on Normandy from 996,600 livres to 363,910 livres. Nevertheless, the deputies from each section cried out that their assessment was too large. The older ratio for dividing the tax was not fair, they charged. "Every section, every province, said that it was too crushed and that it had paid more than its share." There was no one who did not complain except for a small number of men from the Paris section. Even here all was not well, for two deputies from Vermandois repeated unceasingly "have pity, my lords, on the poor bailiwick of Vermandois that has suffered so much; have pity. . . ."[121]

A deputy of the third estate of Languedoc said that for the last two years he had had to pay a taille of over 350 livres. A Norman replied that this was a proof of his prosperity and not evidence that his province had been overtaxed. The Picards complained that the 55,000 livres they were assessed was the same that they had always paid. The council replied that they had been undertaxed in the past, that they were wealthy, and had not suffered any recent devastations. The Picards argued that their province was smaller than the lords thought, that Boulonnais and Artois had been exempted from the taille for five years, that the bailiwick of Amiens and the provostship of Vimeu had been joined with the généralité of Paris, and that much of Picardy was in Vermandois. There remained only 170 villages to support the entire tax. These villagers, of course, had suffered every form of hardship. So it went. The Picards refused to consent to the levy. The crown offered a reduction of 15,000 livres. But the Picards still refused. A proffered reduction of 20,000 brought no better results. When Masselin left Tours two weeks later, they were still holding out for a two-thirds reduction in spite of the profound irritation of the councilors.[122]

The Normans complained as loudly. They had consented to the taille, they said, only if it were equally divided throughout the kingdom. They were now asked to pay one-fourth of the tax when they made up only one-tenth of the area. (The day before they had admitted to one-eighth. They were growing more desperate.) They were impoverished by taxes, devastated by armies, and the victims of pest and famine. When the financial officials criticized some of their statements, the Norman deputies pretended that they had not heard. The quarrel became louder, and at length Beaujeu ordered the deputies to leave the room in order for the councilors to confer. Later, two of the councilors came to the Norman deputies and said that the crown would remit 13,910 livres, leaving a tax of 350,000 livres, provided they would continue to act discontented, for no reduction was contemplated for the other sections.

After this little aside, Beaujeu summoned the deputies and said that the division prepared by the financial officials seemed just and regular. It would therefore be maintained. The deputies replied that it was necessary for them to consult their colleagues before answering and they retired.[123]

The next day the deputies decided to make a separate assessment for the special one-year tax of 300,000 livres. To establish a single levy of 1,500,000 livres might lead the crown to claim the entire amount for the second year also, rather than only the 1,200,000 livres that had been agreed upon. Some advocated that the estates be held in 1485 to make certain that only 1,200,000 livres were levied. Others, including the Normans and the deputies of Languedoïl, opposed this move as being both useless and expensive.

There was also a movement to ask that no future taxes be imposed in any part of France without the consent of the provincial estates, but the deputies from Normandy did not support this pretension. Their own rights and privileges seemed assured. Why should they strive to win a similar position for other localities? Thus the deputies failed to stand together in a concerted move to establish the provincial estates firmly in those parts of France where they had been abandoned. Others spoke of suppressing the *élus* and the *receveurs* of the taille, arguing that they were as objectionable as the taille itself, but too few deputies could get their minds off of the division of the tax to take heed of the common interests of the estates.[124]

Indeed, the introduction of the financial question had seen the spirit of co-operation between the deputies come to an end. Each section sought the reduction of its taxes at the expense of others. Masselin complained of this, but it is worthy of note that a secret reduction of only 13,910 livres from the Norman share removed their opposition to the division of the tax. The councilors were at the same time forced into the realization that the consent of the Estates General had meant nothing. They had won 1,500,000 livres from the group only to have to enter into negotiations with each individual section. To the Picards, to the Normans, and doubtless to others, they had had to make concessions. The system of Charles VII was revived. First, the national assembly had been held to fix the amount of the levy, then the council had to go to each province for its consent. Small wonder the councilors saw little need to hold the Estates General again, but rather returned to the practice of direct negotiations with the provincial estates and towns.

Meanwhile, a deputation from the estates had been meeting with the chancellor to consider the articles in the cahier on justice. The initial procedure was for the cahier to be discussed article by article by the chancellor and by the eight legal advisors he had brought with him. The representatives from the estates were not permitted to participate; for, as the chancellor explained, they had already considered the matter once, and no one ought to be permitted to vote a second time on the same question.[125] The deputies complained. "Why are we here? Why have you summoned us? Let us retire." [126] The chancellor, as was his wont, gave way before this firm stand and conciliated the deputies by permitting them to engage in the discussion. Articles not desired by the councilors were set aside for further consideration or revision. In the end only three or four were not accepted. With one exception, these had not been approved by the entire estates, but had been slipped in by several individuals to support their own personal interests or those of friends. The exception was, however, of some importance because it pointed once more to the internal divisions brought about by Louis XI. The article in question requested that those officials who had been dismissed without cause during the latter part of his reign be re-established in their offices, or that legal remedy be permitted them. The chancellor, supported by his advisors, protested violently against this proposal, for he was only one among many who held a post that could be claimed by another if the article were accepted. The articles on the council were debated in a similar manner, but without any clear decision being reached. They were turned over to the council intact.[127]

At the same time another delegation from the estates met with Cardinal Bourbon, Archbishop of Lyon and brother of the old duke and Pierre of Beaujeu. The purpose was to discuss the chapter in the cahier on the church, and in place of a battery of jurists, the deputies found themselves confronted by a host of archbishops and bishops. The prelates were irate. A few days earlier they had complained at not receiving individual summons to the estates, but their threat not to accept the conclusions reached by the deputies had not prevented the assembly from barring them from the deliberations unless they were willing to serve without pay. This offer was declined and the prelates turned to the king for permission to sit in judgment on the articles. Their success did not diminish their anger, and Cardinal Bourbon lashed out at the deputies, declaring that they had had no right to speak for the Gallican Church and that the articles they recommended were detrimental to the power of the Holy See. In vain the deputies protested that it was their right to request a return to the Pragmatic Sanction because the step would be beneficial to the kingdom. One of their number had the temerity to say that the prelates who had made the Pragmatic Sanction were more holy than those in his day who were seeking to destroy it. This rejoinder so offended the prelates that the *procureur-général* of the king had to intervene. He argued that the Pragmatic Sanction contributed to the prosperity of the kingdom by preventing the exportation of treasures, and to the spiritual welfare by calling for the election of prelates.

The debate continued intermittently for days. The upper clergy was opposed to any system which removed the royal and papal authority of naming prelates, for most of them owed their own position to this practice. They were especially vehement, Masselin charged, because of the approach of the papal legate who, it was rumored, had been given the authority to select several faithful and devoted servants of the pope for red hats. These ambitious prelates were dangerous because they were the friends and relatives of the princes, and their influence was later demonstrated by the refusal of the council to approve the chapter on the church.[128]

Meanwhile, quarrels between the sections, and even within sections over the assessment of the tax continued; for once the question of money was raised, the deputies lost the ability to reach an accord. Data survives only for the activities of the Norman section, but here Masselin gives a detailed picture of the difficulty, if not of the impossibility, of getting the deputies to agree on the distribution of taxes. The patience of the royal officials and their desire to arrive at a settlement satisfactory to everyone is clearly shown, but they must have considered the estates a terrible nuisance.

On March 4 the Norman deputies met with the Bishop of Coutances, president of the *échiquier* at Rouen, the bailiffs of Rouen, Évreux, and Coutances, and several tax officials to discuss the division among the subordinate jurisdictions of the 350,000 livres they had voted. Coutances opened the meeting by stating that several deputies felt that the former ratio governing the distribution among the bailiwicks was unjust. They ought, he stated, to divide the assessment in accordance with the wealth of each locality.[129]

Immediately the deputies from Rouen and Caux raised a loud cry. They insisted that they had never asked for any changes in the distribution and cast slurs at anyone who might have made secret proposals advocating a new system. The bishop seemed almost convinced when the Vicar of Coutances began to speak of the terrible poverty of the bailiwick of Cotentin which he represented. The taille, plague, and famine, named in that order, had wreaked havoc. In despair, husbands killed their wives; and fathers, their children. Indeed, Cotentin and the neighboring bailiwick of Caen paid half the taille levied on Normandy. This situation, he charged, had been brought about some years before when troops had pillaged the bailiwick of Caux. As a result that jurisdiction had been exempted from the taille for five years, and the Norman quota had been met by a higher levy on Coutances and Caen. This additional charge had been kept after the end of the five-year period. Thus it had come to pass that the two bailiwicks paid half the Norman tax. Would it not be more just for them to pay one-third, Rouen and Caux, one-third, and Évreux, Gisors, and Alençon, one-third? [130]

The deputies of Caen supported this move, but then those from Gisors, Évreux, and Alençon began to relate their tales of woe. "No one fought for glory, but each made every effort to disparage his bailiwick." [131] It was then the turn of the Rouen and Caux deputies to become worried at the obvious move to transfer a larger part of the tax to their bailiwicks. They pointed out that the government had already promised to maintain the old ratio for the division of the tax and that it was therefore useless to debate the matter. They would spare the group a detailed exposition of their miseries—which were infinite.

By now it was apparent why the Bishop of Coutances, the Norman bailiffs, and financial officials of the province had been chosen by the government to work out the new scheme for distribution. Only persons intimately acquainted with the province could hope to form any idea of what each part could pay. No trust could be placed in what the deputies had to say, and it appeared even more certain that, left alone, they would never arrive at a solution. The royal officials clearly thought that Rouen and Caux were paying less than their share and were anxious to equalize the burden. They denied that there had ever been a promise not to make any modification in the distribution and announced their intention to withdraw to deliberate alone.[132]

The deputies of Rouen and Caux became frantic. If a larger percentage of the tax was thrust on them now, they would have to pay it for many years before they could hope for readjustment. They determined to plead as eloquently as the others, although even Masselin from Rouen admitted that his bailiwick was more prosperous than Cotentin or Caen. To leave no doubt in the minds of his constituents that their cause had been vigorously defended, Masselin gave at great length the arguments of their spokesman. There is no need to go into the details of the defense. Suffice it to say that every effort was made to show that the other bailiwicks had minimized their capacity to pay and that it was really Rouen and Caen that suffered. Always they stressed the point that there had been a general reduction of the taille by two-thirds and that every jurisdiction ought to profit from this good fortune.[133]

With sarcasm and scorn the Vicar of Coutances sought to refute the arguments of the spokesman for Rouen and Caen, and when he had done, the debate became louder. Those of the third estate were especially angry, and it was with difficulty that they could be restrained from attacking each other. At length order was restored, and the Bishop of Coutances announced that a decision would be made based on their overlong debate. He appealed to the deputies of Caux to put aside their passions and admit that their bailiwick was better off than Cotentin and Caen. He called on several natives of that district in the council to support his contention, but this appeal was lost on Masselin and his fellow deputies. The Bishop of Coutances was unable to overcome his bias for his diocese, Masselin reported. He could not, or he would not, admit the justice of the bishop's position.

It was an irate nobleman who violated any remaining sense of propriety by laying bare the weakness of the Bishop of Coutances' position. "My lord," he said, "we know that you think and occupy yourself only with the welfare of the people of your bishopric and it is already publicly said that you have promised them this relief. Please pardon me for speaking to you in this manner, but you ought not to be a judge in this affair. . . . If you render a decision against us, we will appeal to the king in council." [134]

While the nobleman was speaking, the bishop and councilors got up and went in the next room to give the appearance of not hearing what was said. Masselin and several of his compatriots quickly joined them to apologize for their colleague's rudeness and to add further arguments to support their cause. When they had finished, the ill-feeling that had been germinated by the discussion was temporarily dissipated by a splendid dinner the bishop had ordered.[135]

The next two days were uneventful; Lombez had ceased to devote much of his attention to the estates, and there was no general assembly to deal with the problem of the division of the taille within the sections. Probably, the government negotiated with each of them separately just as it had done with Normandy, but there is no positive evidence. During this period Masselin and four or five Norman nobles went to Montils to ask the king and council to consider some individual requests of their province. They found that body deliberating on the army question and decided to limit their own requests to the same subject. Interestingly, the Normans set their military needs at 100 *lances* to be commanded by the seneschal, a far cry from the 700 *lances* and unspecified number of foot soldiers recommended by the council. Troops were not even desired by regions exposed to invasion by the English.[136]

On the afternoon of March 7, the king came to Tours to hold the final full meeting of the estates. The deputies assembled about three in the afternoon and the proceedings were opened with an address by the chancellor. Rochefort praised the deputies for their work and the king and the princes for their benevolence. He announced that the king was firmly resolved that none of their requests would be transgressed except for powerful reasons, and he instructed the deputies to praise their sovereign when they returned to their homes. The king, he said, had just been ordered by his doctors to go to Amboise, but the chancellor comforted the deputies with the assurance that a messenger could go to his residence and back to Tours in a day. Any new question that arose could be quickly resolved. When he finished, he turned to the king and asked if he had spoken as directed. The thirteen-year-old Charles who had so often been praised in the assembly for his precocious intellect and wisdom then uttered his only words before the deputies: "Je l'avoue." [137]

Jean de Rély replied for the deputies in his usual scholarly manner. He thanked the king and the princes and pleaded for an early coronation. When he had finished, the meeting came to an end.[138]

The sections returned to the question of taxation on the morning of March 8. The Normans debated on four specific problems. The first was whether the ordonnance for the levy should come from the king or the commissioners of the estates of Normandy. The deputies chose the former because the assembly had met in the presence of the king and outside the province in spite of their privileges. They had no intention of permitting the commissioners to handle the tax just as if it had been approved by their provincial estates. No agreement was reached on the second problem of whether the ordonnance should be addressed to the *élus* or to the lieutenant of the bailiff. The third question of what persons and what towns should pay the taille produced the longest debate. Many men had been ennobled by Louis XI without sufficient cause, at least so some deputies thought, and there was strong sentiment to make them pay. The question of the exempt towns was also discussed, and here the matter came before the general assembly of the estates. Some wanted to exempt only Paris and Rouen, others would add Amiens, Bordeaux, Tours, Orléans, Lyon, or some other place. There were those who would be content if the traditionally exempt towns would pay a share of the tax for the coronation. At length the royal council intervened and as usual defended the privileged. The exempt towns were to remain unassessed. Finally the Norman deputies turned to the question of the duration of the ordonnance, whether they should order the tax for one year or two, and whether, as was decided, two men from each estate should assist the *élus* in the division of the tax among the parishes.[139]

Nearly all the decisions taken by the Norman section came under the criticism of the Bishop of Coutances and other royal Norman officials when the deputies reported to them at Montils the following day. They opposed the provision calling for the members of the three orders to work with the *élus* because it would lead to confusion and differences of opinion, and they were equally adamant against a proposal to abolish the *élus* altogether. When the Normans suggested that the ordonnance be for two years as the majority of the sections had asked, the officials argued that this would violate their charter of privileges because it would have the effect of levying a tax on the province next year without a meeting of the provincial estates. Masselin had no doubt of the true motive behind this stand. The Norman officials wanted the estates to be held in the expectation that they would take part as royal commissioners and receive the handsome fee usually accorded such service. Besides, the government opposed the two-year ordonnance for the same reason the deputies advocated it. The government wanted the opportunity to raise taxes in 1485, the deputies desired to insure the present rate.[140]

Wednesday was spent in more individual conferences between the sections and the royal officials over the cahier and the tax. The deputies worked under the shadow of a rumor that they were about to be dispatched to their homes, and while many were homesick, the majority were anxious to complete the work of the general cahier before leaving.

The appearance of the chancellor before the deputies on the following day removed any lingering doubt as to the intentions of the government. He began by promising that the king would approve the articles concerning the church in spite of the opposition of the prelates, and he pointed out that most of the remainder of the cahier had been acted upon. To remain longer in session would only impose a useless expense on the people.

There was an immediate outcry from the deputies who regarded their financial concession as being very generous, so generous that it seemed unjust to dismiss them until the answers to all the articles had been received. One theologian was especially outspoken. The chancellor sought to escape the storm of protests by referring the deputies to the king and council. He also promised to have the royal replies to the articles read before the estates in the afternoon, but later it was decided to postpone this event until the next day. The Normans profited by the interlude to visit Montils once more where they sought the Bishop of Coutances and were informed that their provincial cahier had been expedited by the council. They were also told that the council had added, or was going to add, ten or twelve deputies to their number. This concession was probably designed to make the deputies more willing to return to their homes in a friendly frame of mind, but actually it meant little, for the complexion of the council was by no means changed. Four of the supposedly new councilors were either former or current members of that body, and of the remainder, only three left any trace in its records. These men, the Bishop of Rieux, Guillaume de Montmorency, and Philippe Pot were probably chosen because the first was a partisan of the independents, especially from the south, the second of Orléans, and the third of the Beaujeus. The delicate balance between the various factions that had been established soon after the death of Louis XI was maintained.[141]

The Bishop of Lombez was one of the former councilors who was reappointed. His new duties, and the arrival of an embassy from Spain, made it necessary for him to excuse himself from presiding over the estates on the following day. The deputies took this action as indicating that he had renounced the presidency of the estates, and the Bishop of Lavour was chosen in his stead.[142] This prelate had the clerk of the chancellery read the royal reply to the cahier. Unfortunately, it had been written in haste and with so many abbreviations that the clerk had difficulty in deciphering them. Worst of all, the replies were too vague to give any confidence that they would ever be enforced.

The deputies decided to appeal to the chancellor and council to make more precise answers to the articles in the cahier and to have the royal judges enforce them in the same manner as other ordonnances. The judge of Forez was given the task of selecting the most important articles for immediate consideration. The deputation that awaited the chancellor the next day at Montils was rebuffed on the grounds that the council had other pressing matters to discuss. However, eventual approval was promised. Meanwhile, each section was asked to leave three or four deputies at Tours until the council could complete its work on the cahier, and the remaining deputies were instructed to return to their homes.

Some of the deputies wanted to stay, but the majority longed for their native provinces or wished to please the princes by departing. A committee was chosen by each section to remain with instructions, at least in the case of the Normans, to continue to work together. The remaining deputies, including Masselin, departed "content," feeling that they had achieved a thorough reformation of the government, had substantially reduced taxes, and had a definite pledge that the Estates General would meet again in two years.[143] One wonders how long the deputies remained satisfied, and why the Estates General promised for 1486 did not materialize. Speculation on these two problems really centers on the basic question of what benefits each of the three rival parties and the public felt that they had obtained from the long and costly meeting at Tours.

The Beaujeus could hardly have been happy with the results. They had been largely responsible for the convocation of the estates and had hoped that the deputies would free them from the council of fifteen set up by the princes after the death of Louis XI. Instead, the estates had been unwilling to support them in the matter, and they found themselves no better off than before. Indeed, they were forced to make their greatest concession, the surrender of Armagnac, several weeks after the closing of the estates. It is difficult to believe that the Beaujeus did this willingly even though their action gave them enough support among the great nobility to keep custody of the king. They must have realized that in a few years the youthful Charles would assert his authority, and a transient control of the crown was hardly worth the sacrifice of the domains Louis XI had granted them.[144]

The Duke of Bourbon and his fellow independents had no reason to be any more favorably impressed by the usefulness of the Estates General. They had done much to bring about the meeting only to have their position in the council challenged, the army reduced, and their pensions curtailed. Like the Beaujeus, they had no reason to advocate another meeting of the Estates General, with the months of deliberating and continual bickering that it entailed.

The Duke of Orléans was initially the most irritated of all the critics of the estates. He was particularly disgruntled at not being given the regency to which he felt his rank entitled him.[145] However, in January, 1485, and again in February, 1487, he advocated a second assembly.[146] This change of heart was the result of a change in his position. Nothing seemed to have been altered in the months that immediately followed the Estates General. The Duke of Orléans continued to lead from strength. In May he took the confiscated lands of the hated barber of Louis XI, Olivier le Daim, and added them to his already extensive domains.[147] This victory failed to reconcile him to the existing situation; and he renewed, with other members of his house, the intrigues with the Duke of Brittany, Richard III of England, and the Habsburg, Maximilian. The dangerous possibilities of this coalition were temporarily dissipated by the recall of the nobles from Nantes to attend the coronation of the king at Reims on May 30. Here a new danger confronted the Beaujeus. Charles became infatuated with the athletic prowess of his cousin of Orléans and may have pleaded to be freed from the domination of his sister. The duke began to hope for a bloodless coup and plotted to abduct the king. The Beaujeus could not temporize before this threat, and after the middle of September, fled with their charge from Paris to the security of the small fortified town of Montargis. There Guyot Pot and two other nobles of the Orleanist faction were dismissed from the entourage of the king. This precipitous action drove Orléans and his followers into open alliance with Brittany and led to further negotiations with England and the Archduke Maximilian.[148]

The Beaujeus also sought allies. They took full advantage of their control of the person of the king and had him give back lands taken by Louis XI in return for support. Lorraine won Bar and a promise that his claims to Provence would be considered when the king was older. The duchy of Nemours was surrendered to the eldest son of the late rebellious duke and the county of Guise, to a second child. The Duke and the Cardinal of Bourbon agreed to add their support, and the fiery Alain le Grand and the Count of Comminges joined the alliance. Alain had supported the claims of his cousin, the Count of Armagnac, and after Pierre de Beaujeu had surrendered the county, he took it from his now insane relative. More important, the Beaujeus had aided Alain in his efforts to marry his eldest son to the heir of the county of Foix and the kingdom of Navarre. The lands of the Albrets now extended from the Garonne to the Ebro, and their power in the south was brought to redress that of the rebellious nobility in the north and west. The able Louis de La Trémoille was won by the offer of the hand of Gabrielle de Bourbon, and some rebellious Breton nobles and three towns in Flanders were added to the coalition to weaken the Duke of Brittany and Maximilian. The period of conciliar government was coming to an end. In its place, two rival factions were poised to struggle for control of the kingdom.[149]

At this point, the Dukes of Orléans and Brittany made their proposal for a new meeting of the Estates General, a proposal undoubtedly intended to win popularity for themselves and to embarrass the Beaujeus on whom any criticism of the government was likely to fall, since they held custody of the king. Their suggestion failed to produce the desired results, in part because neither of them had an enviable record in connection with the estates of Tours. Brittany had not even bothered to have his duchy represented and Orléans had not paid much attention to its proceedings. He had even agreed in August, 1484, before the final break with the Beaujeus, to keep the taille at 1,500,000 livres for the following year, this in violation of the promise that had been made to the deputies that the total would be reduced by 300,000 livres.[150] Yet the principal reason for the failure of the two dukes to win popular acclaim for their stand must certainly have been the lack of desire of the people to undertake the trouble and expense of another meeting of the Estates General.

It is difficult to document the position taken by the public on political issues during this period. We can only guess that the electorate despaired of winning general administrative reforms through action of the Estates General. No ordonnance combining all the articles of the cahier submitted in 1484 was ever promulgated, although directives on this or that action requested by the estates were issued now and then for over a quarter of a century. The council did reply to the cahier soon after the deputies departed, but in a vague and indirect manner.[151] Whether this reply was universally considered to have the force of law is not known. The deputy of the third estate of Amiens thought it worthwhile to bring home a copy to show his constituents. The seneschal of Beaucaire and Nîmes took steps to have the number of sergeants reduced in Velay following the directives of the deputies, but the estates of Languedoc found it necessary to get a royal ordonnance issued in September, 1485, ordering officials to honor the replies given at Tours. They had not been enforced because they were not in the proper form.[152] The very fact that Charles VIII and Louis XII later made ordonnances based on individual articles suggests enforcement was lax. In January, 1485, the Dukes of Orléans and Brittany charged that the wishes of the estates had not been carried out. While there were propaganda advantages to be achieved by taking this position, there is no doubt that there was some justice in their assertion.[153] The failure to secure administrative reform was coupled with a mixed feeling among the people of disillusionment over the possibility of the Estates General ever winning effective control over the amount of taxation, contentment at seeing the government reduce the taille to a third or a half of what it had been a few years earlier, and a strong conviction that it was best for each province or other locality to set the amount of its tax in direct negotiations with the royal council.

This frame of mind is best illustrated by the relations between the council and the provincial estates during the years immediately following the Estates General. In August, 1484, the council announced that the taille for 1485 would be 1,500,000 livres in spite of the fact the Estates General had granted only 1,200,000 livres for that year. On May 4, 1485, an additional 463,500 livres was requested. The council returned to the figure of 1,500,000 livres for 1486,[154] but the Estates General had made no offer at all for that year. Would not the provincial estates have protested violently against these and the other violations of the agreement made at Tours if they had any desire to force the convocation of another national assembly? Let us examine their attitude on this question.

The three estates of Dauphiné met in May, 1484, to vote the 20,000 livres they had been assessed as their share of the levy established at the Estates General. In 1485, and again in 1486, the procedure was repeated without any known remonstrance, although the anticipated reduction was not given in the former year and the sum voted in the latter had not been approved by a national assembly.[155]

Indeed, the provincial estates were more worried about the Estates General having helped set the amount of the tax than they were when the council alone set it. They evidently feared that the consent of the national assembly might be used as a substitute for their own. The Burgundian deputies at Tours went to great lengths to establish that they had taken no action at the Estates General that in any way affected the privileges of the duchy. They even obtained a letter from the king stating that they had not consented to any tax while there and that all levies had to be approved by the three estates of the province.[156] The crown had had to abandon any hope of getting final consent from Burgundy at the national assembly, but to make matters worse the estates of the duchy met in June and refused to vote the 45,000 livres that had been assigned as their share of the 1,500,000 livres agreed on at Tours. There is no precise information as to why the Burgundians adopted this attitude. The 45,000 figure was far less than their just portion. The most logical explanation is that the Burgundians feared that to vote anything might establish the precedent of future taxes accepted by the Estates General being levied on them. Such was the power of provincialism! In August they refused once more, with considerable talk of their "ancient privileges," but finally in September the estates met a third time and agreed to contribute 30,000 livres. There is proof of only 10,000 livres being voted by Burgundy in 1485, of nothing being voted in 1486, and of a refusal to give anything towards the 48,000 francs requested by the king in January, 1487. That the intransigent attitude displayed on the last date did not reflect that the Estates General had not been called to consent to the taille for that year is indicated by the vote of 40,000 francs in another meeting some months later, and by sums granted in future years without mentioning the government's failure to consult the national assembly.[157]

The estates of Normandy met in the early fall of 1484 to consent to their part of the tax voted by the Estates General, and again in May, 1485, to approve their share of the 463,500 livres that the crown felt necessary to request in addition to the 1,500,000 livres already demanded for that year. The government made elaborate preparations before approaching the three estates on the latter occasion. The need for the additional revenue was carefully explained and the king appeared in person before the deputies at Rouen to insure a minimum of protest. Normandy had at times paid nearly one-third of the taxes in the kingdom and at Tours had been persuaded to accept about one-fourth of the total burden. The crown could not risk a refusal, and its efforts were rewarded by a vote of 117,000 livres. The Norman estates met twice in 1486, but there is no evidence that those who attended took any steps to insure a new convocation of the Estates General as had been promised.[158]

Languedoc had no less hesitation in putting provincial advantage ahead of national considerations. The cahier prepared by the deputies from that province while at the Estates General specifically asked that no taxes be levied without the consent of the estates of Languedoc and the crown granted this request.[159] However, it was not until February–March, 1485, that the estates voted 145,803 livres as their share of the taille of 1484, and 124,345 for 1485. The reduction in the amount for the second year suggests that the estates had not forgotten that their representatives at Tours had won an agreement that the levy would be reduced by 300,000 livres in 1485. In July, 1485, Languedoc accepted an increase in the tax as Normandy had done, and in the spring of 1486, and again in March, 1487, her estates voted money for the crown.[160] There is no evidence of any move to force the promised convocation of the Estates General by the refusal to vote taxes or by any other means. The provincial estates of France abandoned the Estates General because of a preference for local consent, and the government abandoned that same institution because it was of too little use to justify the work and trouble it caused. Many years were to pass before there was another meeting of the Estates General, but meanwhile the popular, consultative tradition of the Renaissance Monarchy was maintained by meetings of small advisory groups.

FIVE

𝒯he Assemblies, 1484-1515

The Consultative Assemblies

The Estates General of 1484 marked but a brief break in the practice of summoning small advisory groups in lieu of the large unwieldy assemblies that had characterized the two decades before 1440. Except for a short period of personal government by Charles VIII, the rulers for the next generation had a sincere interest in the welfare of their subjects; and the monarchy, which had been cordially abhorred during the reign of Louis XI, reached the peak of its popularity under Louis XII. Throughout the sixteenth century the reign of Louis XII was looked upon as a golden age, an age of ever increasing prosperity that was paralleled by reduction in taxation. The taille, which had stood at 4,400,000 livres during the last year of the reign of Louis XI, was reduced to 1,500,000 livres for 1484 and was limited to this figure again as late as 1507.

Most of the assemblies which met under the auspices of Charles VIII or his sister were concerned with the confused state of the currency or with the financial requirements produced by the Breton and Italian Wars. The first of these meetings resulted from letters issued on December 10, 1484, ordering the inhabitants of the towns to elect deputies experienced in currency matters. These deputies were to meet with the king's council and royal financial officials the following February to give advice on what to do about the varying metallic content of foreign and domestic coins.[1] In January, 1487, members of the Parlement and financial officials joined the princes of the blood and other notable persons to deal again with the currency situation.[2] Late in 1489 or early in 1490 a large assembly met at Orléans to tackle this problem once more. Present were the princes of the blood, members of the council, financial officials from the various courts, and deputies from the towns.[3] In 1493 the crown considered forbidding the circulation of foreign currency and the "churchmen, nobles, bourgeois, men, and inhabitants" of the towns were directed to name representatives to meet on August 15 to give advice on the matter.[4]

War sometimes made necessary taxation of a sufficiently extraordinary nature for the government to convoke relatively large assemblies to explain its needs. On July 1, 1489, the Parlement of Paris was ordered to send its first president and six elected representatives to attend an assembly at Amboise with important prelates and other royal advisors to discuss a levy on the clergy to help meet the costs of the Breton War.[5]

The needs of the treasury in 1494 at the eve of the invasion of Italy were even greater. The expedition itself was unpopular and the people were thought likely to resist additional financial demands. To overcome the anticipated opposition, Charles VIII decided to hold assemblies on March 17 and April 7 in Lyon, prior to his departure. The first was attended by important seigneurs, prelates, and members of the Parlement, and the second by the deputies of the towns. Few details are known of the earlier assembly, however in the later the government sought to justify the Italian expedition on the grounds that Naples belonged to the crown of France and that its conquest would further plans for a Crusade against the Turks. No request was specifically made for money or other sacrifices during either of the meetings. The plan was to convince those who attended of the wisdom and justice of the royal cause and then to take the unpopular steps of increasing the taille, imposing new aides, farming the royal domain, reducing court salaries, and suspending pensions. Where it was necessary, the consent of the provincial estates and the towns was solicited, but Paris, Orléans, and perhaps other localities were not swayed by the arguments heard at Lyon and refused to make any special contributions to the Italian adventure. Fortunately for the king, the three estates of Languedoc were a little more generous.[6]

The government of Charles VIII was not noteworthy for its reforms, but it did produce one great ordonnance designed to improve the administration of justice, and it attempted to reorganize the whole system of tax assessment. The ordonnance was published in July, 1493, as a result of the deliberations of "the princes and seigneurs of our blood and line, prelates, barons, chevaliers, our presidents, councilors, advocates and *procureurs* of our court of Parlement, and other people of our council. . . ."[7]

The attempted tax reform is of greater interest to the student of representative assemblies. For a long time there had been complaints from certain provinces that they had been paying more than their share of taxes. The matter had been discussed at length in the Estates General of 1484 but without result. Soon thereafter, the question was raised again by Normandy and Languedoc. The Normans claimed that they were paying 10 livres per head while the inhabitants of the more fortunate region of the Seine and Loire contributed only 3 or 4 livres per head. The people of Languedoc also made strong representations against the injustices of the existing system.[8]

The crown determined to investigate, and during June and July, 1491, letters were issued ordering each of the four généralités to choose eight deputies and a clerk to assemble at Angers at the end of September to study the question. The deputations from the généralités of Normandy and Languedoc were elected by their provincial estates, but as there were no comparable institutions in the généralités of Languedoïl and the Outre-Seine, instructions were sent to the *élus* to assemble representatives from the principal towns of each *élection* to elect someone to meet with the deputies chosen from the other *élections* of their généralité. At the assembly of the généralité, deputies to the national meeting at Angers were to be elected. This action by the crown was undoubtedly hailed with delight in Normandy and Languedoc, but there was a storm of protest from the more favored généralités who feared any talk of a tax reassessment. The deputies from the *élections* in Outre-Seine were careful to prepare a long list of their sufferings to confront anyone who suggested that they could possibly pay more. They expected an onslaught from Normandy on whom they blamed the investigation.[9]

The assembly at Angers ran into difficulty almost immediately. Any readjustment of the taille between the généralités involved determining the number of hearths in each, since the hearth was the basis of the levy. But what hearths should be counted? Languedoc wanted to include those in the free towns that were exempted from the taille and the nonnoble holdings of the nobles and ecclesiastics. This policy would favor Languedoc for there were fewer free towns there than in the northern provinces, and there the nobles and ecclesiastics paid the taille on their common lands. For the same reasons the plan was opposed, and opposed successfully, by the other généralités. At length the assembly decided to break up into four groups consisting of two deputies from each généralité. Each group established itself in a different généralité to carry on its investigation. The work proceeded slowly, being constantly delayed by certain localities anxious to preserve their special privileges and by royal tax officials who were opposed to change. At length the young king became impatient, and on February 7, 1494, he halted the work of the commission and arbitrarily granted Normandy an annual rebate of 30,000 livres and Languedoc one of 20,000 livres. Thus ended one of the most unusual experiments in the use of national representative assemblies in France.[10]

Charles VIII held several great judicial assemblies during the winter of 1487–88 concerning legal action to be taken against the Dukes of Orléans and Brittany who were then in rebellion. The princes of the blood, peers of France, archbishops, dukes, counts, chevaliers of the Order of Saint-Michel, members of the Parlement, bailiffs, seneschals, and other royal officials attended.[11]

Louis XII continued his predecessors' policy of holding assemblies whenever he needed advice. If it were a question of judicial and administrative reorganization, he might summon some prelates, members of the various Parlements, seneschals, bailiffs, and great nobles, with the usual members of the council as he did at Blois in March, 1499.[12] For a matter more purely judicial, such as the creation of a Parlement for Provence in July, 1501, it was "several princes and seigneurs of our blood and line, and other great and notable persons of our grand council, courts of *Parlement,* and others of several and divers estates. . . ." who were consulted.[13] If it were a matter as involved as the Pragmatic Sanction, members of the various Parlements, financial officials, and leading prelates might be called upon for advice, as at Lyon in June, 1510. The French clergy was assembled later that year at Tours and again at Lyon in 1511 to discuss similar problems. The first of these two ecclesiastical assemblies was particularly large. All bishops, two representatives from each cathedral chapter, and delegates of the diocesan clergy were convoked. Indeed, every year or two during the reigns of Charles VIII and Louis XII some sort of assembly was held.[14] There was little system or order about these meetings. The king simply summoned whom he chose, but their very existence proves the consultative nature of the Renaissance Monarchy.

The Estates and Treaties

Charles VIII and Louis XII also continued the policy of associating certain elements of the nation with their treaties. Most frequently this was done by having the great lords and towns furnish sealed oaths that they would support a given treaty and by having the treaty registered by the Parlement of Paris. The towns, of course, had to hold assemblies to ratify the treaty, a copy of which was always sent them by the king. They and the Parlement could make remonstrances, but obviously they could change nothing in the agreement. Nevertheless, this practice furnishes one more example of how the Renaissance Monarchs attached various elements of the population to their policies.

There is no need to discuss each of the numerous instances that the nobles, the towns, and the Parlement were asked to act on a treaty.[15]

As examples let us consider the agreements made with Maximilian of Austria at Senlis in May, 1493, and with Ferdinand and Isabella at Barcelona a few months earlier. The guarantees furnished were so similar that it is sufficient to quote only from the one made with Maximilian. Here it was stated that the French king, "for the security of this peace would give to the said King of the Romans and Archduke the letters and seals of mylords the Dukes of Orléans, Bourbon, Nemours, and the Counts of Angoulême, Montpensier, Vendôme, the Prince of Orange, the marshals and admiral of France, the cities, towns, and communities of Paris, Rouen, Lyon, Poitiers, Tours, Angers, Orléans, Amiens, and Tournai." Maximilian was likewise to furnish guarantees by his principal vassals and towns.[16] Charles VIII used the assembly of the towns at Lyon in April, 1494, prior to the invasion of Italy to explain the need for the two treaties and then wrote the municipalities that they were to hold meetings to give "promises to maintain the peace, alliances, and confederations . . ." made with the two foreign powers.[17] In addition, the treaty was to be registered by the Parlement of Paris and the *Chambre des comptes* for France and by comparable institutions for Maximilian.[18]

The ratification of the Treaty of Étaples in 1492 with England is of greater interest because the terms provided that within a year the agreement would be submitted to the English Parliament and the three estates of France. Then, less than two months later, the two monarchs decided to postpone this part of the ratification until the next meeting of the three estates and Parliament.[19] We suspect that Henry VII instigated, or at least welcomed, this new arrangement. He had won a grant from Parliament to invade France to save Brittany, and now he was being paid by France to make peace after an extremely brief campaign in which he had not prevented the duchy and her ruler from falling into the hands of the French. It was well to let time calm any ill-feelings in England before convoking Parliament to ratify the treaty. Not until October, 1495, did the wily monarch finally assemble Parliament for this and other reasons.[20]

Charles VIII began to take steps to have the treaty ratified a little earlier. He followed the procedure established by Louis XI in regard to the Treaty of Arras in 1482 of holding bailiwick assemblies except in such places as Languedoc and Normandy where there were provincial estates. In his letters Charles directed that the estates swear "to confirm, ratify, and approve, and to observe, maintain, and keep" the treaty without making any limitations or difficulties.[21] This form was followed with minor variations by the three estates of at least eighteen bailiwicks and provinces.[22]

The three estates could also be used to break a treaty as Louis XII clearly demonstrated in 1506 when he decided to marry his eldest daughter, Claude, to Francis, Count of Angoulême, rather than to Charles of Luxemburg, a young Habsburg prince to whom she was betrothed. At one time the Habsburg alliance had seemed most desirable from the dynastic point of view. Louis had wanted imperial investiture for Milan, and this favor was best obtainable in conjunction with a marriage alliance. Then too, Louis had been pleased at the thought of his daughter married to Charles, who, as heir to the Spanish kingdoms and many lands in the empire and Italy, was potentially the most powerful sovereign since Charlemagne. The Habsburgs were equally anxious for the alliance. Claude was the richest heiress in Europe unless she had a brother. To her would go Milan, Asti, Genoa, claims to Naples, Brittany, and rich lands in Orléanais. Of her parents' possessions only the crown of France would be denied her, for it could pass only to a male. Louis' wife, Anne of Brittany, had also been happy at these prospects. Besides providing a glittering future for her daughter, the marriage would prevent her beloved duchy from being swallowed in the mammoth domain of the crown of France. It was, therefore, with mutual anticipation that the treaties arranging the marriage had been signed in 1501 and again in 1504.

Soon thereafter Louis began to change his plans for his daughter. His health was quite poor, and it was increasingly apparent that he would have no son. If the marriage were allowed to take place, the Habsburgs would get the Valois claims in Italy and an important voice in the internal affairs of France. Besides, he had finally been given imperial investiture of Milan in 1505, and the emperor's friendship was now less necessary. The marriage was exceedingly unpopular in France with only the queen and the powerful Cardinal of Amboise lending support. Soon the problem became one of how he could most graciously break his word, and it was here that the estates became of use.

During 1505 a rumor was spread that the French people were strongly opposed to the marriage, but still the king and queen gave the Habsburgs assurances of their intention to honor the treaties. At the same time they were careful to mention the opposition of the French people. Thus Louis began to build the idea that in the long run he might not be able to persuade his subjects to accept the marriage, an important point because the treaties provided that should the nuptials not take place through the fault of the king, queen, or princess Claude, Burgundy, Milan, and Asti would go to Charles of Luxemburg anyway. But there was the possibility of placing the blame for the breach on the French people. Sometime in 1505 or early in 1506 Louis XII began to work toward this end.[23]

Then, quietly, between April 23 and 28, 1506, the towns began to elect deputies to go to the king. There had been no royal letters of convocation sent to the mayors and *échevins*. At Paris and Abbeville nothing occurred that would lead one to believe that the whole affair was not spontaneous. At Amiens and Troyes the municipal councils stated that the lieutenant generals of the king in their respective provinces had given them orders to act. A certain Abbot of Fécamp passed the instructions along to Rouen. Sometimes, as at Amiens, Troyes, and Abbeville, the towns did not seem to know why they were to elect deputies to go to the king other than it was for the good of the kingdom. From other places, like Paris, Rouen, and Lyon, the deputies definitely planned to plead with the king to marry his daughter to the Count of Angoulême. In no place was any effort made to assemble all the inhabitants for consultation as had often been done in 1468. Usually, only the bourgeois oligarchy that elected deputations to go to the king about more ordinary affairs participated.[24]

The secrecy, which made the whole affair seem spontaneous, was broken by Louise of Savoy, Countess of Angoulême, who had other plans for her son. She betrayed the role of Louis on May 11 when she belatedly wrote the mayor, *échevins,* and councilors of her town of Angoulême that "the king wanted to discuss some matters for which he had ordered the inhabitants of the principal towns of his kingdom . . ." to elect deputies to meet him at Tours on the tenth. Angoulême was instructed to do likewise.[25]

The leader in organizing the deputies of the twenty towns that were represented at Tours was Eustace L'Huillier, provost of the merchants and deputy from Paris and *maître des comptes ordinaire* of the king. He arranged for the delegates to meet in the town hall on Monday, May 11, no doubt in accordance with previous instructions. Here plans were laid to beg for an audience with the king to ask him to marry his daughter to the Count of Angoulême. Thomas Bricot, doctor of theology at the University of Paris and one of the deputies from the capital city, was elected speaker.[26]

Meanwhile, rumors of what was afoot began to spread in spite of the efforts for secrecy. On May 13 a Habsburg ambassador reported from Tours that the princes and estates of the realm were assembled and that it was believed their purpose was to plead for a marriage between the princess and the Count of Angoulême. The king, he predicted, would readily grant this request.[27]

On Thursday, the fourteenth, Louis held an audience in the great hall at the château of Plessis-les-Tours. Present in addition to the usual royal councilors and the deputies from the towns were the princes of the blood and many archbishops, bishops, seigneurs, barons, members of the Parlements, and the ambassadors of foreign princes.[28]

The session was devoted to the presentation of the views of the towns by Thomas Bricot. He informed the king that

they were come before him in all humility and reverence to declare certain things of great moment touching the welfare of his person, the profit of his kingdom, and the utility of all Christendom, to wit, that in the month of April of the year last past he had been grievously sick, whereat all his subjects had been sorely grieved, fearing to lose him and calling to mind his singular favours; how he had kept his kingdom and subjects in a peace so good that the like of it had never been seen in times past, for no man durst take aught without payment, and the very hens knew that they were safe from violence; how he had remitted to his people one quarter of the *tailles;* how he had reformed justice in his kingdom, placing upright judges in the *Parlement* of Paris and in all other tribunals; and for these and other like reasons too numerous to rehearse he ought to be styled Louis the Twelfth, the Father of his People.

Then the deputies knelt before the king, and Bricot proceeded: "Sire, we are come here to proffer a request for the general welfare of your kingdom. Your humble subjects beg that it may please you to give your only daughter in marriage to My Lord Francis here present, who is France's son." [29] These and the fair words that followed brought tears to the eyes of the king and all that heard them.

When Bricot had finished, Louis spoke to several of his close advisors and then had the deputies informed that he had heard nothing of the proposed marriage, but would discuss the matter with the princes of his blood.

On the following Monday, another great assembly was held in which the king asked for the advice of the Cardinal of Amboise, the Bishop of Paris, and the Presidents of the Parlements of Paris and Bordeaux. They all agreed that the request of the towns was reasonable. The next day the chancellor informed the estates that the king would authorize the marriage in response to their suggestion, the advice of the princes and his councilors, and the desires of the representatives from the duchy of Brittany, who had petitioned separately. Furthermore, the king wanted the deputies and the inhabitants of their towns to swear to see that the marriage was performed and consummated when the children were of age, and to recognize the Count of Angoulême as their sovereign lord in the event that he died without male issue. A written copy of the oath to be taken was issued. Bricot gave thanks to the king in the name of the estates and leave was given for the deputies to return to their homes, but before their departure they witnessed the espousal of the two royal children. The princes and barons took the required oath at this time, and during May, June, and July the towns held very large assemblies in which they gave their approval.[30] Thus Louis XII was able to use the desires of his people as expressed in an assembly of the estates to justify breaking his treaty with the Habsburgs.

The decision of the king was widely hailed in 1506 and since that date has received the unanimous approval of French historians, but one cannot help but speculate what would have happened if the future Charles V had been permitted to marry Claude of France as the earlier treaties had promised. Would her dowry of the Italian duchies, Brittany, and lands in Orléanais have permitted the future emperor to swallow France? Might not even the Salic law have been set aside, as Maximilian suggested on one occasion, to permit the offspring of the union to inherit nearly all of western Europe thereby making the idea of a united Christendom a reality? Probably none of these conjectures would have borne fruit. Louis XII was nearer the truth when he pointed out to the mayor and *échevins* of Saint-Omer that a similar marriage had caused the Hundred Years War.[31] Of one fact we can be sure. The most beloved king of his age had associated the desires of his people with his actions, and the popular and consultative traditions of the Renaissance Monarchy were handed over to his successor unimpaired.

SIX

Francis I, Henry II, and the Estates

The Monarchy of Francis I

"Francis I and Henry II were as powerful as any other kings of France; it was at the beginning of the sixteenth century that the absolute monarchy triumphed." [1] So wrote Georges Pagès, one of the leading authorities on French constitutional history. There is certainly evidence to support his position. The assemblies of the three estates of the kingdom virtually ceased, the towns were not convoked after 1517, the notables were summoned less often to give advice, the estates were not asked to ratify treaties after 1544, and there was a growth of absolutist political theory. Furthermore, the Concordat of 1516 gave the crown effective control over appointments to important church positions, the seizure of the bulk of the Bourbon inheritance in central France removed the greatest of the French nobles from the scene, and the reorganization of the administration of finance further strengthened the crown. Yet with all these changes, the popular, consultative nature of the monarchy continued unmodified for the first third of the period and was only mildly altered thereafter.

Francis I had "neither the strength of mind nor the steadfast will to apply himself to a systematic transformation of society and institutions." [2] He was preoccupied with foreign affairs and war. The few changes he instituted arose largely from the need for money for foreign enterprises. He sincerely believed the Bourbon inheritance to be his; he was so far from trying to destroy Charles of Bourbon, the greatest of his vassals, that he named him Constable of France and Governor of Languedoc and Milan soon after he came to the throne. Indeed, Francis I loved his nobility as no other French king had. On them he heaped honors, pensions, and court positions. It was the nobility who profited most from the Concordat, for they received the finest ecclesiastical benefices. It was in part to have them near him that he built huge châteaux. They were his companions in arms and in the chase. The

126

young king was knighted by the bravest of their number and asked no better than to be called "the first gentleman of France."

Nothing could be more erroneous than to accept the statements of several Venetian ambassadors that Francis I could tax his subjects as much as he pleased. It is true that wars and extravagance made an increase in the taille necessary. The revenue from this tax stood at 2,400,000 livres in 1517 and was gradually increased to 4,600,000 by 1543, a figure no higher than that reached under Louis XI in 1481. During the intervening sixty years, prices had nearly doubled, and the capacity of the French people to pay had grown considerably. But the ability of Francis I to tax, like that of his predecessors, was dependent on public opinion. There was an ill-defined, but nonetheless definite point beyond which he could not go without provoking revolt. When he reached that point, he had to turn to expedients, and this he did early in his reign. Substantial parts of the domain were sold, as were the crown jewels, and even some of the treasures of the churches; offices were created and made venal, wages of officials were taxed, loans were demanded, and a system of public credit was instituted.[3] Such measures, though sometimes arbitrary, were not those of an absolute monarch who could tax at will. Only the favored nobility escaped almost intact from the financial manipulations of the king, and they were the principal beneficiaries of his largess.

The Decline of the Consultative Assemblies

The first few years of the reign of Francis I saw the most important administrative changes that were made between his succession to the throne in 1515 and the death of his son in 1559. During this period there was a large amount of consultation. On September 10, 1516, Francis ordered the towns to send deputies to Paris on October 15 to give advice on what should be done about the perennial currency problem.[4] The deputies met several times with Chancellor Duprat in the *hôtel de ville,* but according to Jean Barrillon, the secretary of that official, no solution was reached and the deputies returned to their homes having accomplished nothing.[5] Whether the deputies really contributed anything or not, cannot be said, but on November 27 an ordonnance was issued upon the advice of the council, the various financial courts, and "some delegates of several of our good towns of our kingdom" which set the value on various coins.[6]

Francis instructed the towns to send deputies to Paris on March 15, 1517, to give advice on how the kingdom could be enriched. Seventeen towns and the provincial estates of Provence and Brittany responded to his summons.[7] This time the government took steps to ensure orderly proceedings, a precaution one suspects that had been neglected in the

October assembly. The letters of convocation stipulated that one or two economic experts be chosen, and efforts, for the most part unsuccessful, were made to get the towns to comply with this regulation. When Troyes elected an advocate, the *procureur* of the town, and a seigneur, the chancellor asked the municipality to send instead two merchants, whom he named, because they knew more about the matters to be discussed than anyone else. A similar fate may have befallen Dijon, for the municipal council reduced the original delegation from seven to two, but then in a show of independence elected the town scribe and a councilor to accompany them. Nevertheless, in spite of the royal directives, less than half the towns limited themselves to one or two deputies and most of those chosen were municipal officials, not merchants. Indeed, many deputies were nobles, a few being of the sword, and clergymen were in the delegations from Rouen, Tours, and Bayonne.[8]

The first meeting of the assembly was held on March 21 at the court of Parlement. The judges had been carrying on a battle against the Concordat that the king had just concluded with the papacy, and it had been decided to explain the new policy to the deputies and the members of the sovereign court at the same time. The crown hoped to rally the support of the towns as a counterweight to the opposition that was being offered by the judiciary and some ecclesiastics.[9]

Chancellor Duprat initiated this policy. Before Francis I, several princes, the Parlement, and the deputies, he began by pointing to the domestic problems and foreign enemies the king faced on his succession to the throne. He glorified the great victory that the young ruler had won at Marignano. He argued that the enemies of France had persuaded the pope to abolish the Pragmatic Sanction and assume control over appointments to benefices in the French church. To halt these evils, the king had concluded the Concordat which, it is true, made some changes in the matter of ecclesiastical elections, but nevertheless preserved the essential features of the Pragmatic Sanction and made possible peace with the papacy.[10]

The restoration of peace, the chancellor continued, had freed the king to turn his attention to domestic affairs. The principal persons of the various courts of the realm had been assembled to evaluate old ordonnances and recommend new ones, expenses had been reduced, and an assembly of the deputies of the towns had met to advise on the preparation of a decree establishing the value of the currency. The present meeting was designed to secure the enrichment of the people.[11] Duprat's ideas on how this enrichment should be accomplished were purely mercantilistic. He spoke of the fertility of France which produced all that was needed and made imports unnecessary. He admitted that there were several gates through which money was brought into the kingdom, but added that there were several through which it left. The latter were, for the most part, unwarranted and ought to be closed to allow money to be drawn from but not returned to neighboring states. To secure this enviable situation, the king desired that certain proposals be placed before the assembly.[12]

These proposals were not submitted to the deputies of the towns on that day, but rather were read to them on March 25 in a meeting held in the *hôtel de ville*. They consisted of nine articles designed to prohibit the importation of foreign goods, ensure the use of French ships in foreign trade, set the value of French currency, establish a single system of weights and measures, limit the use of luxury goods, and the like.[13]

After the articles had been read, they were discussed for two days without any agreement being reached. Instead of giving advice, many deputies wanted to submit cahiers bearing on the needs of their individual towns. At length, the government decided to break up the assembly. The deputies were sent home with copies of the articles to be debated in assemblies of the larger and wiser part of the inhabitants of their towns. The conclusions were to be transmitted to the king to be utilized in the preparation of an ordonnance for the enrichment of the kingdom. Steps were also taken to communicate the articles to the smaller, unrepresented towns in the bailiwick of Dijon and possibly elsewhere to secure their opinions.[14]

Jean Barrillon reports that when the letters containing the advice of the towns reached the capital, they were placed unopened in a big leather sack and spoken of no more. Perhaps the secretary of the chancellor exaggerated a little in his disgust at the work of the assembly, but no ordonnance emerged based on its deliberations and no further calls were made on assemblies of the towns for advice during the reign. Barrillon leaves no doubt as to the reasons for his unhappiness over the outcome of the meeting. The government had presented a mercantilistic program designed to stop the flow of money out of France by halting the importation of goods, and the deputies had opposed this move in favor of a policy which permitted greater freedom in trade. This attitude, to Barrillon, indicated that the deputies preferred their individual profit to the general good. Another thing that irritated him was the tendency of some of the deputies to insist that their individual complaints be satisfied before they would pay attention to the proposals of the king. On this last point, we suspect, there was justice in Barrillon's position. When asked to make recommendations on what should be done to enrich the kingdom, the deputies from Troyes could only suggest that the holding of the *Grand jours* of Champagne and Brie in their town be confirmed and that they be given permission to have another fair. The problem of fortifications seems to have dominated the ideas of Bayonne.[15] To the bureaucratic Barrillon, the towns were too motivated by self-interest to make it worth-while to consult them. It was for officials like himself, who presumably were above local prejudice and had only the general good in their hearts, to prepare ordonnances for the government of the kingdom. He gave no indication that he feared representative assemblies. Rather he opposed them because he thought they were useless. One suspects that his attitude was shared by many.[16]

There were no further assemblies of the towns during the reign of Francis I, but it would be virtually impossible to prepare a list of all the nonrepresentative assemblies. Ordonnances were usually made and issued on the advice of great nobles and the regular members of the council, though vague references to "other notable persons" were not infrequent. In addition, specialists were consulted now and then. For example, some captains took part in the preparation of the army regulations issued in June, 1526, and financial officials helped prepare an ordonnance forbidding the export of gold in December, 1529.[17] Records have usually survived only for assemblies held in conjunction with the Parlement of Paris, where the clerk of the court carefully noted who attended. Often these assemblies took the form of a *lit de justice.* Present would be the king, prelates, great nobles, bailiffs, members of the Parlement, and others in widely varying numbers. In his *Recueil de rangs des grands de France,* the clerk, Jean Du Tillet, listed more than twelve meetings during the reigns of Francis I and Henry II as examples, but on the whole there was a marked decline in the use of large consultative assemblies after the first few decades of the period.[18]

The Estates and Treaties

There were many interesting meetings concerned with foreign affairs and treaties. They began with a series of assemblies on the Concordat made with the pope in 1516. This treaty was to be ratified by the French church and the various courts of Parlement within six months, but it was unpopular because it gave the king effective control over important ecclesiastical appointments and made probable the revival of the *annates* abolished by the Pragmatic Sanction. With a degree of caution, Francis approached the problem of ratification. Twice he had it approved by his council, with several ecclesiastics and members of the sovereign courts being present. Then on February 5, 1517, he appeared before the Parlement of Paris accompanied by several great nobles, important ecclesiastics, canons of Notre Dame, and representatives of the University of Paris to ask that the Concordat be registered by

Parlement and ratified by the clergy. After some speeches, the members of Parlement and the clergy separated to discuss their replies. When the two groups reassembled, the Cardinal of Boissy reported in the name of the ecclesiastics that the entire French church was interested in the Concordat and that it could be ratified only by a general assembly of the clergy. The king was angered, for he had hoped that this rump assembly would serve as the means of satisfying his agreement with the pope to get the consent of the clergy. The reply of the Parlement was noncommittal.[19]

On March 21 the matter was placed before a joint meeting of the deputies of the towns and the members of Parlement in the hope of rallying public opinion to the side of the new arrangement.[20] On May 29 the king renewed his demands on the Parlement for ratification, but after much debate the court refused. For nearly a year the quarrel continued, until, at length, the Parlement abandoned its stand before the threat of the king to reduce its jurisdiction by creating a new court at Orléans. Immediately after his victory, Francis took steps to secure ratification by the provincial courts.[21] The University of Paris continued to resist for a short time, but eventually it too was silenced, and the Concordat of 1516 became one of the principal decrees which regulated the French church.[22] The consultative traditions of the monarchy had been violated, not so much by the enforced registration of the Parlement—for here the king was clearly within his constitutional rights—but by the failure to get the consent of all the French clergy as had been agreed with the pope. Francis' action was undoubtedly caused by the belief that the Gallican Church could not be persuaded to accept the proposed changes. The affair is of interest because it shows that in the ratification of treaties, the Parlement and the other institutions consulted were no mere rubber stamps, even though they were eventually persuaded to accede to the royal desires.

Francis encountered little difficulty in the ratification of the other treaties he made during the first decade of his reign. The rank and number of the guarantors varied considerably. In the treaties of Paris in March, 1515, and Noyon in August, 1516, with the future emperor, Charles V, the great nobles and twelve towns were to promise their support, and the agreements were to be enregistered by the Parlement of Paris and the *Chambre des comptes*.[23] Two letters sent by Francis I on December 20, 1516, to the town of Bayonne provide an excellent indication of what was expected of an individual or community chosen to swear to support a treaty. The first letter was general in nature and explained the treaties. The second stipulated that in event Francis broke the treaty, Bayonne was to furnish him no assistance, but instead was to support Charles notwithstanding the oaths of fidelity taken to the French crown. On January 8, 1517, Bayonne made the required pledge.[24]

The five-year period following the capture of Francis in February, 1525, at the battle of Pavia was marked by several large assemblies and some interesting examples of how and why the estates and towns were asked to ratify treaties.

The queen mother and regent, Louise of Savoy, found herself in a difficult position when the news of the capture of the king reached France early in March. Public opinion had never been enthusiastic about the Italian Wars, nor was the young king popular. His extravagances and lack of prudence had won him few friends among the people. His arbitrary action in regard to the Concordat and his efforts to curtail the expansion of the role of the Parlement of Paris in the government had cost him some support among the clergy and jurists. A reaction was sure to set in because he had become a captive and his policy, a failure. This situation was not helped by the strong feeling that a woman should not rule.[25]

Louise of Savoy was quick to recognize the weakness of her position and took measures to enlarge the council to include fifteen or sixteen great nobles and prelates, members of the Parlements of Paris, Rouen, and Bordeaux, and several representatives of the town of Paris. This council was sometimes referred to in contemporary documents as the estates of Lyon, but only in the broadest sense did it contain representative elements, the deputies from Paris being present only for a short time. What the regent had really done was to associate her government with men like the Duke of Vendôme. Such men were in strong positions to challenge her authority. One of the most striking aspects of Francis' year in captivity was the loyalty of the great nobles.[26]

The Parlement of Paris was more willing to take advantage of the situation, and although the majority of its members were loyal to the regent, the court sought to expand its prerogatives into the political sphere. Early in March, it delegated eight of its number to meet with members of the *Chambre des comptes* and leading ecclesiastics and officials of the town of Paris to prepare the defense of the city and the provinces to the north. Near the end of July, these meetings came to an end largely because of jealousy between the component parts. At first, Louise of Savoy encouraged the activities of the Parlement, but during the spring and summer of 1525 the court expanded its activities into military and financial spheres and sought mild political reforms. At length, the regent was forced to try to limit these usurpations of authority.[27]

During this period there was some talk of convoking the Estates General. The matter came up in the Parlement on March 23, but it was decided not to press for a meeting at that time.[28] Louise of Savoy was definitely opposed to the idea because the three estates had in times past claimed the right to name the council during a regency. It seemed to her that those who sought a meeting of the Estates General could only desire her removal, and on October 8 she reproached a member of the Parlement saying that several councilors of that court wanted to see the estates of the kingdom assembled to diminish her authority. This charge the Parlement steadfastly denied.[29]

The unfavorable attitude of Louise of Savoy towards convoking the Estates General should not be interpreted as a general policy of the monarchy; it only meant that she did not feel the moment was opportune. A decade earlier, when Francis had named her regent during his first Italian campaign, he had issued two orders defining her powers. In the first, dated July 15, 1515, he had included a vague statement that she could do whatever was necessary for the good of the kingdom. This phrase he clarified that same day in the second order giving her authority to make ordonnances and "to assemble . . . the people of the estates of our kingdom. . . ." [30] When he again named her as regent on August 12, 1523, he gave her the power to summon the members of the sovereign courts, other crown officials "and likewise the mayors, *échevins,* councilors, bourgeois, men, and inhabitants of the towns of our kingdom, and our other subjects . . . in order to have their council and advice. . . ." [31] Later in the same document and with almost the same phraseology as in 1515, the queen mother was given authority to convoke "the people of the estates of our kingdom. . . ." [32] Would Francis have authorized his mother to hold meetings of the estates if he had feared these assemblies? Would not the easiest way to protect her from such demands have been specifically to deny her this right? Yet in 1515 in order that there be no uncertainty in his first declaration of her powers, he had issued a second statement specifically giving her the authority to consult the estates. No less a person than Chancellor Duprat advocated assembling the three estates when news of the disaster at Pavia reached the court. Later, Francis was made so desperate by the demands of the emperor that he issued a letter from captivity ordering that his eldest son be crowned king and that his mother act as his regent. To inform the people of these changes, he further directed that the three estates be assembled.[33]

Additional information on the attitude of the government is supplied by the negotiations and ratification of treaties. The defeat at Pavia made it necessary for France to seek allies, and negotiations with England to this end were terminated with the Treaty of Moore in August. This treaty involved the payment by France of nearly 4,000,000 livres over a period of years, but in return it brought peace with England

and the entrance of England into a defensive alliance against the emperor. The English, naturally enough, wanted every assurance that they would be paid, and from the beginning there was difficulty on this score. Did the regent have the authority to negotiate a treaty that would bind her son after he had regained his freedom? The answer was in doubt, and Cardinal Wolsey determined to tie as much of the French population to the agreement as possible. In addition to securing a promise that Francis would ratify the treaty on his release, the Cardinal insisted that the regent, certain of the great nobles, and some towns guarantee the payments, and that the various courts of Parlement and the estates of the kingdom undertake to support the arrangement.

Louise of Savoy was opposed to the estates being asked to give guarantees because she anticipated difficulty in getting them to ratify a treaty involving heavy payments to a foreign prince, and hence causing further taxation. At length, it was agreed that only the estates of Normandy and Languedoc would give approval, and the regent turned to the question of securing the required ratifications, a task which was supposed to be completed within three months.[34]

The great nobles saw the advantage of buying English friendship rather than running the risk of a joint invasion by Henry VIII and Charles V. Without argument they approved the treaty and guaranteed that the payments would be made. The estates of Languedoc at first refused to comply, but quickly reversed itself when the necessity for the treaty was recognized. The Parlement of Paris fought the arrangement for a long time, but at length agreed "to read, publish, register, and approve" the treaty, and the provincial Parlements also agreed, although several failed to meet the three-month deadline. Four of the towns gave their pledges with little or no persuasion, but the other five—Paris, Orléans, Tours, Rouen, and Bordeaux—refused to do so, and they were followed by the estates of Normandy. The towns objected to the large payments. Normandy argued that since the treaty concerned everyone, it should be approved by the estates of the kingdom. This opposition made it necessary for the regent to ask the English for additional time and for a modification of the type of guarantee demanded of the towns. These concessions were granted, and they were sufficient to bring the recalcitrant municipalities into line. The regent decided against approaching the estates of Normandy again on the subject, but the return of Francis to France and his acceptance of the treaty were enough to satisfy the English.[35]

The negotiations for Francis' release offer another interesting example of the role of the people in foreign affairs. In March, 1525, Charles V demanded the return of Burgundian territories taken by France in 1482, the surrender of French claims in Italy, and other concessions. He insisted that these terms be ratified and approved by the French estates, the Parlement of Paris, four provincial Parlements, the various *Chambres des comptes,* and the members of the council.[36] Francis replied in April. He balked especially at the surrender of Burgundy on the grounds that it was allied to the crown of France, and stated that ratification by the estates, the Parlements, and the *Chambres des comptes* was impossible unless the terms of the treaty were modified.[37] Whether Francis' refusal to secure the ratification of the treaty in the desired manner was based on his belief that the estates would not consent to the dismemberment of the kingdom as he said, or whether his attitude resulted from a desire to use the estates as an excuse not to make major concessions, cannot be determined; but he was not motivated by fear of consulting the assemblies because he made counter proposals that included winning the approval of the Parlement of Paris and the estates of France.[38]

By December, 1525, Francis was desperate enough to move a long way toward meeting the territorial demands of the emperor and expressed his willingness to see the treaty ratified by the courts of Parlement and the three estates of France.[39] The final terms of the Treaty of Madrid of January, 1526, provided for freeing the king in return for the surrender of two of his sons and twelve great nobles as hostages. These hostages were to be returned as soon as Burgundy had been delivered to Spain; the Estates General had promised the perpetual observance of the treaty; and the various courts of Parlement and the *Chambre des comptes* of Paris had registered it.[40]

How soon after his release Francis and his advisors resolved not to honor their treaty obligations is difficult to say, but this decision was made public in a meeting of the council at Cognac in May. The problem then was how to justify this action before European public opinion and how to effect the return of the royal hostages. To accomplish the first, the belief that a subject should not be transferred from one ruler to another ruler without his consent and the doctrine that the domain was inalienable were brought into play. In June the estates of Burgundy and Auxonne were asked to choose between a Habsburg and Valois lord. With little persuasion, the estates of both localities expressed a preference for the Valois, and the young king did not hesitate to use the desires of his subjects as justification for keeping these lands in spite of his pledges to the contrary.[41]

Having decided to refuse to surrender Burgundy and other territories because of the desires of the inhabitants, it remained for Francis to effect the release of his two sons and the other hostages. This task was commenced by trying to strengthen the country through a system of alliances in which England played a key role. Then negotiations were begun to ransom the princes. As Charles V slowly came to realize that he could not get Burgundy, he became more willing to accept financial payment in compensation. This meant that Francis had to prepare his subjects for new sacrifices.[42]

On December 16, 1527, the king assembled at Paris twenty-three archbishops and bishops, about twelve great nobles, some bailiffs, seneschals, and the members of his household, sixteen presidents and councilors of the provincial Parlements, members of the Parlement of Paris, and the provost of the merchants and four *échevins* of that city; in all there were some two hundred persons. After the chancellor had made a few introductory remarks, the king took the floor and pointed out that he needed the aid and advice of his loyal subjects on some very important matters. He justified his previous policies in a manner that did little credit to his honesty. The blame for the Italian War and his defeat he placed on others. He himself had always worked for peace. The Treaty of Madrid for his release had been the doing of his mother and the French ambassadors. He, on the contrary, had prepared an edict in captivity ordering that his eldest son be crowned, for he would have preferred to remain a prisoner than to surrender Burgundy. With rather specious arguments he sought to excuse himself for accepting the treaty when in the hands of the Spanish and then refusing to ratify it on his release. Recently, he continued, the king of England had joined him in sending ambassadors to the emperor offering peace and 4,000,000 livres, of which 2,400,000 livres were to ransom the royal children. If the emperor refused this offer, which seemed unlikely, the money would be needed anyway for war. The royal treasury was, of course, in no position to meet either of the contingencies. Having presented this obvious hint that financial assistance was needed, Francis offered to return to captivity to secure the release of the two princes; that is, if those present found it impossible to recommend that extraordinary taxes be levied.

When he finished, he directed the clergy, nobility, members of the Parlement, and the town of Paris to deliberate apart to determine what advice to offer him in his difficulty. The clergy met that same day. The judicial officials and the town of Paris deliberated on the seventeenth and eighteenth. Nothing is known of the activities of the nobility.[43]

The estates assembled together again on the twentieth to give their replies. The Cardinal of Bourbon, speaking for the first estate, favored ransoming the two princes and offered 1,300,000 livres to be divided among the clergy in provincial assemblies of that order. In return, the king was asked to succor the pope who was then a captive of the emperor, to stamp out Lutheranism, and to maintain the liberties and rights of the Gallican Church. The Duke of Vendôme offered the king the goods and lives of the nobles who were present and he expressed the hope that those of the second estate who had not been summoned would do likewise. To secure their consent he recommended that assemblies be held in the bailiwicks and seneschalsies. President de Selve spoke for the Parlements. His address was in two parts. First he declared that the Treaty of Madrid was null and that the duchy of Burgundy, as the first peerage of France, could not be alienated. Secondly, he recommended that the king levy a tax of 4,000,000 livres on the nobility, clergy, free towns, and the people of the kingdom to ransom his children. The members of the Parlements would contribute with their lives and their goods. Neither proposal came as a surprise, for the court at Paris had issued a decree two days before exonerating the king for breaking his oath and recommending that the tax be divided between the various orders of the kingdom by five or six prelates, some nobles, and "those of the sovereign courts." The provost of the merchants, speaking for the town of Paris, also offered to pay part of the ransom.[44]

When they had finished, the king thanked those present for their friendship and fidelity. He did not ask money for himself, but for the kingdom. He granted the three requests of the clergy. To the nobility he pointed out that he himself was but a gentleman and he promised to protect and observe their privileges. To the town of Paris he likewise rendered his thanks, and the meeting came to an end.[45]

The nature of this assembly is difficult to determine. Far more notables were present than in the usual *lit de justice,* but the king made a special point of indicating that the meeting took place in the chamber where the *lit de justice* was held and that it was not organized as the estates.[46] It seems useless to assign the name of any particular institution to the meeting; the king could summon whom he pleased to give advice, and this was the group he had chosen. The towns, other than Paris, were probably omitted because they had shown so little enthusiasm when consulted in regard to the Treaty of Moore. The capital had since been chastised for its bad behavior and then could be safely admitted to give the municipalities a spokesman. The presence of the Parlements was dictated by Francis' desire to secure legal justification for his conduct. He took his profession of knighthood seriously and was deeply embarrassed by the questionable position in which the failure to ratify the Treaty of Madrid had placed his honor. The upper clergy and nobility had proved their loyalty during the regency. He did not fear their advice. The one thing Francis did not want was for someone to recommend that he carry out the Treaty of Madrid or return to captivity. He had chosen his assembly accordingly.

The emperor refused to accept the offer to ransom the two princes;

war continued and the French were again defeated. At length the Turkish threat at Vienna led Charles V to relinquish his demands for Burgundy in return for the proffered ransom, and with these changes in the Treaty of Madrid he consented to make peace at Cambrai in August, 1529. The two treaties were to be ratified and approved by the provincial estates and registered by all the Parlements and by the *Chambre des comptes* at Paris before the hostages were delivered.[47] This time the French proceeded with the ratification; during the fall and winter of 1529 and 1530 the three estates of Normandy and Languedoc and of at least thirty-five bailiwicks and seneschalsies assembled and swore to observe and maintain perpetually the treaties.[48]

Ratification of the treaties brought forward the question of money to pay the ransom. The government began to work towards solving this problem even before the assembly of December, 1527, but stringent measures had to be taken in the last of 1529 and early in 1530 to get the necessary sum. Where there were provincial estates, they were summoned to consent to taxes during these trying years. The clergy usually voted its share of the ransom money in provincial or diocesan assemblies. The nobles argued that they owed only military service in spite of the generous offer the Duke of Vendôme had made in their name.[49] At length the second estate in the Île-de-France was summoned to meet at Paris on September 28, 1529, to hear a royal plea for assistance. Francis pointed out that on his return from captivity he had summoned the princes, great seigneurs, prelates, and principal towns of the kingdom to explain his difficulties. They had promised to aid and succor him with all their power to free his children. He had turned first to the clergy and the towns, but now it was necessary to ask the nobility for assistance. They were accustomed, he admitted, to serve only with their persons, and he had always tried to spare them from the *arrière-ban;* but what he now asked would help preserve their own liberty. Certain evil men had dared spread the rumor that he wished to make gentlemen subject to the taille, but the charge was false. He would not do such a thing against himself for "I am a gentleman; it is the principal title I bear and the one I esteem the most. As a gentleman and your king, I speak to you as gentlemen. I pray you . . . to offer me such gifts and presents that will enable me to know the love and affection you bear me." [50]

The nobles of the Île-de-France responded in the amount of one-tenth of the annual revenue of their fiefs and rear-fiefs. The victorious monarch now turned to the other provinces, hoping that this gift would become the national pattern. On October 5 letters were issued to the bailiffs to convoke all nobles and other persons holding fiefs and rear-fiefs from the crown. On the twenty-fifth and twenty-sixth the nobility of Touraine met and decided to offer a "free gift" similar to that granted by the Île-de-France, and the nobility of other areas followed suit.[51] The king had managed to extract money from the nobility, but he had done so only after two years of persuasion in both national and local assemblies. Ransoming a lord was among the most deep-rooted of the obligations of a vassal. Clearly Francis I was far from being able to dominate his nobility.

The towns were also subjected to special levies. On February 26, 1528, the king asked Paris for 200,000 livres. An assembly was held, and in spite of the generous offer made in December to ransom the two princes, it was decided to name a delegation to go to the king to ask for a reduction. The mission was successful, and the assessment was reduced to 150,000 livres, but the king requested that this favor be kept secret so that the other free towns would not ask for like consideration.[52]

Well might the king plead for secrecy, but he did so in vain. When Lyon was asked to furnish 35,000 livres, the town protested against the size of the assessment and asked the king for a reduction of one-fourth "such as he had granted the town of Paris." [53] The royal commissioners asked Rouen for 75,000 livres on May 2, and the town dispatched a deputation to court to plead for a reduction. At Paris the deputies quickly learned that the capital city had won a 50,000 livres rebate, but when cornered on his return from Mass the king escaped making a similar commitment by referring them to his council. Here they were confronted by the chancellor, who said that the tax was just, that the king could make them pay without their consent but didn't want to, and that everyone was contributing—he himself having been assessed for his house in Paris. The deputies held their ground before this tirade, stoutly maintaining that the sum was intolerable. There the matter remained for some months. The town refused to consent to the tax. The government refused to reduce it. Finally, in January, 1529, Rouen was prodded into making an offer of 30,000 livres, and deputies were again dispatched to the king. When this amount was refused, they raised the offer to 40,000 livres, and then finally to 50,000 livres when friends at court hinted that the king might be content with that amount. He was, and on September 8, 1529, the offer was approved. After nearly a year and a half of negotiations, Francis had finally obtained two-thirds of what he had asked. Some other towns were still more fortunate. Orléans won a reduction from 30,000 to 20,000 livres, Bourges from 15,000 to 7,500 livres, and Beauvais from 12,000 to 4,000 livres.[54]

The history of this tax is very revealing. No request Francis ever made for financial assistance was more legitimate. The obligation to ransom a lord was steeped in tradition, and he had won acceptance of the levy in an exceptionally large consultative assembly. Nevertheless, the consent of local assemblies of the clergy and nobility, interminable negotiations with the privileged towns, and reductions in the sums demanded, had been necessary. The chancellor had told the deputies of Rouen that the king could tax them without consent; this and similar remarks were undoubtedly overheard by the Venetian ambassadors who reported that the French ruler could levy what he pleased, but a glance at the archives shows how false their reports were.

The next great treaty of the Habsburg-Valois Wars was signed at Crépy in September, 1544. As at Cambrai the terms called for ratification and approval by the provincial estates and for registration by all the Parlements and the *Chambre des comptes* at Paris.[55] In spite of similarity in the phraseology concerning the method of ratification in the two treaties, it seems probable that this time approval was given by the provincial estates as stipulated, rather than by the estates of the bailiwicks and seneschalsies. The agreement was ratified by the estates of Languedoc, Burgundy, Normandy, Picardy, and presumably other provinces.[56]

The final treaty in the long wars between the two dynasties was signed at Cateau-Cambrésis in April, 1559. This time the approval of the provincial estates was not required, only that of the Parlements and the *Chambre des comptes* was retained.[57] Did this omission mark the growth of absolutism and a decline in the popular, consultative nature of the Renaissance Monarchy? This is possible, but one suspects that estates were also dropped because European rulers had come to believe that their oaths to support and maintain treaties were useless. Time and again the estates had made these vows, sometimes even swearing to help the Habsburgs against their own king, but we do not know of a single instance of their doing anything when their king broke the treaty, as he invariably did. Philip II knew what his father had never learned, that a people can be as warlike and as dishonest as a king. It is true that registration by the Parlements and the *Chambre des comptes* had not prevented violation of treaties by French kings either, but registration was advisable for legal as well as diplomatic reasons and was therefore retained.

The Growth of the Theory of Absolutism

The decline of the number of assemblies and the failure to use the estates to ratify treaties was paralleled by a growth of absolutism in political thought. The theorist par excellence of the earlier stages of the Renaissance Monarchy had been Claude de Seyssel. His *La Grand' Monarchie de France* was written to instruct Francis I, who had reigned only four years when it was first published. Following the general pattern of the medieval theory of kingship, he depicted the ruler as being limited by the religious life of the state, *la justice,* and *la police.* The religious check not only required the king to conform to the rules of the Catholic Church, but also bound him to adhere to the general principles of justice. *La justice* involved more specific limitations on the authority of the crown and empowered the courts to give redress when the king encroached on the rights of his subjects. *La police* included the fundamental laws governing the succession to the throne and the inalienability of the royal domain as well as the rights, privileges, and customs of the various social groups. The king, Seyssel admitted, could annul or change bad customs and laws, but one of his primary duties was to maintain those that were good. Taxes should be light, but for taxing he did not require popular consent. He also closely followed the practices of the early Renaissance Monarchs by insisting that rulers get advice before taking important action. In addition to the small, frequently consulted *Conseil Ordinaire* and *Conseil Secret* to handle ordinary affairs, he discussed the larger general councils which were of two types. The one, known as the *Grand Conseil,* consisted of the leading clergymen, nobles, great officers of the crown, and members of the sovereign courts. The other, which he referred to as the *Assemblée Casuelle,* included, in addition, the deputies of the principal cities and towns of the kingdom. It would be inconvenient, he thought, to summon either of the general councils too often, and he relegated to them only matters of great consequence to the whole kingdom: the question of war or peace, the preparation of laws and ordonnances concerning justice and administration, and the like.[58]

However, during the two or three decades which preceded the outbreak of the Wars of Religion, a new group of jurists headed by Grassaille, Rebuffi, and Chasseneuz began to advocate a theory of kingship that permitted some expansion of royal power. The checks of religion, *la justice,* and fundamental law were maintained in a slightly altered form, but there was a marked tendency to give the king more authority to override customary law, and much less was said about the various types of consultative assemblies that Seyssel had treated in some detail, though, of course, the advisability of taking council was still insisted upon.[59]

The Survival of the Renaissance Monarchy

The Renaissance Monarchy was threatened, but one must not exaggerate the danger. The new developments in political theory had little immediate influence on the thinking of the average Frenchman. One strongly suspects that the jurist was read only by his fellow jurists. Neither nobles nor burghers were affected as their behavior in the Wars of Religion was to prove. Nor was the decline in the use of the various types of national consultative assemblies paralleled by a fundamental change in all the other popular aspects of the government. The two reigns actually saw the development of diocesan assemblies of the clergy and the occasional use of provincial and even national clerical assemblies. The cause of the innovation was the need for the clergy's consent to taxation. At first Francis asked the clergy for financial assistance about every third year, but between 1541 and 1558 royal demands were annual. The amounts involved were substantial. Henry II never asked for less than 4 décimes, or about 1,600,000 livres, except in 1550 when he contented himself with half that amount. Consent was most often given by diocese, a procedure that led this type of local assembly to flower at the very time the large consultative meetings became less frequent. Not until 1561 did the first estate get its assemblies organized on a national basis, but the idea had slowly developed during the preceding half century.[60]

There was no comparable system of assemblies for the nobility during the period, because the kings were either unwilling or unable to get them to pay taxes. The only time they were assessed, and therefore assembled, was to free the royal hostages held by the emperor. For this purpose, as we have seen, both a national and many local assemblies of the nobility were held between 1527 and 1529.[61]

The declining use of the assemblies of the towns did not mean that the municipalities were cut off from the central government. Letters were frequently sent back and forth between officials at the capital and those in the towns. More significant was the constant flow of deputies from the towns to court. Hardly a year went by but that a municipal council had occasion to send someone to the king concerning the privileges of the town, to request that some restriction be removed, or to ask that a tax be reduced.[62]

Amiens can be used as an example. On March 6, 1539, the *échevins* heard the report of the town clerk who had been to the king at Fontainebleau on various affairs. On May 8 another official was paid for a visit to the king to prevent the transportation of wheat. On June 3 an Italian inspected a gun emplacement between a tower and one of the gates of the town on order of the crown. An anticipated royal visit was discussed, and plans were made to help the royal harbingers when they came looking for lodging. On July 3 it was once more necessary to pay deputies who had been to Paris on the business of the municipality. On September 18, it was the king who summoned representatives from the town to him about some matter. On October 23 an *échevin* and a companion who had been to court made their report. Among the privileges they had won was the right to levy a sales tax in the town for ten years without assembling the people, a real triumph for the municipal oligarchy. On December 12 a deputy was dispatched to Paris to see about a case before the Parlement which concerned the town.[63]

It made no difference whether Amiens sent deputies to assemblies with the other towns of France or the three estates of the kingdom. The representatives of Amiens were as likely to be heard by the king if they were dispatched when the *échevins* felt the need. More likely, indeed, for then they could get the undivided attention of the monarch. To suppose that only the three estates meeting together could get a reduction in taxes is to misconstrue the nature of the Renaissance Monarchy. Actually when a town petitioned a king—even Francis I—and asked with good cause that a tax be removed or diminished, it was more than likely to receive a favorable reply. After all, it cost the king far less to reduce the taxes on a single town than on his entire kingdom.[64]

Another way in which the kings maintained contact with the townsmen, as well as their other subjects, was through travel. Rarely did one of the Valois stay more than a month or two in the same place. This itinerant life gave many of their subjects chances to see their king and perhaps to petition him. These wanderings gave the rulers personal knowledge of the condition of their kingdom and the problems of each locality, an advantage that the eighteenth century kings who shut themselves up at Versailles sadly lacked.[65]

Then there were always the provincial assemblies. It is not necessary to prove that the three estates of Brittany, Normandy, Burgundy, Languedoc, Dauphiné, Provence, and some smaller outlying provinces met regularly during these years, that they kept their right to consent to taxation, often reducing the amount requested, and that they performed many other services useful to themselves and to their king. It is true that a few historians of the estates have professed to see the decline of these institutions during the period of the Renaissance Monarchy, but we can only agree with Henri Prentout that they have offered no real evidence to substantiate their conclusions. Indeed, the period of the Italian Wars brought increased financial demands, and the provincial estates were summoned more often than before.[66]

One only criticizes Prentout for not going further. He failed to stress the development of the assemblies of the clergy and he failed to note the meetings composed primarily of the third estate. The thirteen towns of Basse-Auvergne met regularly to vote taxes during the sixteenth century. What happened between 1451, the date Antoine Thomas chose for the demise of the provincial estates, and the reign of Francis I, we can only guess, but the existence of the assemblies is beyond dispute.[67] In Guyenne there was a representative institution composed primarily of the deputies of the third estate from eleven seneschalsies and numerous local assemblies as well. The early history of these estates is not known, but they were flourishing in 1561 and were still functioning in 1616. The conquest of Piedmont provides further evidence of how little the principles of the monarchy had changed, for Francis continued to summon its estates to vote taxes and to perform other duties.[68]

In spite of the continued vigor of the provincial estates, the decline in the use of national consultative assemblies would in the long run have led to significant changes in the nature of the Renaissance Monarchy had not other factors intervened. Just as the divorce question and the Protestant Reformation brought about a revival in the use of the English Parliament under Henry VIII, so military defeat, financial exhaustion, and religious disunity led to the revival of the large assemblies in France. This revival began near the end of the reign of Henry II and offered the last great opportunity for the establishment of the Estates General prior to the Revolution.

The Estates of 1558

On August 10, 1557, the French were completely defeated by the Spanish at Saint-Quentin. The people of Paris and the Île-de-France were panic stricken at the prospect of invasion, but Henry II acted with firmness. He recalled the Duke of Guise from Italy and planned to attack Calais.[69] There was desperate need for money to pay an enlarged army; and in December the closed towns were asked for substantial contributions, that of Rouen coming to no less than 45,604 livres. The town complained that its inhabitants were too poor to meet the levy and elected three deputies to go to the king to ask to be exempted from the tax, or at least to be given a reduction. Amiens was asked for 15,000 livres, and the closed towns of the provostship of Paris for 100,000 livres. It was in this era of military preparations and financial demands that on December 15 Henry II ordered the towns to send their mayors to Paris on Christmas eve.[70]

The letters of convocation sent to the towns said nothing about the purpose of the assembly except that those who came were to be informed about the nobility of the province; this indicated that the king was as interested in where to find troops as in how to pay them. An Italian ambassador suggested that the purpose of the meeting was to approve the marriage of the dauphin to Mary Stuart, but neither the letters of convocation nor the events of the assembly give support for this view.[71] For some reason the king sent for the mayors of the towns instead of a specific number of elected deputies. This directive inhibited no one. The mayor of Amiens saw to it that he was instructed by an assembly just as if he had been freely chosen. Data elsewhere show that towns selected whom they pleased, as they had always done. Troyes sent three deputies; Carcassonne, a simple bourgeois; Toulouse, a former *capitoul;* and Rouen probably had no specially elected proctors, but came to be represented by three deputies, who had already been sent to Paris to protest against the tax on the closed towns.[72]

There is no evidence to suggest how many municipalities elected deputies, nor is there any way of knowing who else was summoned except from the incomplete list of those who attended.[73] Five cardinals and thirty-three archbishops and bishops were present. Only a handful of nobles were named, but we are told that others attended in great numbers. They were reinforced by the presence of gentlemen from the household of the king and the Chevaliers of the Order. Members of the various sovereign courts of Paris and the first presidents of the provincial Parlements also came. The fact that, in Burgundy at least, the president's expenses were paid by the province suggests that in some way they were regarded as standing for the area as a whole. Certainly the meeting was considered to be an assembly of the estates by contemporaries, and the presence of so many officials from the Parlements and the other sovereign courts even led the king to refer to it in December, 1558, as a "general convocation of the four estates." [74]

Although the king had ordered the deputies to meet in Paris on Christmas eve, the formal opening of the assembly was delayed until January 5. Late arrivals may have been a factor in the postponement, but there must have been other causes as well. By January 1 sufficient representatives were present for an attempt to be made to hold the meeting on the following day.[75] Meanwhile, the individual estates met separately to elect their orators and to discuss what to offer the king.

On January 5 the deputies of the towns reported to the Sainte Chapelle at 7:00 A.M. where they were joined an hour later by the Cardinal of Lorraine and the *Conseil privé*. The procession then began to move toward the hall of Saint Louis in the palace of justice, only to be caught in a crowd of onlookers who pressed in so vigorously that even the assistance of the guard could not prevent the deputies from having to change their course. When, at length, they reached their destination, they found the other orders were already seated.

The king spoke first. He pointed out that since his advent to the throne he had been forced to fight continually against England and the Habsburgs. To pay for the wars he had had to sell his domain and tax his subjects heavily. The time had come, he argued, to make a last great effort in the hope of bringing about a good peace. Since money was the sinew of war, he asked those present what assistance they could offer.[76]

The Cardinal of Lorraine made an hour's speech in the name of the clergy in which he reported that they offered their lives and their goods.

The Duke of Nevers was more brief, but he stated that the nobility was willing to be equally generous. He was followed by the spokesmen for the royal officials and the towns who did likewise, though the latter did not hesitate to add that the people already suffered heavily from the war. Some recalcitrance on the part of the towns had evidently been expected, for immediately the keeper of the seals asked that the deputies from each town submit a list of complaints and promised that the king and his council would consider the suggested reforms before they departed. With this inducement to generosity the assembly came to an end.

The glorious promises and fulsome flattery indulged in by the four orators should be taken no more seriously than the offers to pay the ransom of Francis I in 1527. The basic problem of who was to contribute, and how much, was decided later behind the scene of negotiations. The plans of the government were unfolded on January 8 when the Cardinal of Lorraine summoned the deputies of the towns to appear before him at the *hôtel* of the Cardinal of Sens. He reported that the purpose of the assembly was to raise 6,900,000 livres and that it had been decided to do so by finding 3,000 persons to loan 2,300 livres each. The clergy had offered to furnish 1,000 contributors, and the towns were asked to name the other 2,000. In return, interest at a rate of 8⅓ per cent was promised. To mitigate the effect of this request, the cardinal expressed the king's desire to see a reduction of the taille and of the tax on commodities. As a further concession, he suggested that they attach their cahiers to the roll of donors when they were submitted. The crown asked nothing better than to make a gesture towards the redress of grievances in return for money. Evidently the nobility and royal officials had decided to contribute nothing in spite of the generous promises their spokesmen had made in the full assembly a few days earlier. The two strongest elements of sixteenth century society were to escape once more, thereby throwing the entire burden on the weaker clergy and bourgeoisie.

When the deputies left the *hôtel de Sens,* they discussed the demands of the cardinal and reached the conclusion that no roll of lenders should be submitted because they had no way of knowing the capacity of various individuals to pay. They reported their conclusions to the cardinal, who submitted the matter to the *Conseil privé.* That body at length decided to direct each town to raise a certain sum, and that if there were not enough persons who could loan 2,300 livres, two donors at 1,150 livres each would be accepted instead.

What the reaction of the deputies of the towns would have been to this suggestion will never be known, for during the afternoon of January 9 news reached Paris that the Duke of Guise had taken Calais. The last

English stronghold in France had fallen, and the royal policy of making a final great effort to win a good peace was vindicated. Amidst a burst of enthusiasm the king, queen, and court heard Mass at Sainte Chapelle, the clergy offered a gift of 2,300,000 livres in addition to the regular décimes, and the towns proffered 4,600,000 livres. On the fifteenth, the king appeared before the estates and Parlement to publish several edicts. Action on the petitions of the estates was postponed, and Henry departed for Calais. A month later he abolished many of the restrictions on foreign trade, but most of the requests of the estates were never acted upon.[77]

The nobility and royal officials had offered nothing, and it is likely that the reckless generosity of the third estate on the tenth was short lived. Even the crown recognized that their offer of a gift of 4,600,000 livres was in reality only the acceptance of an obligation to loan that amount. By January 14 the councilors of Troyes were deliberating on the loan of 36,000 livres requested from their town. Someone proposed dividing the amount among three hundred persons, but the motion was defeated. There were complaints about the heavy burden already imposed on them as one of the closed towns that had been asked to help support the enlarged army, and arguments were heard that the simple merchant did not have 200 or 300 livres left. Finally, it was decided to raise the money by surrendering gold and silver plate and jewels. In return, the king promised to pay 3,000 livres per year interest, that is the 8⅓ per cent he had originally proposed.[78]

There were signs that the Estates General of 1558 was not to be an isolated assembly, and that the consultative nature of the Renaissance Monarchy was to be restored to its primitive vigor at the national level. The financial predicament of the crown was unsolved, the Protestant movement was becoming politically dangerous with a sudden increase in noble converts, a rapid rise in prices was leading to economic unrest, and the desire of the vocal elements of the population to return to the former system of government was reflected by new editions of Claude de Seyssel's, *La Grand' Monarchie* in 1557 and in 1558, the first since 1541. Only a strong effort by the crown to enlist popular support could save the kingdom from civil war. This situation led to a second flowering of representative institutions that will be the subject of a later study.

Reference Matter

APPENDIX

Assemblies of The Estates General and the Estates of Languedoïl, 1421-1615

Date	Location	Type of Meeting
May, 1421	Clermont in Auvergne	Estates General
Jan., 1423	Bourges	Estates of Languedoïl
Aug., 1423	Selles	Estates of Languedoïl
Mar., 1424	Selles	Estates General ?
Oct., 1424	Poitiers	Estates of western Languedoïl
Nov., 1424	Riom	Estates of eastern Languedoïl
Mar., 1425	Chinon	?
May, 1425	Montleul	?
Oct., 1425	Poitiers	Estates General ?
Nov., 1426	Mehun-sur-Yèvre	Estates of western Languedoïl
Dec., 1426	Montluçon	Estates of eastern Languedoïl
Apr., 1428	Chinon	Estates of western Languedoïl
?, 1428	?	Estates of eastern Languedoïl [1]
Sept., 1428	Chinon	Estates General
Mar.–Apr., 1431	Poitiers	Estates of Languedoïl ?
Nov., 1431	Amboise	Estates of Languedoïl ?
June–July, 1432	Amboise	?
Sept.–Oct., 1433	Tours	Estates of Languedoïl
Aug., 1434	Tours	Estates of Languedoïl
Jan., 1435	Poitiers	Estates of western Languedoïl
Apr., 1435	Issoudun	Estates of eastern Languedoïl [1]
Apr., 1435	Tours	?
Feb., 1436	Poitiers	Estates of Languedoïl
Oct.–Nov., 1439	Orléans	Estates General ?
Feb.–Aug., 1440	Bourges	Estates General [2]
Apr., 1444	Tours	?
June, 1448	Tours	?
Dec., 1463—Jan., 1464	Montferrand	Estates of eastern Languedoïl
Jan., 1464	Tours	Estates of western Languedoïl

? Type of assembly unknown or in doubt.
[1] There may not have been an assembly.
[2] The king never met with the assembled deputies.

151

Date	Location	Type of Meeting
Apr., 1468	Tours	Estates General
Jan.–Mar., 1484	Tours	Estates General *
May, 1506	Tours	Estates General **
Jan., 1558	Paris	Estates General **
Dec., 1560—Jan., 1561	Orléans	Estates General *
Aug., 1561	Pontoise	Estates General * [3]
July–Aug., 1575	Paris	Estates General **
Dec., 1576—Mar., 1577	Blois	Estates General *
Oct., 1588—Jan., 1589	Blois	Estates General *
Jan.–Aug., 1593	Paris	Estates General * [4]
Nov., 1596—Jan., 1597	Rouen	Estates General **
Oct., 1614—Mar., 1615	Paris	Estates General * [5]

* Election by bailiwick.

** Restricted assembly: Only a limited number of clergymen, noblemen, and deputies of the towns were summoned.

[3] The deputies elected by the bailiwicks went to assemblies of the governments where in turn deputies were elected to the Estates General.

[4] This assembly was convoked by the Duke of Mayenne, not the king. He ordered the estates to meet in 1590, 1591, and 1592, but postponed them each time. Some bailiwicks held electoral assemblies for these earlier meetings.

[5] This was the last meeting of the Estates General before the Revolution. The assemblies of Rouen in 1617 and Paris in 1626–1627 did not contain representative elements. The Estates General was convoked in 1649 and 1651, but both meetings were canceled. Elections, however, were held in many provinces and bailiwicks.

ABBREVIATIONS

AC	Archives Communales
AD	Archives Départementales
AN	Archives Nationales
BEC	*Bibliothèque de l'École des Chartes*
Bernard	*Procès-verbaux des États généraux de 1593. CDI,* ed. Auguste-J. Bernard (Paris, 1842)
B. Mun.	Bibliothèque Municipale
BN	Bibliothèque Nationale
BN, MS. fr.	Bibliothèque Nationale, Manuscrits français
BN, MS. n. a. fr.	Bibliothèque Nationale, Manuscrits nouvelles acquisitions françaises
BR	Charles-A. Bourdot de Richebourg, *Nouveau Coutumier général* (Paris, 1724), 4 vols.
CDI	*Collection de documents inédits sur l'histoire de France*
Dumont	*Corps universel diplomatique du droit des gens . . . ,* ed. Jean Dumont (Amsterdam, 1726–31), 8 vols.
FGC	*Forme générale et particulière de la convocation et de la tenue des assemblées nationales ou États généraux de France,* eds. Lalourcé and Duval (Paris, 1789), 3 vols.
HL	Claude de Vic and Jean Vaissete, *Histoire générale de Languedoc* (Toulouse, 1874–1905), 16 vols.
IAC	*Inventaire sommaire des archives communales antérieures à 1790*
IAD	*Inventaire sommaire des archives départementales antérieures à 1790*
Isambert	*Recueil général des anciennes lois françaises depuis l'an 420 jusqu'à la révolution de 1789,* eds. François-A. Isambert and others (Paris, 1821–33), 29 vols.
Masselin	Jehan Masselin, *Journal des États généraux de France tenus à Tours en 1484. CDI,* ed. A. Bernier (Paris, 1835)
Mayer	*Des États généraux et les autres assemblées nationales,* ed. Charles J. Mayer (Paris, 1788–89), 18 vols.
RCG	*Recueil des cahiers généraux des trois ordres aux États généraux,* eds. Lalourcé and Duval (Paris, 1789), 4 vols.

RPO	*Recueil de pièces originales et authentiques, concernant la tenue des États généraux,* eds. Lalourcé and Duval (Paris, 1789), 9 vols.
SHF	*Société de l'histoire de France*
Thierry	*Recueil des monuments inédits de l'histoire du tiers état. CDI,* ed. Jacques Augustin Thierry (Paris, 1853–70), 4 vols.

NOTES

Chapter One

1. Henry Lemonnier, *Histoire de France illustrée depuis les origines jusqu'à la Révolution,* ed. Lavisse (Paris, 1911), V, pt. I, 211.

2. I have adopted the term "Renaissance Monarchy" in preference to the more common "New Monarchy" in order to emphasize that the type of government herein described existed in the same age which saw the artistic and intellectual innovations that have long gone under the name of the "Renaissance." For an excellent discussion of recent works on the nature of the post-Medieval–pre-Revolution monarchies see F. Hartung and R. Mousnier, "Quelques problèmes concernant la monarchie absolue," *Relazioni del X congresso internazionale di scienze storiche, IV, Storia Moderna* (Florence, 1955), 1–55. See also J. R. Major, "The Renaissance Monarchy: A Contribution to the Periodization of History," *The Emory University Quarterly,* XIII (1957), 112–24. I am indebted to the *Quarterly* for permission to reprint part of this article here.

3. The dynastic motivation in Renaissance diplomacy has recently been stressed by Garrett Mattingly, *Renaissance Diplomacy* (London, 1955), esp. pp. 121–90.

4. Roland Mousnier, *Histoire générale des civilisations,* ed. Maurice Crouzet (Paris, 1954), IV, 99.

5. Édouard Perroy, *La Guerre de Cent Ans* (Paris, 1945), pp. 262–70.

6. Roger Doucet, *Les Institutions de la France au XVIe siècle* (Paris, 1948), I, 210–28, 284–90.

7. In an excellent article Prof. J. P. Dawson presents as a paradox the escape of private law from the control of the sovereign at the very time that political absolutism was triumphing in France. In fact, the development in private law was but another aspect of the general acceptance of decentralization by the Renaissance Monarchs. See Dawson, "The Codification of French Customs," *Michigan Law Review,* XXXVIII (1940), 765–800.

8. Doucet, I, 229–44. G. Zeller, "Gouverneurs de provinces au XVIe siècle," *Revue historique,* CLXXXV (1939), 225–56.

9. Doucet, I, 360–402. Émile Chénon, *Histoire générale du droit français public et privé des origines à 1815* (Paris, 1926–29), I, 858–59; II, 488–90.

10. Armand Brette, *Atlas des bailliages ou juridictions assimilées ayant formé unité électorale en 1789* (Paris, 1904).

11. Étienne-Denis Pasquier, *A History of My Time* (New York, 1893), I, 50.

12. Ch. Petit-Dutaillis, *Histoire de France illustrée depuis les origines jusqu'à la Révolution,* ed. Lavisse (Paris, 1911), IV, pt. II, 94–101, 405. Doucet, II, 608–51. Vallet de Viriville, "Mémoire sur les institutions de Charles VII," *BEC,* XXXIII (1872), 61–84.

13. Lucien Romier, *La Conjuration d'Amboise* (Paris, 1923), p. 199. Théophile Boutiot, *Histoire de la ville de Troyes et de la Champagne méridionale* (Paris, 1873), III, 389. Doucet, I, 385.

14. Preserved Smith, *The Age of the Reformation* (New York, 1920), p. 549.

15. Roland Mousnier, *La Vénalite des offices sous Henri IV et Louis XIII* (Rouen, 1945), pp. 63–65, 309–11.

16. There is no adequate study of how the nobility escaped most taxation, but see Paul Viollet, *Histoire des institutions politiques et administratives de la France* (Paris, 1903), III, 473–77; François Olivier-Martin, *Histoire du droit français des origines à la révolution* (Paris, 1951), pp. 584–87; and René Gandilhon, *Politique économique de Louis XI* (Paris, 1941), pp. 116–20, 273–75, 450–52. Doucet has shown that Louis XI conferred many favors on the nobility. Only those who betrayed him in the War of the Public Good felt his anger. He even checked the encroachment by his officials on seigneurial privileges. "Le Gouvernement de Louis XI," *Revue des cours et conférences,* XXV (1923–24), 240–48. Doucet, *Les Institutions* . . . , II, 835.

17. Gaston Du Fresne de Beaucourt, *Histoire de Charles VII* (Paris, 1891), VI, 349–51. Gandilhon, p. 89.

18. Antoine Thomas, *Les États provinciaux de la France centrale sous Charles VII* (Paris, 1897), I, 273–365. Mousnier, *La Vénalité* . . . , pp. 17, 524–27. For Louis' use of the nobility see Doucet, *Revue des cours et conférences,* XXIV (1922–23), 737–46; XXV, 247–48.

19. Pierre de Vaissière, "Les Marillac et Richelieu. La journée des Dupes," *Revue des questions historiques,* XCVIII (1923), 257–59.

20. Gaston Roupnel, *La Ville et la compagne au XVIIᵉ siècle. Étude sur les populations du pays Dijonnais* (Paris, ed. 1955), pp. 173, 190. Thomas, I, 274–78.

21. André Viala, *Le Parlement de Toulouse et l'administration royale laïque 1420–1525 environ* (Albi, 1953), I, 179–84, 247.

22. Doucet, *Les Institutions* . . . , I, 252.

23. Henri Drouot, *Mayenne et la Bourgogne* (Paris, 1937), I, 48–55. Édouard Maugis, *Recherches sur les transformations du régime politique et social de la ville d'Amiens* (Paris, 1906), pp. 30–38.

24. Henri Prentout, *Les États provinciaux de Normandie* (Caen, 1926), II, 87–89, extract from *Mém. de l'académie nationale des sciences, arts et belles-lettres de Caen,* N.S. II. Doucet, *Les Institutions* . . . , I, 366–67.

25. Édouard Maugis, *Histoire du Parlement de Paris* (Paris, 1913), I, 517–631. Roger Doucet, *Étude sur le gouvernement de François Iᵉʳ dans ses rapports avec le Parlement de Paris* (Paris, 1921–26), 2 vols.

26. *Relations des ambassadeurs vénitiens sur les affaires de France au XVIᵉ siècle. CDI,* ed. Niccolò Tommaséo (Paris, 1838), II, 27.

27. Niccolò Machiavelli, *The Prince,* chap. iv.

28. Robert W. and Alexander J. Carlyle, *A History of Medieval Political Theory in the West* (Edinburgh, 1936), VI, 225, 239–40.

29. Machiavelli, esp. chaps. iii and xviii. Time and again in the meetings of the Estates General, high government officials expressed the belief that the power of the state rested upon popular support. For one example, see J. R. Major, *The Estates General of 1560* (Princeton, 1951), pp. 32–37.

30. *Mémoires de Philippe de Commynes,* bk. V, chaps. ix and xii. On the whole Commynes thought that Louis was a far wiser ruler than his Burgundian rival.

31. Cardinal Richelieu, *Testament politique,* ed. Louis André (Paris, ed. of 1947), p. 326.

32. *Relations des ambassadeurs vénitiens* . . . , I, 403.

33. *Ibid.,* I, 509. Richelieu also complained about this situation. He wrote: "L'entrée de votre Cabinet a été permise à tout monde, non seulement au préjudice de votre dignité, mais, qui plus est, au mépris de la sûreté de votre personne.

"Les ambassadeurs se sont souvent trouvés plus pressés des valets de pied, des pages et autres menus officiers que des grands de votre État en leurs audiences. Et cependant votre dignité et l'ancienne Coutume du Royaume veulent qu'en telles occasions, V. M. soit accompagnée des princes, des Ducs et Pairs et des officiers de sa Couronne et autres grands de son État." *Testament politique,* p. 282.

34. François Olivier-Martin, *Histoire du droit français des origines à la révolution* (Paris, 1950), p. 345.

35. Commynes, bk. IV, chap. i. In this and the following paragraphs on the estates in other European countries I am repeating in a slightly modified and abbreviated form the arguments I used in my *Estates General of 1560,* pp. 7–12. I am indebted to the Princeton University Press for permission to reproduce these pages.

36. A. F. Pollard, *Henry VIII* (London, 1905), p. 258.

37. G. Barraclough, *The Origins of Modern Germany* (Oxford, 1947), pp. 320–52.

38. *Ibid.,* p. 347.

39. H. Pirenne, "The Formation and Constitution of the Burgundian State," *American Historical Review,* XIV (1909), 477–502.

40. *Ibid.,* p. 500. H. G. Koenigsberger points out that there is no evidence that Duke Philip the Good deliberately created the Estates General to unify his dominions, but he agrees that later dukes often preferred to deal with the Estates General rather than the individual provincial estates. See "The States General of the Netherlands before the Revolt," *Studies Presented to the International Commission for the History of Representative and Parliamentary Institutions* (Louvain, 1958), XVIII, 141–58.

41. Henri Pirenne, *Histoire de Belgique* (Brussels, 1912), III, 195–206. For more recent surveys of the estates of the Low Countries see John Gilissen, *Le Régime réprésentatif avant 1790 en Belgique* (Brussels, 1952); and Gordon Griffiths, "Representative Institutions in the Spanish Empire in the Sixteenth Century: The Low Countries," *The Americas,* XII (1956), 234–43.

42. Roger B. Merriman, *The Rise of the Spanish Empire* (New York, 1918), II, 126–28.

43. *Ibid.,* III, 155–63.

44. G. Desdivises du Dezert, "Les Institutions de l'Espagne au XVIIIᵉ siècle," *Revue hispanique,* LXX (1927), 57–61.

45. Merriman, IV, 422–24.

46. Michael Roberts, "The Constitutional Development of Sweden in the Reign of Gustav Adolf," *History,* XXIV (1940), 329. For further details see Roberts, *Gustavus Adolphus* (London, 1953), I, esp. 283–315.

47. E. H. Dunkley, *The Reformation in Denmark* (London, 1948), pp. 73–76.

48. Joseph Billioud, *Les États de Bourgogne aux XIVᵉ et XVᵉ siècles* (Dijon, 1922), pp. 345–62.

49. Léon Cadier, *Les États de Béarn depuis leurs origines jusqu'au commencement du XVIᵉ siècle* (Paris, 1888), pp. 186, 200–201, 312, 351.

Chapter Two

1. For an old discussion of the different interpretations of the character of Charles VII, see Gaston Du Fresne de Beaucourt, *Histoire de Charles VII* (Paris,

1881), I, introduction. A recent character sketch may be found in Édouard Perroy, *La Guerre de Cent Ans* (Paris, 1945), pp. 231–33.

2. Beaucourt, I, 391–92.

3. *Ibid.*, I, 344–88. Perroy, pp. 226–33. A. Thomas, "Nouveaux documents sur les États provinciaux de la Haute-Marche, 1418–1446," *Annales du Midi*, XXV (1913), 430–43.

4. J. R. Strayer, "Philip the Fair—A 'Constitutional' King," *American Historical Review*, LXII (1956–57), 18–32. G. Post, "Plena Potestas and Consent in Medieval Assemblies," *Traditio*, I (1943), 355–408; "A Romano-Canonical Maxim, 'Quod Omnes Tangit,' in Bracton," *Traditio*, IV (1946), 197–251; "A Roman Legal Theory of Consent, Quod Omnes Tangit, in Medieval Representation," *Wisconsin Law Review* (1950), 66–78; and "The Two Laws and the Statute of York," *Speculum*, XXIX (1954), 417–32. Joseph R. Strayer and Charles H. Taylor, *Studies in Early French Taxation* (Cambridge, 1939).

5. Strayer and Taylor, pp. 171–72. J. Viard, "Un Chapitre d'histoire administrative. Les Ressources extraordinaires de la royauté sous Philippe VI de Valois," *Revue des questions historiques*, XLIV (1888), 167–218.

6. Roland Delachenal, *Histoire de Charles V* (Paris, 1909), I, 119–22, 138–40, 172–74.

7. *Ibid.*, I, 264–65, 353–54.

8. Léon Mirot, "Les États généraux et provinciaux de l'abolition des aides au début du règne de Charles VI (1380–81)," *Revue des questions historiques*, LXXIV (1903), 398–455.

9. Alfred Coville, *Les Cabochiens et l'ordonnance de 1413* (Paris, 1888), p. 142, n. 1.

10. For the estates at Clermont in 1421, see A. Thomas, "Le Midi et les États généraux sous Charles VII," *Annales du Midi*, I (1889), 288–309; "Les États généraux sous Charles VII. Étude chronologique d'après des documents inédits," *Le Cabinet historique*, ser. 2, II (1878), 124–25, 212; and "Les États généraux sous Charles VII. Notes et documents nouveaux," *Revue historique*, XL (1889), 55–57. C. de Grandmaison, "Nouveaux documents sur les États généraux du XVe siècle," *Bul. de la soc. archéologique de Touraine*, IV (1877–79), 139–51. Beaucourt, I, 359–63.

11. Antoine Thomas, *Les États provinciaux de la France centrale sous Charles VII* (Paris, 1879), I, 223. Louis Caillet, *Étude sur les relations de la commune de Lyon avec Charles VII et Louis XI* (Lyon, 1909), pp. 19–22.

12. Thomas, *Les États provinciaux . . .* , I, 184–85, 223, 240, 261. Beaucourt, I, 358, 363–64. *HL*, IX, 1072. The estates of Poitou voted 100,000 francs in 1422, but Beaucourt gives no date for this meeting, I, 358. For the consent of the town of Lyon to taxes during the reign of Charles VII, see Caillet, pp. 19–89. On the role of the seigneurs in taxation, see Gustave Dupont-Ferrier, *Études sur les institutions financières de la France à la fin du moyen âge* (Paris, 1932), II, 33–39.

13. Thomas, *Annales du Midi*, I (1889), 309–10; *Le Cabinet historique* (1878), 125–28, 213; *Revue historique*, XL (1889), 58.

14. Thomas, *Annales du Midi*, I (1889), 310–11; XXV (1913), 440–47; *Revue historique*, XL (1889), 59; *Les États provinciaux . . .* , I, 225, 240–41. Caillet, pp. 28–35.

15. Thomas, *Revue historique*, XL (1889), 58–62. Grandmaison, pp. 152–53. Beaucourt, II, 579–81. The provincial estates of Auvergne, Touraine, Poitou, Limousin, and perhaps others tried to change or reduce their share of the tax. Thomas,

Les États provinciaux . . . , I, 187, 224, 241–61. Beaucourt, II, 581. For actions of Lyon, see Caillet, pp. 35–36.

16. Thomas, *Le Cabinet historique* (1878), 213–14.

17. Thomas, *Les États provinciaux* . . . , II, 31, 32. Grandmaison, pp. 154–55.

18. Thomas, *Le Cabinet historique* (1878), 156–57; *Annales du Midi,* I (1889), 311. Beaucourt, II, 581. The best authorities believe that only Languedoïl participated.

19. *HL,* IX, 1077–78. A. Dussert, "Les États du Dauphiné aux XIVe et XVe siècles," *Bul. de l'ac. Delphinale,* ser. 5, VIII (1915), 183. The provincial estates of Auvergne, Haut-Limousin, La Marche, and no doubt others consented to their portion of this tax. Thomas, *Les États provinciaux* . . . , I, 186, 242, 262.

20. Thomas, *Annales du Midi,* I (1889), 311; *Le Cabinet historique* (1876), 158–60. Beaucourt, II, 582–84. Dussert, p. 184. *HL,* IX, 1081–82. For the division of this tax among the parishes and seigneuries of Poitou, see René Lacour, "Documents sur les États généraux de Poitiers de 1424 et 1425," *Archives historiques du Poitou,* XLVIII (1934), 91–111.

21. Thomas, *Annales du Midi,* I (1889), 312–15.

22. Thomas, *Le Cabinet historique* (1878), 160–62, 215–17. Beaucourt, II, 584–87; III, 500–509. Interesting documents on the division of these taxes between the towns and *plat pays* in Lyonnais and Poitou may be found in Caillet, pp. 42–56, 358–66, and Lacour, pp. 111–17.

23. Thomas, *Les États provinciaux* . . . , I, 243, 262–63; *Revue historique,* XL (1889), 62–63. Beaucourt, II, 588.

24. Thomas, *Revue historique,* XL (1889), 63–65. Beaucourt, II, 589–90. Caillet, pp. 56–64.

25. Thomas, *Annales du Midi,* IV (1892), 1–4; *Le Cabinet historique* (1878), 166–67, 217–19. *HL,* IX, 1095. Beaucourt, II, 591–92.

26. For the estates of Chinon, see especially Thomas, *Annales du Midi,* IV (1892), 1–12; *Le Cabinet historique* (1878), 167–69, 218–19; *Revue historique,* XL (1889), 66–68. *HL,* IX, 1096–1100; X, 2077–89.

27. *HL,* X, 2081.

28. Dussert, p. 186.

29. *HL,* IX, 1098, n. 3; X, 2079.

30. Thomas, *Annales du Midi,* IV (1892), 12–13.

31. Thomas, *Revue historique,* XL (1889), 69–70.

32. Between October, 1428, and August, 1434, the estates of Auvergne met ten times and on nine occasions voted money, Thomas, *Les États provinciaux* . . . , I, 189–94. Lyon was asked for 400 *écus* to provision Orléans, Caillet, p. 86.

33. Thomas, *Revue historique,* XL, 71–82. See also *Le Cabinet historique* (1878), 169–70; *Les États provinciaux* . . . , I, 190, 245, 263; Beaucourt, II, 594–97; and Caillet, pp. 69–72.

34. Thomas, *Annales du Midi,* IV (1892), 14.

35. Thomas, *Le Cabinet historique* (1878), 202–4.

36. *Ibid.,* 204–5. Beaucourt, II, 599.

37. Thomas, *Le Cabinet historique* (1878), 220–21; *Annales du Midi,* IV (1892), 15.

38. Thomas, *Le Cabinet historique* (1878), 205–6; *Revue historique,* XL (1889), 82–84; *Annales du Midi,* XXV (1913), 447–50. Caillet, pp. 78–82.

39. Thomas, *Revue historique,* XL (1889), 84–88; *Le Cabinet historique* (1878), 207–8, 221. Caillet, pp. 82–83. Beaucourt, III, 434–36.

40. Thomas, *Les États provinciaux* . . . , I, 128–38.

41. A. Spont, "La Taille en Languedoc de 1450 à 1515," *Annales du Midi,* II (1890), 365–70.

42. Dussert, pp. 200–201. *HL,* IX, 1124–25; X, 2127–28.

43. Thomas, *Le Cabinet historique* (1878), 208–10. Recently Jacques Garillot has attacked the erroneous interpretation of the Estates General of 1439. See his *Étude de la coutume constitutionnelle au XVᵉ siècle. Les États généraux de 1439* (Nancy, 1947). In the introduction there is a brief résumé of the position of various historians on this question.

44. The letter of convocation has been published by Garillot, pp. 88–89, and by Beaucourt, III, 526–27.

45. Garillot, pp. 1–7.

46. Thomas, *Annales du Midi,* IV (1892), 15–16. Beaucourt, III, 528–29. Jules Flammermont, *Histoire des institutions municipales de Senlis* (Paris, 1881), 261–62. Garillot, pp. 8–10. Isambert, IX, 58.

47. Garillot, pp. 11–49. The text of the Ordonnance of 1439 may be found in Isambert, IX, 57–71, and *Ordonnances des rois de France de la troisième race,* eds. Louis G. Vilevault and Louis-G. Bréquigny (Paris, 1782), XIII, 306–13. Abbé Pierre-L. Péchenard, *Jean Juvénal des Ursins* (Paris, 1876), pp. 193–207. *Histoire de Charles VII, Roy de France par Jean Chartier, Jacques le Bouvier, dit Berry . . . et autres . . . ,* ed. Denys Godefroy (Paris, 1661), pp. 404–5.

48. Thomas, *Annales du Midi,* IV (1892), 16–24. Beaucourt, IV, 442–44, 528–29. T. Boutiot and A. Babeau, "Documents inédits tirés des archives de Troyes et relatifs aux État généraux," *Collection de documents inédits relatifs à la ville de Troyes et à la Champagne méridionale* (Troyes, 1878), I, 1–2. Garillot, pp. 15–19. Isambert, IX, 77–79. For activities of Charles VII during the first half of 1440, see *Chronique de Mathieu d'Escouchy. SHF,* ed. Beaucourt (Paris, 1864), III, 4–16.

49. *Chronique de Mathieu d'Escouchy,* III, 75. See also pp. 28–29 and 58.

50. *La Chronique d'Enguerran de Monstrelet. SHF,* ed. Louis-C. Douët-d'Arcq (Paris, 1862), VI, 39. For a general discussion of the assembly of Nevers, see Beaucourt, III, 194–231.

51. Thomas, *Annales du Midi,* IV (1892), 17, n. 1.

52. The clergy of Dauphiné consented to a tax at Bourges in September, 1440. This opens the possibility that the province was represented at the earlier meeting of the Estates General. Isambert, IX, 77–79.

53. Thomas, *Annales du Midi,* I (1889), 311, n. 3, and IV (1892), 14.

54. Thomas, *Le Cabinet historique* (1878), p. 157; *Revue historique,* XL (1889), 79.

55. Thomas, *Revue historique,* XL (1889), 83.

56. Thomas, *Les États provinciaux* . . . , I, 118–20; II, 144–53.

57. *Mémoires de Philippe de Commynes,* bk. V, chap. xix.

58. Thomas, *Les États provinciaux* . . . , I, 69–72, 190, 225, 240, 262–64.

59. Caillet, pp. 19–22, 28–84, and numerous documents in the *pièces justificatives,* pp. 299–652.

60. Thomas, *Les États provinciaux* . . . , I, 261, n. 3; *Annales du Midi,* XXV (1913), 443–47.

61. Perroy, p. 265.

62. Caillet, pp. 85–87.

63. Thomas, *Les États provinciaux* . . . , I, 70–72, 117–20, 220–22.

64. Isambert, VIII, 834–42. Dupont-Ferrier, II, 85–96.

65. Thomas, *Les États provinciaux* . . . , I, 100–113. During the Renaissance

there were *élus* in some of the provinces that had estates. Hence the same province was often both a *pays d'états* and a *pays d'élections*.

66. *Ibid.*, I, 128–34. Dupont-Ferrier, II, 130–33.

67. André Marchadier, *Les États généraux sous Charles VII* (Bordeaux, 1904), pp. 95–96, 99, 152–53. Paul Dognon, *Les Institutions politiques et administratives du pays de Languedoc* (Toulouse, 1896), pp. 247, 498–500. *HL*, IX, 1124–25, 1132, 1148–52; X, 2127–28, 2144–67, 2190–91, 2197–2210.

68. Dupont-Ferrier, II, 131.

69. Thomas, *Les États provinciaux . . .* , I, 152–61, 217.

70. *Ibid.*, I, 161–62, 164–65.

71. *Ibid.*, I, 165–67.

72. Henri Prentout, *Les États provinciaux de Normandie* (Caen, 1925), I, 221, extract from *Mém. de l'ac. nationale des sciences, arts et belles-lettres de Caen*, N.S. I.

73. Caillet, pp. 43–62, 358–61, 382–85.

74. Thomas, *Les États provinciaux . . .* , I, 167–74.

75. Caillet, pp. 127–53, 293.

76. Théophile Boutiot, *Histoire de la ville de Troyes et de la Champagne méridionale* (Troyes, 1872), II, 544–45. Charles Petit-Dutaillis, *Histoire de France*, ed. Lavisse (Paris, 1902), IV, pt. II, 247. Beaucourt, III, 435–36.

77. Prentout, I, 156–81; II, 216–29; III, 23–26.

78. Louis D. Brissaud, *L'Administration anglaise et le mouvement communal dans le Bordelais. Les Anglais en Guyenne* (Paris, 1875), pp. 272–86. Eleanor C. Lodge, *Gascony under English Rule* (London, 1926), pp. 146–47.

79. Petit-Dutaillis, IV, pt. II, 251. *Comptes consulaires de la ville de Riscles de 1441 à 1507*, eds. Paul Parfouru and J. de Carsalade du Pont (Paris, 1886), I, xvii–xxxiv, extract from *Archives historiques de la Gascogne*, Fasc. XII.

80. Léon Cadier, *La Sénéchaussée des Lannes sous Charles VII, administration royale et états provinciaux* (Paris, 1885), 40–44; extract from *Revue de Béarn, Navarre et Lannes*, III.

81. Beaucourt, V, 40–53, 261–86. Brissaud, pp. 285–86. Robert Boutruche, *La Crise d'un société. Seigneurs et paysans du Bordelais pendant la Guerre de Cent Ans* (Paris, 1947), pp. 399–422.

82. Peter N. Riesenberg, *Inalienability of Sovereignty in Medieval Political Thought* (New York, 1956). J. Declareuil, "Le Traité de Madrid et le droit public français," *Recueil de législation de Toulouse*, ser. 2, IX (1913), 96–122. Émile Chénon, *Histoire générale du droit français public et privé* (Paris, 1926–29), I, 898–902; II, 339–41. René-A.-M. de Maulde-la-Clavière, *La Diplomatie au temps de Machiavel* (Paris, 1893), 212–18. Garillot, pp. 53–61.

83. Dumont, II, pt. II, 144, art. 27. See also art. 11.

84. *Ibid.*, II, pt. II, 145, art. 32.

85. Georges Picot, *Histoire des États généraux* (Paris, ed. of 1888), I, 284–90. When the Duke of Burgundy changed from the English to the French side in the war, he felt it necessary to hold an assembly to justify his action. Joycelyne G. Dickinson, *The Congress of Arras, 1435* (Oxford, 1955), pp. 53–77.

86. Beaucourt, II, 81–82, 367; III, 500. Caillet, pp. 109–10.

87. Thomas, *Le Cabinet historique* (1878), 200–202, 219–20; *Revue historique*, XL (1889), 79–80. Thomas argues that this meeting was only an assembly of notables because the towns were not instructed to give the deputies full powers. However, the fact that deputies were elected is enough to make the meeting a representative assembly. The failure to demand that full powers be given probably resulted from the king's desire for advice, not money.

88. Beaucourt, II, 307. Thomas, *Revue historique*, XL (1889), 84.
89. Beaucourt, IV, 418, n. 1. Godefroy, p. 346. *La Chronique d'Enguerran de Monstrelet*, VI, 96.
90. An assembly was held at Tours in June, 1448, that voted money, but there is not sufficient evidence to show what provinces or estates were convoked. A few other large regional assemblies also took place after 1440, but it appears certain that as the English Wars drew to a close, the number of assemblies declined. Beaucourt, IV, 418. Petit-Dutaillis, IV, pt. II, 244, 247–48.
91. Beaucourt, III, 352–53; V, 208–19.
92. *Ordonnances des rois de Frances . . .* , XIV, 285.
93. Beaucourt, VI, 187–89.

Chapter Three

1. Charles Petit-Dutaillis, *Histoire de France illustrée depuis les origines jusqu'à la Révolution*, ed. Lavisse (Paris, 1911), IV, pt. II, 321–42. R. Doucet, "Le Gouvernement de Louis XI," *Revue des cours et conférences*, XXV (1924–25), 240–48. For the confirmation of privileges see *Ordonnances des rois de Frances de la troisième race*, ed. Claude-E. Pastoret (Paris, 1811), XV.
2. René Gandilhon, *Politique économique de Louis XI* (Paris, 1941), pp. 273–84. Henri Prentout, *Les États provinciaux de Normandie* (Caen, 1925–27), I, 181–87; II, 229–31, extract from *Mém. de l'ac. nationale des sciences, arts et belles-lettres de Caen*, N.S. I–III. A. Spont, "L'Équivalent aux aides en Languedoc de 1450 à 1515," *Annales du Midi*, III (1891), 243–48.
3. Gandilhon, pp. 284–96. Louis Caillet, *Étude sur les relations de la commune de Lyon avec Charles VII et Louis XI* (Lyon, 1909), pp. 165–75, 257–58. Doucet, XXV (1924–25), 375–84.
4. AC, Poitiers, registre 4, pp. 239–40. T. Boutiot and A. Babeau, "Documents inédits tirés des archives de Troyes et relatifs aux États généraux," *Collection de documents inédits relatifs à la ville de Troyes et la Champagne méridionale* (Troyes, 1878), I, xvii, 2–3. Just Paquet, *Institutions provinciales et communales et des corporations des pays de l'ancienne France* (Paris, 1835), pp. 126–27. Caillet, p. 176. *Lettres de Louis XI, Roi de France. SHF*, eds. Joseph Vaesen and Étienne Charavay (Paris, 1883–1909), II, 155–57. Gandilhon, p. 101. L. de Cardenal, "Catalogue des assemblées des États de Périgord de 1378 à 1651," *Bul. philologique et historique du comté des travaux historiques et scientifiques* (1938–39), 251.
5. Paquet, pp. 135–36. See also documents and references to the estates of Guyenne in Henri Stein, *Charles de France* (Paris, 1919). Charles of France was exceptionally interested in the estates and appears to have been on the verge of increasing their role in Normandy when he was transferred from that duchy. Prentout, I, 190–92; III, 111–12.
6. The frugal Louis XII managed to increase the revenue from the domain to 330,000 livres. A. Spont, "La Taille en Languedoc de 1450 à 1515," *Annales du Midi*, II (1890), 365–84, 497–500. Petit-Dutaillis, IV, pt. II, 405–7. Doucet, XXV (1924–25), 524–32, 661–69. Charles Samaran, *La Maison d'Armagnac au XVe siècle* (Paris, 1908), pp. 223–29.
7. Petit-Dutaillis, IV, pt. II, 400. Doucet, XXIV (1923), 1010–19.
8. *Ordonnances . . .* , XV, 16.
9. Petit-Dutaillis, IV, pt. II, 339. *Journal de Jean de Roye. SHF*, ed. Bernard de Mandrot (Paris, 1894–96), I, 161–62. Doucet, XXIV (1923), 1016–17.
10. *Ordonnances . . .* , XVII, 293.

11. Doucet, XXIV (1923), 1018.

12. *Ordonnances* . . . , XVIII, 167. *Journal de Jean de Roye,* II, 4–5.

13. *Lettres de Louis XI,* VII, 146–47. *Journal de Jean de Roye,* II, 77–78.

14. Édouard Maugis, *Histoire du Parlement de Paris* (Paris, 1913), I, 634–35.

15. Henri Sée, *Louis XI et les villes* (Paris, 1891), pp. 197, 203. *Lettres de Louis XI,* III, 74–75. Gandilhon, pp. 326, 424–26.

16. *Lettres de Louis XI,* IV, 146–47. Sée, pp. 340–41. Gandilhon, pp. 374–76, 431–33. *Ordonnances* . . . , XVII, 332–34, 353–57.

17. Théophile Boutiot, *Histoire de la ville de Troyes et de la Champagne méridionale* (Paris, 1873), III, 97.

18. *Lettres de Louis XI,* VIII, 4–6. Gandilhon, pp. 329, 336–37, 340.

19. The towns of Champagne and the Île-de-France were to meet at Paris; those of Dauphiné, Languedoc, Auvergne, Bourbonnais, Forez, Beaujolais, and Lyonnais, at Lyon; those of Touraine, Anjou, Maine, Berry, Blésois, and Orléanais, at Tours; those of Normandy and Évreux, at Rouen; and those of Angoumois, Saintonge, Limousin, and Poitou, at Saint-Jean-d'Angély. *Lettres de Louis XI,* VIII, 19–21. Gandilhon, pp. 124–31.

20. *Lettres de Louis XI,* IX, 122–27. Sée, pp. 339–40, 406–9. Gandilhon, pp. 256–58.

21. *Lettres de Louis XI,* X, 115–16. Thierry, II, 406–11. Twenty-three towns sent deputies including Bordeaux and others whose deputies arrived late. The marriage was celebrated but never consummated. The dauphin, Charles, finally married Anne of Brittany.

22. Stein, pp. 69, 106. Petit-Dutaillis, IV, pt. II, 343–56.

23. The letters of convocation to Poitiers have been published in *Lettres de Louis XI,* III, 198–201 and *Archives historiques du Poitou,* I (1872), 168–70; to Agen, in *Archives historiques du département de la Gironne,* XXXV (1900), 26–27; to Lyon, in *BEC,* XXVII (1866), 24–25.

24. See letters of convocation cited above. Tournay sent four laymen. It is conceivable that one was intended to represent the clergy, *Oeuvres de Georges Chastellain,* ed. Joseph B. Kervyn de Lettenhove (Brussels, 1864), V, 387, n. 1.

25. For Tours, P. Viollet, "Élection des députés aux États généraux réunis à Tours en 1468 et en 1484," *BEC,* XXVII (1866), 25, 27–28; for Troyes, Boutiot, III, 83–84 and Boutiot and Babeau, pp. 3–5; for Chartres, Eugène de Lépinois, *Histoire de Chartres* (Chartres, 1858), II, 116–17, 601–2; for Rodez, AC, Rodez, BB 3, fol. 47v; for Châlons-sur-Marne, AC, Châlons-sur-Marne, BB 4, fols. 145–48; for Agen, *Archives historiques . . . de la Gironde,* XXXV (1900), 26–27; for Évreux, Stein, p. 237, n. 9; and for Périgueux, *IAC, Périgueux,* ed. Michel Hardy (Périgueux, 1894), p. 116. Périgueux sent three laymen to the estates in spite of the royal directives.

26. For Blois see Alexandre Dupré "Étude sur les institutions municipales de Blois," *Mém. de la soc. archéologique et historique de l'Orléanais,* XIV (1875), 525–26; for Senlis, Jules Flammermont, *Histoire des institutions municipales de Senlis* (Paris, 1881), pp. 276–78; and for Millau, Jules Artières "Documents sur la ville de Millau," *Archives historiques du Rouergue,* VII (1930), 381–82.

27. Viollet, pp. 22–30. Caillet, pp. 195–96. Alfred Richard, "Les Maires de Poitiers," *Mém. de la soc. des antiquaires de l'Ouest,* ser. 2, XX (1897), 436–37. See also documents cited in footnotes 24 and 25.

28. Caillet, pp. 571–72. AC, Rodez, BB 3, fols. 66–68v.

29. *Mémoires de Philippe de Commynes,* bk. III, chap. i. Commynes also erred when he said that the assembly of the estates in 1470 was the only one during

Louis' reign. It should be remembered that he did not enter the king's service until 1472, that he did not begin his memoires until 1488, and that he probably had no documents to refresh his memory. Paul Pélicier, *Essai sur le gouvernement de la dame de Beaujeu* (Chartres, 1882), p. 13, n. 1. Stein, p. 237, n. 3 argues in favor of the thesis of royal interference in the elections, but he offers no additional evidence beyond a statement by Barbot who wrote 150 years after the elections. Barbot had access to the now lost communal archives of La Rochelle; therefore he may have had proof that Louis indicated whom he wished to be elected by that town, but there is no reason to believe that he had information concerning other localities.

30. *Lettres de Louis XI,* III, 378–79.

31. *Documents historiques inédits tirés des collections manuscrites de la bibliothèque royale. CDI,* ed. Jean-J. Champollion-Figeac (Paris, 1847), III, 494. AC, Rodez, BB 3, fol. 52.

32. Champollion-Figeac, III, 494–97. Mayer, IX, 204–10. As has been indicated the towns sent from two to four deputies each, and not three as the *procès-verbal* states, Mayer, IX, 210.

33. Mayer, IX, 204–12. Champollion-Figeac, III, 497. AC, Rodez, BB 3, fols. 50v–53v.

34. AC, Rodez, BB 3, fol. 53v. For a list of the king's councilors who attended the estates, see Stein, p. 236 or Mayer, IX, 209.

35. AC, Rodez, BB 3, fols. 54–58. For biographical sketch see *Lettres de Louis XI,* II, 215, n. 3, for Cousinot; V, 169, n. 1, for Bernard; II, 102, n. 2, for Doriole; and II, 297, n. 1, for Estouteville.

36. Pierre Champion, *Louis XI* (Paris, 1928), II, 3. For a biography of Jean Jouvenel see the study of Pierre-Louis Péchenard. This speech has been published in Charles P. Duclos, *Histoire de Louis XI* (Amsterdam, 1746), III, 233–48; and Mayer, IX, 231–46. It was not regarded too highly by the assembly if we may judge by the scant attention the deputies of Rodez gave to it. AC, Rodez, BB 3, fol. 56v.

37. A summary of the important speeches may be found at AC, Rodez, BB 3, fols. 54–59v.

38. AC, Rodez, BB 3, fols. 59v–61v. Champollion-Figeac, III, 498–99.

39. At least two towns copied the advice given by the estates in their registers. See AC, Rodez, BB 3, fols. 61v–66; and AC, Poitiers, carton 98, reg. 5, fols. 115–19. The advice has been printed in Mayer, XI, 212–26. Georges Picot, *Histoire des États généraux* (Paris, ed. of 1888), I, 342, n. 1, argued that the material printed in Mayer, XI, 146–48 was part of this document, but this is doubtful as it was not included in the registers located in the archives of Rodez and Poitiers.

40. Mayer, XI, 223–26. Stein, pp. 250–54, 261–63. Doucet, XXIV (1923), 1014–16.

41. Dumont, III, pt. II, 107. In 1475 Louis had had the prelates, barons, and towns swear to uphold a treaty with Castile, *Lettres de Louis XI,* X, 461–62.

42. *Lettres de Louis XI,* X, 27–31.

43. *Mémoires de messire Philippe de Comines,* pub. by Jean Godefroy (Brussels, 1723), V, 326.

44. *Ibid.,* V, 324–25. For a letter to a town concerning the ratification see *Lettres de Louis XI,* X, 36–37, and to a peer, X, 37–38. There are some discrepancies between the list of towns that were supposed to swear to support the treaty and those that actually did.

Chapter Four

1. Later under Charles IX this Ordonnance was interpreted to mean that the king need be only in his fourteenth year, but no one in 1483 and 1484 appears to have questioned that Charles VIII was a minor. Paul Pélicier, *Essai sur le gouvernement de la dame de Beaujeu* (Chartres, 1882), p. 69.

2. *Ibid.*, pp. 33–46. René-A.-M. de Maulde-la-Clavière, *Histoire de Louis XII* (Paris, 1890), II, 38.

3. There has been some debate on this last question. See John S. C. Bridge, *A History of France from the Death of Louis XI* (Oxford, 1921), I, 49–53.

4. Maulde-la-Clavière, II, 44.

5. Pélicier, p. 49, n. 2.

6. Charles VIII alone signed an order confirming the privileges of the *Chambre des comptes* on September 11, a fact which indicates that the magnates had not yet arrived; Jean-Marie de La Mure, *Histoire des ducs de Bourbon et des comtes de Forez* (Paris, 1868), II, 327.

7. Maulde-la-Clavière, II, 44.

8. *Ibid.*, II, 49–50. Noël Valois, "Le Conseil du roi et le grand conseil pendant la première année du règne de Charles VIII," *BEC*, XLIII (1882), 600–601.

9. Maulde-la-Clavière, II, 45–50. Achille Luchaire, *Alain le Grand, sire d'Albret* (Paris, 1877), pp. 63–64. Pélicier, p. 118. *Gallia Regia*, ed. Gustave Dupont-Ferrier (Paris, 1954), IV, 256–58.

10. *Gallia Regia*, IV, 297. Maulde-la-Clavière, II, 53.

11. *Gallia Regia*, II, 314; IV, 86. Pélicier, p. 91, n. 3.

12. Pélicier, pp. 36–41.

13. Bridge, I, 35–46.

14. "Procès-verbaux de cinq séances du grand conseil du roi Charles VIII tenues au mois de décembre 1483 . . . ," *Bul. du comité de la langue, de l'histoire et des arts de la France*, III (1855–56), 248–58.

15. Pélicier, pp. 58–61. Isambert, XI, 119–24. Bridge, Heyns, and Tixier also accept this point of view. Bridge, I, 48–49. Garrett Heyns, *The Estates General of 1484* (Unpublished dissertation, University of Michigan, 1928), pp. 15–16. Octave Tixier, *Les Théories sur la souveraineté aux États généraux de 1484* (Paris, 1899), pp. 12–18.

16. Masselin, p. 122. The phrase in italics is mine.

17. Joseph B. Kervyn de Lettenhove believed that Commynes suggested the convocation of the Estates General to Orléans, but he published a letter clearly connecting Commynes with Alain d'Albret at the time of the death of Louis XI, and he admitted that Commynes remained with the government after Orléans had broken with the Beaujeus. It is therefore almost certain that Commynes had not yet joined the Orleanists. See Lettenhove, *Lettres et négociations de Philippe de Comines* (Brussels, 1867–74), II, 1–36; III, 88–89.

18. Maulde-la-Clavière, II, 54–55.

19. *Ibid.*, II, 54, n. 7.

20. The letters of convocation sent to Montargis have been published in *Annales de la soc. historique et archéologique de Gâtinais*, XII (1894), 105; to Agenais in *Archives historiques du département de la Gironde*, XXXV (1900), 29–32; to Vermandois in G. Hérelle, "Documents inédits sur les États généraux tirés des archives de Vitry-le-François," *Mém. de la soc. des sciences et arts de Vitry-le-François*, IX (1878), 198–200; and to Lannes in P. Viollet, "Élection des députés

aux États généraux réunis à Tours en 1468 et en 1484," *BEC*, XXVII (1866), 33.

21. For arguments that the change in electoral procedure was dictated by the desire of the Beaujeus to control the elections, see Tixier, pp. 21–23, 36–38; and Heyns, p. 18.

22. C. H. Taylor, "Assemblies of French Towns in 1316," *Speculum*, XIV (1939), 287, n. 1; and "The Composition of the Baronial Assemblies in France, 1315–1320," *Speculum*, XXIX (1954), 436. Thierry, I, 552.

23. Antoine Thomas, "Le Midi et les États généraux sous Charles VII," *Annales du Midi*, I (1889), 300–307, 315, n. 3; and IV (1892), 1–12; *Les États provinciaux de la France centrale sous Charles VII* (Paris, 1879), I, 84–88. Thomas says that there was no meeting of the estates at Tours in 1435, but Beaucourt has shown that there was an assembly there that spring to discuss the approaching Treaty of Arras. Gaston Du Fresne de Beaucourt, *Histoire de Charles VII* (Paris, 1882), II, 307.

24. Joseph Billioud, *Les États de Bourgogne aux XIVe et XVe siècles* (Dijon, 1922), p. 393.

25. *HL*, X, 2080–81. Thomas, *Annales du Midi*, IV (1892), 12–13.

26. Valois, pp. 602–4. Valois is, I feel, incorrect in his assumption that the vote of a judicial or financial expert in the council was regarded as being of equal importance to that of a great noble. The former was to advise and the latter to make decisions. The mere counting of heads was not enough to decide a Medieval or Renaissance ballot. It was "la plus grande et sayne partie," and not necessarily the majority, that ruled.

27. Maulde-la-Clavière, II, 42–49.

28. Viollet, pp. 22–58.

29. La Mure, II, 331. Maulde-la-Clavière, II, 55.

30. *Archives municipales de Bayonne. Délibérations du corps de ville. Registres Gascons, 1474–1514,* ed. Édouard Ducéré, P. Yturbide, and Ch. Bernadou (Bayonne, 1896), I, 282.

31. P. Pélicier, "Voyage des députés de Bourgogne à Blois (1483). Élection des députés de la Bourgogne aux États généraux de 1484. La Bourgogne aux États généraux de 1484," *BEC*, XLVII (1886), 357–63.

32. Pélicier, *Essai . . . ,* p. 73, n. 3. Hélène Bouchard, "Philippe Pot et la démocratie aux États généraux de 1484," *Annales de Bourgogne*, XXII (1950), 33–35.

33. Georges Picot, "Le Parlement sous Charles VIII," *Ac. des sciences morales et politiques, séances et travaux*, XXXVII (1877), 805–6.

34. Masselin, pp. 739, n. 1.

35. A. Dussert, "Les États du Dauphiné de la Guerre de Cent Ans aux Guerres de Religion," *Bul. de l'ac. Delphinale*, ser. 5, XIII (1922), 84–85.

36. Picot, pp. 788–94.

37. Among the deputies who were to obtain concessions were the Abbot of Cîteaux, who was able to win favorable treatment for his abbey; Philippe Pot, who was given a mission to the Low Countries; the Abbot of Saint-Antoine, who won partial satisfaction in a case he presented before the council and the office of chancellor of Dauphiné; and Pierre Charreyron, who was made lieutenant general in Limousin. *Gallia Regia*, III, 553. Pélicier, *Essai . . . ,* pp. 220, 222–25, 230.

38. Some of the cahiers were actually petitions on special local grievances prepared and submitted by the deputies while at the Estates General. There is no way to tell to what degree they followed the instructions given in the electoral assemblies. For Burgundy, see Pélicier, *BEC*, XLVII (1886), 366–67; for Dauphiné, Dussert, pp. 325–28; for Languedoc, Pierre de Caseneuve, *Le Franc-Alleu de la province de*

Languedoc (Toulouse, 1645), pt. II, 43–70; and for Lannes, *Archives Municipales de Bayonne. . . . Registres Gascons*, I, 285–88.

39. *Lettres de Charles VIII, Roi de France. SHF*, ed. P. Pélicier (Paris, 1898), I, 28–29.

40. Pélicier, *Essai* . . . , p. 287.

41. Masselin, ii–vi. C. de Robillard de Beaurepaire, "Notice sur Maître Jean Masselin," *Mém. de la soc. des antiquaires de Normandie*, XIX (1851), 268–302. Henri Prentout, *Les États provinciaux de Normandie* (Caen, 1925), I, 205–6, 209–11, 239–41, extract from *Mém. de l'ac. nationale des sciences, arts et belles-lettres de Caen*, N.S. I.

42. Thierry, II, 419. Masselin, p. 2. Pélicier, *Essai* . . . , p. 78, n. 3.

43. Maulde-la-Clavière, II, 66–68.

44. Masselin, pp. 4–37. Thierry, II, 419. *RPO*, I, 42.

45. Rochefort was also something of a classical scholar. He was the only participant in the Estates General who displayed a knowledge of Plato's *Republic*, which was then available in Latin translation only in manuscripts. J. C. Naber, "Platon et les États généraux de 1484," *Revue historique de droit français et étranger*, ser. 4, VII (1928), 5–10.

46. Masselin, pp. 36–65. Thierry, II, 419–20.

47. Masselin, pp. 66–67. Valois, p. 604. *Bul. du comité de la langue, de l'histoire et des arts de la France*, III (1855–56), 248–58. The decision to deliberate and vote by section or province was less of an innovation than has sometimes been imagined. In the estates of 1346 and perhaps on other occasions a similar practice was followed. Henri Hervieu, *Recherches sur les premiers États généraux* (Paris, 1879), pp. 65, 218–20.

48. Masselin, pp. 66–73. Masselin sometimes refers to the Aquitaine section as Guyenne, but to avoid confusion, we have used Aquitaine throughout.

49. *Ibid.*, pp. 72–73. Valois, p. 610. Maulde-la-Clavière, II, 61–62. Charles Samaran, *Jean de Bilhères-Lagraulas, Cardinal de Saint-Denis* (Paris, 1921), extract from *Le Moyen âge*, ser. 2, XXII (1920).

50. Masselin, pp. 72–75, 304–5.

51. Georges Picot, *Histoire des États Généraux* (Paris, ed. of 1888), I, 358, n. 1. Masselin, pp. 74–77.

52. Masselin, pp. 76–81, 718, n. 3. Louis Moréri, *Le Grand dictionnaire historique* (Paris, 1759), IX, 119. Beaurepaire, p. 291. For Rély's role in the reform movement, see Augustin Renaudet, *Préréforme et humanisme à Paris* (Paris, ed. of 1953).

53. Masselin, pp. 80–83.

54. *Ibid.*, pp. 82–85, 661–66. *Bul. du comité de la Langue* . . . , III (1855–56), 248–53.

55. Masselin, pp. 84–85, 666–69.

56. *Ibid.*, pp. 84–85, 88–89, 669–80.

57. *Ibid.*, pp. 84–93, 138–39, 680–98.

58. *Ibid.*, pp. 698–701.

59. *Ibid.*, pp. 86–87. Moréri, IV, 293. On February 19 the ambassador from Flanders renewed the appeal to the estates that justice be given Croy and the other relatives of Constable Saint-Pol. Masselin, pp. 322–29.

60. Masselin, pp. 86–89. Pélicier, *Essai* . . . , p. 37. The spokesman for Armagnac was probably Pierre d'Absac, Bishop of Rieux, and not the Bishop of Riez as Bernier reported in his edition of Masselin. See Charles Samaran, *La Maison d'Armagnac au XVᵉ siècle* (Paris, 1907), p. 242, n. 3.

61. Masselin, pp. 132–35. Pélicier, *Essai* . . . , pp. 38–40.

62. Masselin, pp. 92–97, 697. The deputy of the third estate of the bailiwick of Amiens was careful to report the pleas of the great nobles. Thierry, II, 421.

63. Masselin, pp. 80–83. This message to the deputies was delivered only in the names of "the Dukes of Orléans and Alençon, the Counts of Angoulême, Foix, and Dunois, and several other illustrious seigneurs."

64. *Ibid.*, pp. 76–81.

65. On pp. 80–81 Masselin dates the visit of Le Mans as being between January 27 and 31, but on pp. 116–17 he puts the date on January 24. If the latter date was correct, it was the first specific suggestion that the deputies deal with the question of the council. However, the problem always lay in the back of the minds of the deputies and was mentioned as early as January 17 by Jean Henri, a probable supporter of the Beaujeus. Masselin, pp. 66–67. Valois, p. 604.

66. Masselin, pp. 92–93. Maulde-la-Clavière, II, 38–39, 77. Le Blanc was made bailiff of Troyes in June, 1484, as a reward for his services. Orléans, who was governor of Champagne, was undoubtedly responsible for the appointment. *Gallia Regia*, III, 549.

67. Maulde-la-Clavière, II, 55, 63. Masselin, pp. 230–31.

68. Masselin, pp. 230–31.

69. *Ibid.*, pp. 100–105. Maulde-la-Clavière, II, 78–79.

70. Masselin, pp. 108–11, 116–21.

71. *Ibid.*, pp. 106–9.

72. *Ibid.*, pp. 108–9.

73. *Ibid.*, pp. 110–11. Valois, p. 603.

74. Masselin, pp. 110–13.

75. Valois, p. 602.

76. Masselin, pp. 112–15.

77. *Ibid.*, pp. 114–21. It is well to remember that Masselin is our only source for the episode and he was strongly prejudiced against Lombez.

78. *Ibid.*, pp. 122–27.

79. *Ibid.*, pp. 126–31, 138–39.

80. *Ibid.*, pp. 130–31.

81. *Ibid.*, pp. 128–33, 136–37.

82. *Ibid.*, pp. 136–41.

83. *Ibid.*, pp. 140–57. I have used the excellent, but abridged translation of Bridge with minor changes especially in spelling and capitalization. Bridge, I, 77–80. This speech should not be interpreted as an effort to raise the authority of the estates against the crown. Rather it represented an attempt by the Beaujeu faction to win the support of the estates against their rivals. The theories enunciated were not new. They reflected twelfth and thirteenth century legal thought and had long been taught at the University of Paris and elsewhere. See Pélicier, pp. 73–76; and Bouchard, pp. 33–40.

84. Masselin, pp. 156–57.

85. *Ibid.*, pp. 156–63, and pp. 106–7 for the Norman proposal.

86. *Ibid.*, pp. 162–65. A few days later Masselin specifically accused the princes of interference in Languedoc, pp. 222–25.

87. *Ibid.*, pp. 167–219.

88. *Ibid.*, pp. 218–27.

89. *Ibid.*, pp. 226–29.

90. *Ibid.*, pp. 228–31.

91. *Ibid.*, pp. 230–33.

92. *Ibid.*, pp. 232–35.

93. *Ibid.*, pp. 701–3.
94. *Ibid.*, pp. 298–301.
95. *Ibid.*, pp. 234–37, 702.
96. *Ibid.*, pp. 236–71.
97. *Ibid.*, pp. 270–99. For the accuracy of the Armagnac charges, see Charles Samaran, *La Maison d'Armagnac au XVe siècle* (Paris, 1908), pp. 220–23, 242–48. The feud was continued in the estates a week later. Masselin, pp. 318–21.
98. The Beaujeus did receive some financial compensation for the loss of Armagnac. Samaran, pp. 248–53, 442–49.
99. Masselin, pp. 298–303.
100. *Ibid.*, pp. 302–5.
101. *Ibid.*, pp. 304–11.
102. *Ibid.*, pp. 310–19.
103. *Ibid.*, pp. 328–35.
104. *Ibid.*, pp. 334–39.
105. *Ibid.*, pp. 320–29, 339–45.
106. *Ibid.*, pp. 344–49. A. Spont, "La Taille en Languedoc de 1450 à 1515," *Annales du Midi*, II (1890), 367–68.
107. Masselin, pp. 350–61.
108. *Ibid.*, pp. 360–85.
109. *Ibid.*, pp. 384–85.
110. *Ibid.*, pp. 384–91, and note. Spont estimated the taille as being only 3,900,000 livres in the last year of Louis' reign. Spont, p. 498. In either case the offer of the government was indeed generous.
111. Masselin, pp. 390–93.
112. *Ibid.*, pp. 398–407, 410–11.
113. *Ibid.*, pp. 410–21.
114. *Ibid.*, pp. 420–23. I have used the translation of Bridge, I, 100–101. Bridge, however, has lifted the quotation out of context.
115. Masselin, pp. 422–23.
116. *Ibid.*, pp. 422–27.
117. *Ibid.*, pp. 426–31.
118. *Ibid.*, p. 443. For speech, see pp. 430–47.
119. *Ibid.*, pp. 446–53.
120. *Ibid.*, pp. 452–59.
121. *Ibid.*, pp. 460–63.
122. *Ibid.*, pp. 462–77.
123. *Ibid.*, pp. 476–87.
124. *Ibid.*, pp. 486–89.
125. *Ibid.*, pp. 488–93.
126. *Ibid.*, pp. 492–93.
127. *Ibid.*, pp. 492–95.
128. *Ibid.*, pp. 392–95, 406–9, 510–19, 704.
129. *Ibid.*, pp. 518–21.
130. *Ibid.*, pp. 520–25.
131. *Ibid.*, pp. 524–25.
132. *Ibid.*, pp. 524–29.
133. *Ibid.*, pp. 528–81.
134. *Ibid.*, pp. 586–89.
135. *Ibid.*, pp. 588–91.
136. *Ibid.*, pp. 314–15, 590–95.

137. *Ibid.*, pp. 594–605.

138. *Ibid.*, pp. 604–25.

139. *Ibid.*, pp. 624–29.

140. *Ibid.*, pp. 628–39.

141. *Ibid.*, pp. 640–49. Valois, pp. 610–11.

142. Masselin, pp. 648–49. Masselin's bitterness against Lombez was largely unjustified. He had been ambassador to Spain, and his presence at the negotiations with the new Spanish ambassadors was probably ordered by the council. See Charles Samaran, *Jean de Bilhères-Lagraulas . . . ,* pp. 33–41. It is interesting that in May Lombez became president of the Norman *Échiquier*. Later, after the Beaujeus had established their control over the central government they had Masselin appointed a councilor in the same body. The two ecclesiastics apparently got along much better at this time. Beaurepaire, p. 292.

143. Masselin, pp. 648–59. That the royal officials, or at least those in finance, were quite busy during the last days of the estates is proved by a letter of March 12. See *Lettres-missives originales du chartrier de Thouars,* ed. Paul Marchegay (Les Roches-Baritaud, 1873), pp. 80–81.

144. Charles Samaran, *La Maison d'Armagnac . . . ,* pp. 248–58, 442–49. The Beaujeus did get some financial compensation for the loss of Armagnac, but that they were a greedy couple is amply illustrated by the reputation Pierre had achieved during the reign of Louis XI and by their activities after Orléans and Brittany had been defeated in 1486. They helped themselves to the royal treasury, demanded expensive gifts, tried to assure the great Bourbon inheritance for themselves and their heirs, and possibly accepted bribes. Pélicier, pp. 208–12. Bridge, I, 241–52.

145. Pélicier, *Essai . . . ,* p. 78, n. 2.

146. *Ibid.*, pp. 91–98, 247–48, 266–69. Isambert, XI, 119–24. Picot, *Histoire des États généraux . . . ,* I, 398–403.

147. Pélicier, *Essai . . . ,* p. 83.

148. Bridge, I, 103–14. Pélicier, pp. 79–87. Maulde-la-Clavière, II, 85–111. *Procès-Verbaux des séances du Conseil de régence, du roi Charles VIII. . . . CDI,* ed. Adhelm Bernier (Paris, 1836), p. 101.

149. Pélicier, *Essai . . . ,* pp. 87–90. Bridge, I, 114–16. *Titres de la maison ducale de Bourbon,* ed. Albret Lecoy de La Marche (Paris, 1874), II, nos. 6,869 and 6,882. Luchaire, pp. 22–25.

150. Pélicier, *Essai . . . ,* p. 84.

151. Picot, *Histoire des États généraux . . . ,* II, 128–35. Masselin, pp. 704–13.

152. Thierry, II, 422. *Titres de la maison ducale de Bourbon,* II, no. 6,892. Caseneuve, pt. I, 138–40.

153. Picot, *Histoire des États généraux . . . ,* I, 398–403. Isambert, XI, 119–24.

154. Pélicier, *Essai . . . ,* pp. 98–100, 252–55.

155. Dussert, pp. 90–96, 282.

156. *RPO,* IX, 350–54. Billioud, pp. 460–65.

157. Billioud, pp. 412–14. Bernier, 50–51. Pélicier, *Essai . . . ,* pp. 233–34.

158. Prentout, I, 204–9; III, 36–38. Pélicier, *Essai . . . ,* pp. 98–100, 252–55.

159. Caseneuve, pt. II, 48.

160. *HL,* XI, 128–29, 138–39.

Chapter Five

1. *Lettres de Charles VIII, roi de France. SHF,* ed. Paul Pélicier (Paris, 1898–1905), I, 47–49. For related letters see also V, 190–91; and *Ordonnances des rois*

de France de la troisième race, ed. Claude-E. Pastoret (Paris, 1835), XIX, 594–96. *Procès-verbaux des séances du Conseil de régence du roy Charles VIII. CDI*, ed. Adhelm Bernier (Paris, 1836), pp. 211–14. See James R. Major, *The Deputies to the Estates General of Renaissance France* (Madison, 1960), Appendix A.

2. *Ordonnances* . . . , XX, 56–58.

3. *Lettres de Charles VIII*, III, 31–32.

4. *Ibid.*, III, 345–47.

5. *Ibid.*, II, 372–73, 380. Guillaume de Jaligny and others, *Histoire de Charles VIII, roy de France*, ed. Théodore Godefroy (Paris, 1617), pp. 138–39.

6. Henri-F. Delaborde, *L'Expédition de Charles VIII en Italie* (Paris, 1888), pp. 320–21, 327–28. René-A.-M. de Maulde-la-Clavière, *Histoire de Louis XII* (Paris, 1891), III, 7–8. John S. C. Bridge, *A History of France from the Death of Louis XI* (Oxford, 1924), II, 88–89. *Documents historiques inédits tirés des collections manuscrits de la bibliothèques royale. CDI*, ed. Jean-J. Champollion-Figeac (Paris, 1843), II, 477–81. *IAC. Amiens*, ed. Georges Durand (Amiens, 1894), ser. BB, II, 271–72. The Tuscan ambassador gives the impression that the assembly of towns was expected to vote money, but the matter was not raised in the meeting. Indeed, in the letters of convocation the towns were instructed to give their deputies only powers "pour oyr, entendre et vous rapporter ce qui luy sera dit et communiqué de par nous." *Lettres de Charles VIII*, IV, 22–23. *Négociations diplomatiques de la France avec la Toscane. CDI*, ed. Abel Desjardins (Paris, 1859), I, 291–95, 304, 398. *Ordonnances* . . . , XX, 437–38.

7. *Ordonnances* . . . , XX, 387.

8. A. Spont, "Une Recherche générale des feux à la fin du XVe siècle," *Annuaire-bulletin de la soc. de l'histoire de France*, XXIX (1892), 222–26; and "La Taille en Languedoc de 1450 à 1515," *Annales du Midi*, II (1890), 375–81. Henri Prentout, *Les États provinciaux de Normandie* (Caen, 1925), I, 216–18, extract from *Mém. de l'ac. nationale des sciences, arts et belles-lettres de Caen*, N.S., I.

9. Spont, *Annuaire* . . . , XXIX (1892), 226–28; *Annales* . . . , II (1890), 381–83. *Lettres de Charles VIII*, III, 165–67.

10. Spont, *Annuaire* . . . , XXIX (1892), 228–32; *Annales* . . . , II (1890), 383–84. Prentout, I, 219–23. Preliminary figures showed that a taille of 19 sous per hearth was paid in Languedoïl, 27 sous in Outre-Seine, 60 sous 8 deniers in Normandy, and 67 sous in Languedoc, but Languedoc was accused of having false rolls, and there were other complications. Prentout, I, 219–22.

11. Jaligny, pp. 76–79. Paul Pélicier, *Essai sur le gouvernement de la dame de Beaujeu* (Chartres, 1882), p. 140.

12. *Ordonnances* . . . , XXI, 178, 207.

13. *Ibid.*, XXI, 281.

14. *Ibid.*, XXI, 420–36. Roger Doucet, *Les Institutions de la France au XVIe siècle* (Paris, 1948), II, 848. Jean Du Tillet gives the composition of some of these assemblies in *Recueil des rangs des grands de France*, pp. 76–79, published in *Recueil des roys de France* (Paris, 1607).

15. For a brief but very incomplete statement on this subject see René-A.-M. de Maulde-la-Clavière, *La Diplomatie au temps de Machiavel* (Paris, 1893), III, 212–18.

16. Dumont, III, pt. II, 307, art. 39. For treaty with Ferdinand and Isabella, see pp. 297–301.

17. *Lettres de Charles VIII*, IV, 36–38, 116–17. Thierry, II, 463–66.

18. Dumont, III, pt. II, 307, art. 40. For examples of promises to support the treaty see pp. 309–10.

19. For treaty see Dumont, III, pt. II, 291–96. For other documents see Thomas Rymer, *Foedera, conventiones, literae* . . . (The Hague, 1751), V, pt. IV, 48 ff.

20. *Rotuli Parliamentorum* (London, 1832), VI, 507.

21. Rymer, V, pt. IV, 88.

22. They were Ponthieu, Languedoc, Normandy, Rouergue, Quercy, Agenais, Poitou, Périgord, Amiens, Touraine, Anjou, Orléans, Montargis, Meaux, Berry, Saintonge, Boulonnais, and Paris. In addition several subordinate jurisdictions assembled and ratified the treaty. Rymer, V, pt. IV, 80, 88–105.

23. Bridge, III, 204–47.

24. For the elections and the ratification of the marriage see *Registres des délibérations du bureau de la ville de Paris,* ed. François Bonnardot (Paris, 1883), I, 117–20; *IAC. Abbeville,* ed. Alcius Ledieu (Abbeville, 1902), I, 137–38; T. Boutiot and A. Babeau, "Documents inédits tirés des archives de Troyes et relatifs aux États généraux," *Collection de documents inédits relatifs à la ville de Troyes et à la Champagne méridionale* (Troyes, 1878), I, 7–20; *IAC. Rouen,* ed. Charles de Robillard de Beaurepaire (Rouen, 1887), I, 94; Thierry, II, 506–10; and B. Mun., Lyon, MS. 721, fols., 191–201.

25. *IAC. Angoulême,* ed. Émile Biais (Angoulême, 1889), p. 74. The king himself directed Angers to send deputies, but not until May 11, after the other deputies had arrived. AC, Angers, BB 13, fol., 130–30v.

26. The deputies of Amiens arrived at Tours on May 8 and paid their respects to the Cardinal of Amboise. At this time they may have received some instructions. Thierry, II, 507. Boutiot and Babeau, p. 17. *IAC. Rouen,* I, 94. Jean de Saint-Gelais, *Histoire de Louys XII* (Paris, 1622), p. 181. A deputy from Rouen later reported that twenty towns were present, but I have been able to establish the identity of only sixteen. See Major, *The Deputies* . . . , Appendix A for list of towns. For proof see documents cited in footnote 24; the list given in the report of the deputies of Troyes, Boutiot and Babeau, p. 17; *IAC. Dijon,* ed. Louis de Gouvenain (Dijon, 1867), I, 50; *Archives législatives de la ville de Reims. CDI,* ed. Pierre Varin (Paris, 1844), I, pt. II, 570, n. 1; and AC, Angers, B 13, fols. 130v–31. Sens and Montpellier have been added to the list because they took the oath to support the marriage and therefore were almost certainly represented at the estates, Jean d'Auton, *Chroniques de Louis XII. SHF.* (Paris, 1895), IV, 47, n. 2. The towns of Brittany, Dauphiné, and Provence were apparently not represented.

27. André-J. Le Glay, *Négociations diplomatiques entre la France et l'Autriche. CDI* (Paris, 1845), I, 132.

28. *Lettres du roy Louis XII et du Cardinal Georges d'Amboise* (Brussels, 1712), I, 43. Auton, IV, 44. Saint-Gelais, p. 181.

29. *Lettres du roy Louis XII* . . . , I, 43–44. I have used Bridge's translation with minor changes, III, 248–49.

30. *Lettres du roy Louis XII* . . . , I, 44–51. Saint-Gelais, pp. 184–87. Auton, IV, 44–47. Le Glay, I, 136, 138. For the ratification of the towns see the sources cited in footnote 24; AN, J. 951; and Auton, IV, 47, n. 2. These assemblies were far larger than those that had originally elected the deputies. The need for secrecy had passed, and Louis XII now wanted to associate as large a part of the population with his policy as possible.

31. Lauwereyns de Roosendaele, "Une lettre de Louis XII aux maire et échevins de Saint-Omer après les États généraux tenus à Tours en 1506," *Bul. historique trimestriel de la soc. des antiquaires de la Morinie,* VI (1877–81), 610–16; and VII (1882–86), 30–32. In another letter Louis justified his conduct by pointing out

that in his coronation oath he had sworn not to permit a reduction in the size of his kingdom, Mayer, X, 195–96.

Chapter Six

1. Georges Pagès, *La Monarchie d'ancien régime en France* (Paris, ed. of 1946), p. 3.

2. Roger Doucet, *Étude sur le gouvernement de François Ier* (Paris, 1921), I, 349.

3. Henry Lemonnier, *Histoire de France illustrée depuis les origines jusqu'à la Révolution,* ed. Lavisse (Paris, 1911), V, pt. I, 238–42.

4. *Catalogue des actes de François Ier* (Paris, 1887), I, 88, n. 516. This letter was addressed to Angers. Lyon, Troyes, and Bayonne were also summoned; see *IAC. Lyon,* ed. Fortuné Rolle (Lyon, 1865), ser. BB, p. 17; Théophile Boutiot, *Histoire de la ville de Troyes* (Paris, 1873), III, 291; and *Archives municipales de Bayonne. Délibérations du corps de ville. Registres Gascons,* eds. Édouard Ducére and others (Bayonne, 1898), II, 91.

5. *Journal de Jean Barrillon, secrétaire du Chancelier Duprat. SHF,* ed. Pierre de Vaissière (Paris, 1897), I, 248.

6. *Ordonnances des rois de France. Règne de François Ier* (Paris, 1902), I, 474.

7. Barrillon, I, 275, n. 1. BN, MS. n. a. fr. 7,144, fols. 5v–7v. See James R. Major, *The Deputies to the Estates General of Renaissance France* (Madison, 1960), Appendix A for list of towns.

8. For elections see T. Boutiot and A. Babeau, "Documents inédits tirés des archives de Troyes et relatifs aux États généraux," *Collection de documents inédits de la ville de Troyes* (Troyes, 1878), I, 21–24. Joseph Garnier, "Documents relatifs à l'histoire des États généraux du royaume conservés aux archives municipales de Dijon," *Bul. du comité de la langue de l'histoire et des arts de la France,* I (1852–53), 438. *Archives municipales de Bayonne,* II, 100–101, 106. Garnier has incorrectly dated his documents as 1515 and 1516 rather than 1516 and 1517. Dijon and Troyes were told to send two deputies, Bayonne, one or two. For list of deputies see BN, MS. n. a. fr. 7,144, fols. 5v–7v.

9. Barrillon, I, 275. Doucet, I, 77–88.

10. Barrillon, I, 275–79.

11. *Ibid.,* I, 279–82.

12. *Ibid.,* I, 282–83.

13. *Ibid.,* I, 284–302. BN, MS. n. a. fr. 7,144, fol. 1.

14. Barrillon, I, 284, n. 1; 302–4. Garnier, p. 438. Boutiot and Babeau, I, 24.

15. Barrillon, I, 303–4. Boutiot and Babeau, I, 24. *Archives municipales de Bayonne,* II, 113. The replies of the towns to the nine articles are at BN, MS. n. a. fr. 7,144, fols. 9–81v.

16. Barrillon's concluding statements on the assemblies of October, 1516, and March, 1517, were exactly the same. The deputies went home "sans riens faire." I, 248, 304.

17. *Ordonnances des rois de France. Règne de François Ier* (Paris, 1933), IV, 268; V, 283.

18. Du Tillet published the *Recueil* in *Recueil des roys de France . . .* (Paris, 1607). See pp. 79–107 for the assemblies. See also Théodore Godefroy, *Le Cérémonial françois* (Paris, 1649), 2 vols. for the composition and seating arrangement of numerous large gatherings.

19. Doucet, I, 77–87. The *procès-verbal* of Parlement for the meeting of February 5, 1517, has been published by Jules Thomas, *Le Concordat de 1516* (Paris, 1910), II, 361–65, but unfortunately it does not mention the actions of the clergy. Doucet, I, 86, n. 3.

20. Doucet, I, 87–88.

21. *Ibid.*, I, 88–124. Thomas, II, 365–90.

22. Doucet, I, 125–48.

23. *Ordonnances . . . François 1ᵉʳ*, I, 157–58, 429–30. Paris, Poitiers, Nantes, Bayonne, Narbonne, and Reims were among the twelve towns. I, 430, n. 2.

24. *Archives municipales de Bayonne*, II, 97–99.

25. Lemonnier, V, pt. II, 43. *Letters and Papers, Foreign and Domestic of the reign of Henry VIII*, ed. John S. Brewer (London, 1870), IV, pt. I, 604.

26. Doucet, II, 19, n. 1. See Brewer, IV, pt. I, 601, 624–25, and elsewhere for references to the "estates of Lyon."

27. Doucet, II, 33–116.

28. AN, Xˡᵃ 1527, fol. 230–30v.

29. Doucet, II, 114, n. 3. See Brewer, IV, pt. I, 602, for report in May that Louise of Savoy would not hold estates for fear she would be removed. *Captivité du roy François Iᵉʳ. CDI*, ed. Aimé Champollion-Figeac (Paris, 1847), p. 404.

30. *Ordonnonces . . . de François Iᵉʳ*, I, 262, n. 1; 266, n. 2.

31. *Ibid.*, III, 285.

32. *Ibid.*, III, 288.

33. Champollion-Figeac, pp. 83, 423.

34. Gilbert Jacqueton, *La Politique extérieure de Louise de Savoie* (Paris, 1892), pp. 118–47, 323–41. Brewer, IV, xcv; pt. I, 604, 684–86, 688, 711–12. For treaty, see *Ordonnances . . . de François Iᵉʳ*, IV, 92–109.

35. Jacqueton, pp. 155–90. Henri Prentout, *Les États provinciaux de Normandie* (Caen, 1925), I, 263–71, extract from *Mém. de l'ac. nationale des sciences, arts et belles-lettres de Caen*, NS, I. The oaths and guarantees to the treaty may be found in Thomas Rymer, *Foedera, conventiones, literae . . .* (The Hague, 1741), VI, pt. II, 21 ff.

36. Champollion-Figeac, pp. 157–58.

37. *Ibid.*, pp. 166–67.

38. *Ibid.*, p. 171.

39. *Ibid.*, p. 429.

40. *Ordonnances . . . de François Iᵉʳ*, IV, 185–86.

41. Henri Hauser, *Le Traité de Madrid et la cession de la Bourgogne à Charles V* (Paris, 1912). J. Declareuil, "Le Traité de Madrid et le droit public français," *Recueil de législation de Toulouse*, ser. 2, IX (1913), 96–122. Doucet, II, 279–87.

42. François-A.-A. Mignet, *Rivalité de François Iᵉʳ et de Charles-Quint* (Paris, 1875), II, 338–80.

43. AN, Xˡᵃ 1531, fols., 26v–33. A summary of the deliberations has been published in Isambert, XII, 285–301, but there are several errors in dates. Doucet, II, 288–93.

44. AN, Xˡᵃ 1531, fols. 35v–52v. *Registres des délibérations du bureau de la ville de Paris*, ed. Alexandre Tuetey (Paris, 1886), II, 1–4.

45. AN, Xˡᵃ 1531, fols. 52v–53v.

46. *Ibid.*, 29–29v.

47. *Ordonnances . . . de François Iᵉʳ*, V, 251–52.

48. *Ibid.*, VI, 72–76. For the enregisterment of the treaties by the Parlements and the *Chambres des comptes* and the ratification by some of the towns, see

Dumont, IV, pt. II, 18–42; BN, MS, Mélanges de Colbert 366, 369–70, nos. 316–20, 356–75; and MS. fr. 6,199.

49. Roger Doucet, *Les Institutions de la France au XVIᵉ siècle* (Paris, 1948), II, 835. Louis Serbat, *Les Assemblées du clergé de France* (Paris, 1906), pp. 24–27. Mignet, II, 480. *HL*, XII, 487–88. *Catalogue des actes de François Iᵉʳ* (Paris, 1887–1908), I, 661, 663, 667; II, 80, 318, 685; VI, 164; VIII, 620.

50. BN, MS. n. a. fr. 7,678, fols. 195–99v.

51. BN, MS. n. a. fr. 7,678, fols. 240–41, 304–9. Mignet, II, 480–82. *Catalogue des actes de François Iᵉʳ*, I, 534; II, 318, 473; VI, 193, 208; VII, 704; VIII, 203. Jean Bouchet, *Les Annales d'Aquitaine* (Poitiers, 1644), p. 455.

52. *Registres . . . de la ville de Paris*, II, 10–14.

53. *IAC*. Lyon, ed. Fortuné Rolle (Paris, 1865), I, 21–22.

54. *IAC*. Rouen, ed. Charles de Robillard de Beaurepaire (Rouen, 1887), I, 135–38. *IAC. Beauvais*, ed. Renaud Rose (Beauvais, 1887), p. 15. *Catalogue des actes de François Iᵉʳ*, II, 35; VIII, 620.

55. Dumont, IV, pt. II, 283–84.

56. *HL*, XI, 274. *Catalogue des actes de François Iᵉʳ*, IV, 706. Prentout, II, 374. *IAC. Beauvais*, p. 16. *IAC. Amiens*, ed. Georges Durand (Amiens, 1894), II, 361.

57. Dumont, V, pt. I, 41.

58. William F. Church, *Constitutional Thought in Sixteenth Century France* (Cambridge, 1941), pp. 22–42. Claude de Seyssel, *La Grand' Monarchie de France* (Paris, ed. 1557), fols. 9–13v, 19–25v.

59. Church, pp. 43–73.

60. Serbat, pp. 17–30. Doucet, II, *Les Institutions . . .* , II, 834–41.

61. Mignet, II, 480–82.

62. The proof for this statement may be found in the registers of the towns which kept excellent records, e.g., Amiens, Dijon, Lyon, Rouen, etc.

63. *IAC. Amiens*, II, 336–39.

64. Lemonnier, V, pt. I, 240. Paul Dognon, *Les Institutions politiques et administratives du pays de Languedoc* (Toulouse, 1895), pp. 530–31. The communal archives of the various towns offer many examples of the king reducing a tax upon request.

65. The itinerary of Louis XI has been published in *Lettres de Louis XI. SHF*, eds. Joseph Vaesen and others (Paris, 1909), XI, 3–236; of Charles VIII between 1483 and 1491 in Paul Pélicier, *Essai sur le gouvernement de la dame de Beaujeu* (Chartres, 1882), pp. 285–308; and of Francis I in *Catalogue des actes de François Iᵉʳ*, VIII, 411–548.

66. Henri Prentout, "Les États provinciaux en France," *Bul. of the International Committee of Historical Sciences*, I (1928), 642–45; and *Les États provinciaux de Normandie*, II, 498–517.

67. *IAC. Clermont-Ferrand. Fonds Montferrand*, ed. Alexandre-V.-E. Teilhard de Chardin (Clermont-Ferrand, 1902), pp. 18–76. Gilbert Rouchon, "Le Tiers état aux États provinciaux de Basse-Auvergne aux XVIᵉ et XVIIᵉ siècles," *Bul. philologique et historique du comité des travaux historiques et scientifiques* (1930–31), 167–68.

68. *Archives historiques du département de la Gironde*, XXVIII (1893), 44–108. Lucien Romier, *Les Origines politiques des guerres de religion* (Paris, 1914), I, 541.

69. Romier, II, 178–87, 214–17.

70. *IAC. Rouen*, I, 192. *IAC. Amiens*, II, 414. *Registres . . . de la ville de Paris*, IV, 512–13.

71. Thierry, II, 655. Romier, II, 231.

72. *IAC. Amiens,* II, 414. Thierry, II, 655. Boutiot, III, 438. *HL,* XI, 322. *IAC. Rouen,* I, 192.

73. Our knowledge of who attended the estates of 1558 is based on the seating arrangement recorded by the clerk, Jean Du Tillet, in the registers of the Parlement of Paris, AN, X^{1a} 1587. All or part of this material has been published in the various editions of Du Tillet, *Recueil des roys de France;* and in *Godefroy,* II, 379–82; and Mayer, X, 269–78.

74. AD, Côte-d'Or, C 3,469. These documents prove that the decision to hold an assembly must have been taken by November, 1557, for the first president of the Parlement of Dijon departed for Paris on December 5. In addition to the king's reference to the "general convocation of the four estates," the assembly was referred to as a meeting of the Estates General by a royal official. An ambassador also referred to the assembly as a meeting of the Estates General. L. Romier, "Lettres de Giovanni Dalmatio au Cardinal Farnèse (1558–59)," *BEC,* LXXI (1910), 314.

75. *IAC. Rouen,* II, 192.

76. The best account of the events that took place in the estates of 1558 is *Discours des Estatz tenuz à Paris par les tres-chrestien Roy de France, Henry second au moys de janvier, ceste presente année, 1558* (Paris, s. d.), BN, Le^{11} 1. It is the basis of the account in "Commentaires de François de Rabutin," *Nouvelle collection des mémoires pour servir à l'histoire de France,* eds. Joseph F. Michaud and Jean-J. Poujoulat (Paris, 1838), ser. I, VII, 586–89.

77. Isambert, XIII, 506–9.

78. Boutiot, III, 438–39.

INDEX